A COOK'S TOUR
OF IOWA

Susan Puckett

A
COOK'S
TOUR
OF
IOWA

University of Iowa Press
Iowa City

University of Iowa Press, Iowa City 52242
Copyright © 1988 by the University of Iowa
All rights reserved
Printed in the United States of America
Third printing, 1989

Book and jacket design by Sandra Strother Hudson
Typesetting by G & S Typesetters, Inc., Austin, Texas
Printing and binding by Edwards Brothers, Ann Arbor, Michigan

Library of Congress Cataloging-in-Publication Data

Puckett, Susan, 1956–
A cook's tour of Iowa.
(A Bur oak original)
Includes index.
1. Cookery, American.   2. Cookery—Iowa.   3. Iowa—
Social life and customs.   I. Title.   II. Series.
TX715.P9525   1988   641.5973   87-35751
ISBN 0-87745-191-5

Title page: Evelyn and Bob Birkby with their dog Sparkle,
Cottonwood Farm, 1952, photo courtesy of KMA
Broadcasting. Page 1: Hopeville Old Settlers' Reunion.
Page 139: photo courtesy of Miriam Dunlap, Living
History Farms. Page 207: photo courtesy of the
Iowa State Fair Board.

A Bur Oak Original

TO MY MOTHER, NANCY

CONTENTS

ACKNOWLEDGMENTS

I wish to express my deepest thanks to the friends, relatives, and literally hundreds of Iowans who provided the support, advice, and encouragement I needed to make *A Cook's Tour of Iowa* a reality.

J. K. Hvistendahl, chairman of the Iowa State University Journalism Department, gave me the incentive to plant the seeds by allowing me to earn college credit for submitting the earliest draft as part of an independent study course. Dale Boyd went above and beyond the call of duty by acting as my project adviser after the course was over and even after his retirement.

Iowa State University history professor Dorothy Schwieder and Tom Morain of Living History Farms generously shared their Iowa history expertise; Professor Beverly Madden of the School of Home Economics helped me evaluate the recipes.

Finally, I acknowledge the volunteer cooks who assisted me in testing—and tasting!—the recipes: Iris Bailin, Michael Baron, Vera Beck, Parker Bosley, Jeanine Braun, Diane Carman, Holly Carver, Norma Conaway, Bea Delpapa, Madeline Drexler, Becky Freligh, Janet French, Alma Kaufman, Jane Moulton, Okey Nestor, Dan Postotnik, Nancy Puckett, Sharon Rebouche, Edie Roberts, Jerry Sealy, Beth Segal, Shelley Segal, Jan Shane, Bill Sorrell, Paula Tillinghast, and Stevie Voorhees.

INTRODUCTION

Ask about Tex-Mex cooking, Cajun food, or New England fare and chances are most people would be able to reel off half-a-dozen representative dishes without so much as pondering. Ask the same question about Iowa's cuisine, though, and your response is more likely to be a blank stare or a statement something like, "But I didn't know there was an Iowa cuisine."

That's what I thought when I left my home state of Mississippi to pursue a home economics degree at Iowa State University in Ames. Bland, homogeneous, boring, undistinguished: those were my impressions of the ultimate heartland state. But that was before I had the opportunity to feast on savory sauerbraten and dumplings in the historic Amana Colonies; sample the unusual pancakes called aebleskiver at Elk Horn's Danish Inn restaurant, right across the street from an authentic windmill; or share a meal of dried-corn soup and golden fry bread with an Indian family during the Mesquakie settlement's annual powwow.

The idea for this book stemmed from a similar project I'd undertaken as a food writer for the Jackson, Mississippi, *Clarion-Ledger*. My mission was to comb the state for recipes reflecting Mississippi's heritage. The recipes, along with the stories of the people and places that had produced them, evolved into *A Cook's Tour of Mississippi*. The personal rewards from that effort were so great that I began to fantasize about researching a similar book in my new home. Maybe, just maybe, Iowans would be willing to share their recipes with me, and I could help them preserve a piece of their heritage in return.

They did share, generously, and as a result I was able to gather enough material for forty-two chapters, representing the rich diversity of the entire state. Besides revealing their favorite dishes, Iowans took me on tours of their hometowns: on foot, in cars, in pick-ups, and, in Kalona's Amish-Mennonite community, even in a horse-drawn buggy. They set extra places for me at their family dinner tables and invited me to their local celebrations. Despite my unmistakable Southern drawl, they went out of their way to make me feel like a native daughter.

At the Hopeville Old Settlers' Reunion they surprised me with the award for the longest distance traveled to this annual picnic in southern Iowa: a brand-new photo album and a sack of Chuckles candy.

During the Gladbrook Corn Carnival I got my first lesson in speed-shucking in the back of a pick-up truck carrying enough freshly picked ears to feed seven hundred people.

At the majestic governor's mansion, Terrace Hill, then–First Lady Billie Ray took time out of her busy schedule to chat with me over tea and cookies in the family living quarters.

In the Swedish town of Stanton I was greeted at the Senior Citizens' Community Center with freshly brewed coffee and a full spread of Scandinavian treats, including dainty spritz cookies and the rennet-based pudding called ostakaka. They sent me home with an autographed church cookbook and some Christmas ornaments crocheted by one of the ladies.

In Kalona I got to meet the county Pork Queen at the annual Iowa chop dinner put on by the local bank.

In Des Moines I watched the eager anticipation of state fair contestants as a panel of judges put their cookie and candy specialties to the test.

Throughout my travels Iowa citizens opened their homes, frequently offering me, a perfect stranger, overnight lodging. I stayed in farmhouses, country cottages, even a college fraternity house. While working on this project I made some wonderful friends and gained a real sense of belonging. I also came to the conclusion that Iowa cooking is a lot like its people: hearty, homey, unpretentious. Along the way I stumbled upon an eclectic mix of phenomenal food finds that included what must be the world's most fabulous raisin cream pie, local blue cheese as luxurious as any European variety I'd ever tasted, Mulligan stew stirred up by a former hobo king, a traffic light–green soda called a Green River straight out of the 1950's, and a gooey, home-baked cinnamon roll big enough to feed a family of six.

Each of the recipes (with the exception of a few thrown in for amusement or historical reference) has been kitchen-tested by myself and a number of volunteer cooks. While I've tried to preserve the original flavor of both the written recipe and the end result, I have made some minor adjustments or clarifications, when necessary, to aid readers in duplicating these creations in their own kitchens.

If you like to cook, I invite you to capture the taste of this flavorful and distinctive state in your own kitchen as I did. But even if you don't, I hope you'll come along with me anyway to examine this fascinating culinary patchwork—through its people, places, resources, and celebrations.

Part One

FRIENDS
AND
RELATIONS

THE HOPEVILLE OLD SETTLERS' REUNION

The little drum and fife corps didn't march down the streets of Hopeville in 1982 to kick off the town's annual Old Settlers' Reunion. Nor did Socky Smith entertain the crowds with his banjo strumming while his son Paul jigged to the music. The three-day extravaganza, complete with carnival rides, tent shows, three-legged races, and wrestling matches, has shrunk to a lazy Sunday afternoon picnic. The fifty, maybe seventy-five, friends and relatives who share potluck dishes under the aging maples of this tidy, block-square park toward the end of summer call themselves the Old Settlers and Newcomers Association. Yet you'd be hard-pressed to find either an old settler or a newcomer among them.

The founders of this community are all at the top of the hill in the Hopeville Cemetery, resting under stone markers likely tilted by some fierce Iowa winter wind. And with a population of twenty-seven and falling, Hopeville hasn't had a newcomer in ages. Nevertheless, Avis James still drove up from nearby Murray with the chocolate cake everybody raved about last year—a sweet finale to Maud Stroup's fried chicken, Bonnie Reasoner's zucchini casserole, and a helping or two of anything else one could pile on his or her china plate brought from home.

The Country Rhythm Dusters, a group of women identically attired in blue jeans, plaid shirts, and feathered hats, were all set to pick, fiddle, and strum away the afternoon with a full repertoire of bluegrass favorites. And Cousin Poke, Uncle Dale, and Aunt Bessie were among those on hand to provide the rest of the entertainment by spinning tale after tale of a time when their hometown lived up to its reputation as a "robust, hell-for-leather town where anything could happen and usually did."

Those were the days when Puny Smith gave haircuts for a quarter, and a penny would buy a whole sack of candy at the general store. Law and order were maintained by A. B. Small, Hopeville's self-appointed mayor, often acclaimed by the townspeople as their own Wyatt Earp. Rumor has it that the mayor was never seen without his .44 sticking out of his back pocket. And even those who can't remember Prohibition know all about Walt Case, the "Bootleg King" who concocted a brew in the still in the back of his wagon reputed to "make a wren spit in the face of a chicken hawk."

"Hopeville" was the name adopted by the first settlers in the 1850s, signifying their high hopes of watching their town grow and prosper once the railroad came through. They built hotels, churches, schools, blacksmith shops, and mercantiles, patiently awaiting a day when they would no longer have to trudge through the mud, rain, or snow to board the morning train in Osceola.

That day never came.

About all that's flourishing in Hopeville these days are the weeds choking the last general store, which closed its rusty screen door for good in 1977. Most of the businesses were wiped out by fires too cataclysmic for the bucket brigade to extinguish. Others rotted away and were never rebuilt.

"If you look through the trees over there, you can see the steeple of our old schoolhouse," said Alberta Foland, squinting as she pointed to the skeleton of her alma mater. "It used to be a nice, big school. It's not in too good a shape anymore, though."

The dilapidated frame of the two-story Independent Order of Odd Fellows Hall, now used for storing the rickety old tables used for the picnic, was once the site of many square dances. At times, or so it's been said, the floors would bounce so hard with the foot-stomping that the dancers would disperse to the edges for fear of collapse. While the fiddler whined out one lively tune after another, Smoky German called the dances. Old-timers still get a chuckle when they're reminded of the time Charley Guthrie threatened to whip Smoky because he couldn't hear the calls over his incessant gum-chomping.

Some of the older Hopeville citizens, like Floyd and Gladys Reasoner, had to settle for "party games" instead of square dancing. "The Methodists didn't believe in dancing, and fiddling was 'dance music,'" Floyd's wife of more than sixty years explained. "But if we wanted to play a game like, say, 'Skip to My Lou' while somebody else played the guitar or french harp—well, that was different!" she snickered, putting her hand over her mouth. "Then it wasn't dancing; it was a 'party game,' you see."

The white frame church still opens its doors for a handful of worshippers on Sunday mornings and Saturday evenings. Every Memorial Day for years, a special church service was held in honor of the Hopeville citizens who gave their lives for their country. "Our Sunday School teacher had us make wreaths to set on the soldiers' graves," Mrs. Foland recalled. "We'd practice and practice our march to the cemetery. Some

of us got to carry flags. All of us little girls wore white organdy dresses and new shoes; oh, how they'd rub blisters on our feet!"

The park was the hub of entertainment even then, especially during the summers when the traveling shows made their circuit through southern Iowa. Few will forget the time the 9,400-pound elephant broke loose from the Honest Bill Circus and got into a bin of oats, devouring fifteen bushels. The beast paid for his overindulgence, however. En route to the next stop he dropped dead in his tracks.

In the winter the neighbors looked forward to sleigh rides over snow-drifts piled high over fence tops, to taffy-pulling parties, to molasses strippings. "We used to raise our own cane," Gladys Reasoner recalled. "All the neighbors would come over and we'd have a strippin'. We'd run those stalks through a long pan that was metal on the bottom and wooden on the sides. Then we'd let it cook down for three or four days. Sometimes I'd make a molasses cake the kids used to like, or else we'd just pour it over hot biscuits."

"I tell you, there's nobody that knows how to make 'soppin' biscuits' like my wife," Floyd said matter-of-factly. "She'd make eighteen of 'em every morning to serve with some good 'sop,' enough for us and our kids to have two apiece—unless somebody snitched an extra." Gladys made the sop by adding a little milk and cream from their dairy cow to the drippings left over from ham and eggs. At night she'd sometimes make a fancier variation by serving creamed pheasant over biscuits.

"Just about all of us around here like to cook," Maud Stroup said. "In the wintertime, especially. We always found that when it was cold outside and we were stuck in the house with no money we always felt better if we made us something good to eat."

A lot of those dishes, she said, were "poor people's food," such as "phoney" creamed chicken, a white sauce flavored with chicken bouillon served over baking powder biscuits—"things that kinda gave you the impression you were eating something classier than you really were." And if those experiments went over particularly well, it was almost a sure bet that dish would show up on other Hopeville tables. Recipe swapping is still popular among the members of the Ladies' Aid, comprised of present and former Hopeville citizens who get together to "rag rugs, crack walnuts, can peas, dress chickens—maybe play a hand or two of ten-point pitch," Avis James said. They sell Maid-rites and home-baked goods at auctions and at the annual Hopeville Rural Music Reunion, which attracts some 3,500 country music fans to the little park every fall. "That's how we keep our church going," Mrs. Foland said. "We especially get lots of compliments on our pies; they almost always sell out by lunchtime."

Here are some of the dishes that manage to conjure up a memory of an old-time reunion, a molasses stripping, or maybe just a quiet supper at home with the family in the little town whose only hope is that it will never be completely forgotten.

Gladys Reasoner's Molasses Cake

½ cup (1 stick) butter, softened
½ cup granulated sugar
2 eggs
1 cup molasses

2 cups all-purpose flour
2 teaspoons baking powder
1 teaspoon salt
1 teaspoon cinnamon
Whipped cream (optional)

Preheat oven to 350 degrees. In a mixing bowl, cream together butter and sugar until fluffy. (It's easier to do this with an electric mixer.) Add eggs and molasses and beat until smooth. Sift together flour, baking powder, salt, and cinnamon. Stir into egg mixture. Pour into greased 8 × 8 × 2-inch cake pan. Bake in preheated oven 30 to 40 minutes. Serve with whipped cream, if desired. Makes 8 to 10 servings.

Bonnie's Zucchini Casserole

1 medium zucchini, sliced,
  parboiled, and drained
1 large whole tomato, diced
½ medium onion, chopped and
  sautéed in 1 tablespoon butter

½ green pepper, chopped
5 to 6 slices fried bacon, crumbled
½ cup grated cheddar cheese
½ cup buttered bread crumbs

Preheat oven to 350 degrees. In a greased 1-quart casserole, spread alternate layers of zucchini, tomato, onion, green pepper, and bacon. Sprinkle with grated cheese and top with bread crumbs. Bake in preheated oven 20 minutes. Makes 4 servings.

Old Settlers' Fried Chicken

2 cups all-purpose flour
1 teaspoon salt
½ teaspoon pepper
½ teaspoon onion powder

½ teaspoon Italian seasoning
1 teaspoon cinnamon
1 teaspoon garlic powder
Oil for deep frying
2 whole chickens, cut up

Preheat oven to 350 degrees. Dump flour into a large container. Make a tiny hole in the middle of the flour and pour in the spices. Stir mixture thoroughly. In a Dutch oven or deep, heavy skillet, heat oil until hot enough to turn a piece of bread golden brown. Dredge chicken pieces in flour. Deep-fry, a few pieces at a time, until crisp. Drain. Transfer pieces to a baking pan and bake in preheated oven for 20 to 30 minutes, or until tender. Makes 6 to 8 servings.

Avis James's
One-Bowl Chocolate Cake
with Fudge Frosting

2 cups all-purpose flour
2 cups granulated sugar
1 teaspoon baking soda
½ cup (1 stick) butter or
   margarine
½ cup cocoa
1 cup water
½ cup buttermilk
2 eggs, lightly beaten
1 teaspoon vanilla

FUDGE FROSTING:
½ cup (1 stick) butter or
   margarine
¼ cup granulated sugar
¼ cup cocoa
2 tablespoons milk ("just a dab")
1 to 1½ cups powdered sugar
1 teaspoon vanilla

Preheat oven to 350 degrees. In a large mixing bowl, stir together flour, sugar, and baking soda. In a saucepan over medium-low heat, melt butter or margarine with cocoa and water. Make a hole in the center of the dry ingredients. Pour in the hot mixture, then the buttermilk and eggs. Mix together. Stir in vanilla. Pour into a greased and floured 8 × 12-inch pan. Bake in preheated oven 25 to 30 minutes or until cake tester inserted in middle comes out clean.

To make the frosting, melt together the butter, granulated sugar, cocoa, and milk in a saucepan over medium heat. Cook and stir until bubbly. Remove from heat. Beat in enough powdered sugar to make a creamy consistency. Stir in vanilla. Spread over cooled cake immediately. Makes 10 to 12 servings.

Maud Stroup's Home Remedy Soup

"This was something we ate a lot of and I thought as a child I would never feed this to my family when I grew up. However, I've (or so I believe) improved this dish. Mom always made the soup with four or five diced and boiled potatoes, a large diced onion cooked with the potatoes, and a slice or two of bacon chopped into the boiling potatoes and onions. If we had colds she always added more onion! When the potatoes were tender she drained off the water and added milk, butter, salt, and pepper. Then it was heated and served quite hot. I still use this basic idea but add a cup of diced ham, thicken the broth with a little flour, and add ¼ cup Parmesan cheese.

"Most of these dishes were inexpensive yet filling, for we were quite poor and therefore may not have always had a balanced diet. But we sure never left the table hungry."

RADIO HOMEMAKERS

In 1925, housewives all over southwestern Iowa found some new friends to turn to whenever they were in need of a new recipe, a cleaning tip, some child-rearing advice, or just a little companionship. That was the year radio homemaking hit the airwaves.

It all started when Henry Field, owner of a Shenandoah seed company and radio station KFNF, invited his five sisters to "talk to the womenfolk about children and cooking and things" on the air, says Lucile Verness, Field's niece. At first they were reluctant, lamenting that they knew nothing about broadcasting. But in one sentence, Lucile said, Field told them everything they needed to know: "Just open your mouth and let the Lord fill it."

Field's sister, Helen Field Fischer, began emceeing a program called the "Mother's Hour," during which she'd discuss tidbits from her family's daily life with her listeners. Later, upon deciding that her true calling was horticulture rather than homemaking, she started another program called the "Flower Lady" and turned the "Mother's Hour" over to her sister Leanna Field Driftmier. Whenever Mrs. Driftmier needed a sidekick, she would frequently call upon one of her seven children, particularly Lucile, who was then in high school. In no time Mrs. Driftmier and her family were celebrities. They became the local answer to "Dear Abby," receiving floods of letters seeking advice for everything from how to discipline children to what to do with a glut of gooseberries.

Around this time Earl May, who owned a competing seed company and radio station KMA, hired Jessie Young, a young woman who'd been put out of her job when the bank where she worked closed, to write commercials for KMA. By 1926 she had her own radio program, the "Stitch and Chat Club." Like the "Mother's Hour" it, too, was an instant success.

With more words of wisdom than airtime, Leanna Driftmier began writing the *Mother's Hour Newsletter* with the subtitle *Sent Out Every Once in a While.* Years later, with Mrs. Driftmier's encouragement, Jessie

Young launched a similar publication called *Jessie's Homemaker (Radio . . . Visit)*, a family production with issues that included photographs, letters, recipes, patterns, and a column of helpful suggestions called "Katchy Kinks for the Kitchen."

Since then more than a dozen women (as well as a few men) have followed in Leanna Driftmier's and Jessie Young's footsteps, sharing both their recipes and their lives with their listeners on programs with names such as the "Home Hour," "Domestic Science Talks," the "Farmer's Wife," "It's a Woman's World," and "Visit." Some of these programs eventually became syndicated, including the "Kitchen-Klatter Show," formerly Mrs. Driftmier's "Mother's Hour," which holds the record for the longest-running homemaker program in the history of radio. After Leanna Driftmier's death, her daughter Lucile Verness continued to broadcast the program from her home and publish the *Kitchen-Klatter Magazine* with the help of friends and other family members up until January 1986.

Though Lucile claimed the "Kitchen-Klatter Show" always strove to stay abreast of current trends, the character of the broadcasts and publications remained constant. Never did they attempt to shock either listeners or readers with sensational headlines or stir up controversy with scathing editorials. About the closest thing to a mention of violence in an issue of the magazine was Leanna's brother Frederick's losing battle in New England "with the notorious, noxious, odious gypsy moths," or perhaps the tragedy reported in a regular column entitled "Dorothy Writes from the Farm" about a baby duck who met its untimely fate when a cow stepped on it. Added the writer, "The poor mother stayed beside it all night long and I thought that was real touching."

While the "Kitchen-Klatter Show" and KFNF have since become history, radio homemaking remains the backbone of KMA. Each year thousands of Shenandoans attend the KMA Cookie Tea, a tradition started by the homemakers several decades earlier. For these events the public is invited to bring a plate of cookies, along with the recipe, for a giant cookie exchange.

"We started out at a time when there were many lonely people in the countryside," explained Evelyn Birkby, a former radio homemaker and columnist for the *Kitchen-Klatter Magazine* who still does broadcasts for KMA from time to time. "Now the listeners are mostly parents with little children. Our emphasis is still on a strong family life." What were the criteria radio homemakers had to fulfill? "Friendliness, neighborliness, and a willingness to try new things," Mrs. Birkby answered. "They had to be relaxed, at ease, and on the same level with the listeners. We 'neighbored' on the air. It was just like we were sitting down at your kitchen table, having coffee with you."

Perhaps no one has a better grasp of what Iowa cooking's all about than the radio homemakers. "If it's truly Midwestern, it's a very basic, hearty, rather simple type of cooking," Mrs. Birkby explained. "If I'm going to serve an Iowa dinner, the main course would probably be fried chicken with potatoes and gravy, roast beef and noodles, or maybe an extra-thick pork chop—we call them Iowa chops—and corn on the cob fresh from the garden.

"There would be homemade bread with strawberry jam and of course some type of dessert—maybe apple pie. Midwesterners eat lots of desserts: cookies, cakes, pies, homemade ice cream. That's *my* idea of Iowa cooking, although a cook twenty years younger than me may tell you something completely different."

If her husband's tastes are any indication, Iowans generally go for foods that are homey and familiar. "Just the other night, we had a Middle Eastern tabbouleh salad which I thought was quite good. But my husband said, 'I've never tasted anything so silly in my life!' When I asked him what he meant by that, he said, 'My mother never made it.'"

Throughout the years, the radio station has published numerous cookbooks written by the homemakers. The most comprehensive is *Cooking with KMA, Featuring 60 Years of Radio Homemakers* (KMA Broadcasting, Shenandoah, Iowa 51601), written by Evelyn Birkby in 1985. In this gem of a book, Mrs. Birkby traces the history of the homemaking programs from the station's beginning to the present, with biographies, photographs, and recipes depicting the distinctive personalities of each homemaker. Here are some excerpts.

JESSIE YOUNG

"Jessie was the first. The first to become a long-term KMA radio homemaker. The first to broadcast directly from her home. The first of the KMA women broadcasters to share her experiences and her housekeeping, sewing and cooking expertise with her listeners in depth and in detail for many years . . .

"She and her husband Floyd belonged to the Congregational Church Choir in Shenandoah and this is the choir which participated in the very first broadcast on January 17, 1924. . . . By late 1926, Jessie had her own program. 'The Stitch and Chat Club' gradually became 'A Visit with Jessie Young.'

" . . . in 1946 she began publishing 'Jessie's Homemaker (Radio . . . Visit).' . . . Publication continued until 1980 when Jessie's eyesight began to fail. Over the years, Jessie has also published twenty cookbooks and sewing books which sold thousands of copies.

"One of the funniest recipes ever printed appeared in Jessie's Home-maker Magazine. 'I was not well when this particular issue was ready to go to press and I didn't get to proofread it. I don't know what happened to the people who pasted it up and set the type, but it sure got cob-bobled. Don't try to make it!' Jessie chuckles."

Soft Molasses Drop Cookies

2 tablespoons fat	¾ teaspoon cinnamon
1 clove garlic, crushed	¾ teaspoon ginger
1 frying chicken, cut up	¾ cup shortening
1½ teaspoons salt	¾ cup sugar
½ cup water	2 eggs
3 cups sifted flour	½ cup buttermilk
1 tablespoon soda	½ cup molasses
1½ teaspoons salt	1 cup raisins

Sift flour, soda, salt, and spices together. Cream shortening and sugar, add eggs, buttermilk, and molasses. Beat until smooth. Add flour, mixing until smooth . . .

Try this instead.

Cornhusker Salad

Break crisp lettuce into small pieces. Add sliced radishes, cucumbers, a quartered tomato, julienne-cut green pepper, celery, carrots, green onions and ham cut in medium-sized chunks. Toss with salad dressing of your choice.

BERNICE CURRIER

"By 1927, when Bernice moved with her children to Shenandoah, KMA had been on the air for twenty months. In March of that year, Earl asked Bernice to join the radio staff. Since she was a highly trained concert violinist, much of her early airtime was spent as a musician. As was true with most of the earliest performers, however, she served wherever she was needed.

"Bernice's name is listed on the schedule as early as November of 1927 for the 'Home Hour.' She was also involved in the 'Domestic Science' show and one program simply called 'Visit.' She narrated fashion shows (yes, on the radio), gave commercials and had a contest for prune recipes . . .

"After her children were grown, Bernice left KMA to work for stations in South Dakota, Texas and Cairo, Illinois. . . . Following the death of her mother in 1948, Bernice returned to Shenandoah to make a home for her father. Soon she was back on KMA. By then the effects of a long siege of crippling arthritis had eroded her ability to play her beloved violin. Mr. May, who tried to solve as many problems of his faithful staff as he could, suggested that a place be made for Bernice in the women's department. . . . She started her 1948 program, 'A Visit with Bernice,' with the words, 'I've reared a family and managed a home for forty years. Now I would like to share my experiences with you listeners so you can learn easily what it took me years to find out . . .'

"Billie Oakley describes Bernice as 'a gutsy woman, one who was born before her time. She did her own thing without too much concern for public opinion as long as she knew it was right. She resented being paid less than men. She made $50.00 per week and out of that she paid for the food which she was expected to serve the radio visitors who stopped at her house.

"'In fact, so many listeners came that they wore out her living room rug. When Bernice told Earl May about it he realized it was the responsibility of KMA to replace the carpet, and saw it was done.'

"Some of the radio homemakers developed individual styles for giving recipes. As the years went by, Bernice created the A-B-C method of listing ingredients and describing the mixing. Although she used other styles from time to time, Bernice came to prefer the A-B-C technique as simple, direct and easy to follow."

New 24-Hour Salad
with Creamy Dressing

1 cup small green seedless grapes   *1 cup diced orange*
1 cup diced ripe banana   *1 cup cantaloupe balls*
1 cup diced fresh or canned   *2 plums, fresh or canned, sliced*
*   pineapple*   *2 cups miniature marshmallows*
1 cup pitted fresh or canned Bing   *2 8-ounce cartons sour cream (or*
*   cherries*   *   enough to moisten)*

Combine all ingredients except the sour cream, then stir in the sour cream gently but thoroughly (or use the following dressing instead of the sour cream). Spoon the salad into a bowl, cover, and chill for twenty-four hours. At serving time, serve on individual plates garnished with sprigs of mint and more fruit, if desired. Makes about 2 quarts of salad.

Creamy Dressing

A: 2 eggs mixed with fork   *B: 1 tablespoon butter*
*   2 tablespoons granulated*   *   Dash of salt*
*   sugar*   *C: 2 8-ounce cartons sour cream*
*   2 tablespoons orange juice*
*   2 tablespoons vinegar*

Mix A ingredients in a saucepan. Cook over low heat, stirring constantly, until mixture thickens to consistency of sour cream. Remove from heat and stir in B ingredients. Cool thoroughly, then gently stir in C. Stir this mixture gently into the salad ingredients.

LEANNA DRIFTMIER
AND THE "KITCHEN-KLATTER" FAMILY

"The 'Mother's Hour' was a name devised by Helen Fischer [Leanna's sister], not Leanna, and as Leanna felt more at home before the microphone, she wanted a program name of her own. She ran a contest, and a Nebraska listener sent in the winning suggestion, 'Kitchen-Klatter.'

"Another of Leanna's many radio competitions was the Good Neighbor Contest, in which she asked listeners to tell about a good neighbor in a hundred words or less. First prize was a fine pocket-book.

"'Kitchen-Klatter' also sponsored some weight-loss contests. Participants who lost the most pounds were invited to the Driftmier home where they stepped on a scale to prove the pounds were gone, and then celebrated by sitting down to a big, fattening covered-dish dinner."

One of the family's all-time favorite recipes is this delectable yeast roll. Lucile was sold on trying it because the "Kitchen-Klatter" friend who sent it said, "This is a foolproof recipe if ever there was one. It has certainly made the rounds, and girls who have trouble getting light rolls can make them literally fly off the plate."

Fly-off-the-Plate Rolls

2 packages dry yeast
½ cup warm water
2 cups hot water
½ cup granulated sugar

3 tablespoons butter
   (don't substitute)
6 to 6½ cups all-purpose flour
   (approximately)
3 teaspoons salt

Dissolve yeast in warm water. Heat 2 cups of water and pour over the sugar and butter. Add 2 cups of flour, beating as hard as possible after each addition, and when mixture is warm, not hot, add to the dissolved yeast. Add balance of flour to which you have added the salt. Knead well and then place in a greased bowl and let rise until double in bulk. Preheat oven to 375 degrees. Shape dough into rolls or buns, let rise again until double, then bake for about 18 to 20 minutes. Makes 20 to 24 rolls.

Lucile's Tomato Scallop

6 tablespoons butter or margarine
1 cup dry bread crumbs
2 tablespoons minced onion
3 cups canned tomatoes
5 tablespoons minute tapioca

1 tablespoon granulated sugar
Salt and pepper to taste
½ teaspoon paprika
1 cup grated medium cheddar
   cheese
¾ cup sliced stuffed olives

Preheat oven to 350 degrees. In a skillet, melt 4 tablespoons butter or margarine and stir in bread crumbs until they are lightly browned and toasted. Set aside. In a heavy pan, melt the remaining 2 tablespoons butter or margarine and stir in the minced onion. Add tomatoes, tapioca, sugar, and seasonings. Cook for 5 minutes, stirring constantly (it will bubble up violently and splash unless you keep the fire very low and stir energetically). Butter a 1½-quart casserole (not a flat baking-type) and sprinkle in a layer of toasted crumbs. Cover them with a layer of the tomato mixture, grated cheese, and green olives; repeat. Top with quite a thick sprinkling of the buttered crumbs and bake for 40 minutes. Makes 4 to 6 servings.

DORIS MURPHY

"In 1949, Doris took to the air with her 'Party Line' broadcast. It included news, hints, home beautification and recipes. . . . Doris was influential in many of the great homemaker days held in the Mayfield auditorium. For a time they were monthly events, each built around a theme—one time the subject was paint, the next the way to carpet your home; many were built around food preparation . . .

"It was Doris who started the famous KMA Cookie Teas. . . . Said Doris: 'The first tea was held in 1954 near Christmastime, so we called it the "KMA Christmas Cookie Tea." I worked very hard to make the event beautiful, interesting and entertaining.'

"Each of the homemakers made cookies and decorations for display and arranged her own table with some kind of Christmas arrangement. Doris brought pink plastic tablecloths ('pink was "in" for Christmas that year') and borrowed Gertrude May's large silver candelabras. Pink and green candles were placed in the silver holders and evergreens were added to the table centerpieces. Live talent furnished music and a speaker talked about Christmas decorations.

"The first tea was held in the old Elks building located west of the Shenandoah library. Over 300 women came with their cookies and recipes. . . . The Cookie Tea became an annual affair which continued for years under Doris' direction."

Typical of this era, when fluorescent Jell-O desserts were at the height of chicdom, was this candy recipe from Doris's files.

Sea-Green Jelly Squares

1 cup applesauce   *1 3-ounce package*
1 cup granulated sugar   *lime-flavored Jell-O*
                                             Granulated sugar for dipping

In a medium saucepan, combine applesauce, sugar, and Jell-O and bring
to a boil, boiling gently for 2 minutes. Pour into a well-buttered 8 × 4
× 3-inch loaf pan. Chill until set. Cut into pieces with a sharp knife
dipped in hot water. Dip each piece firmly in granulated sugar. Makes
about a dozen pieces. Variations: Replace lime-flavored Jell-O with 1
package raspberry-, cherry-, or strawberry-flavored Jell-O. Follow the
same procedure.

EDITH HANSEN

"Two world wars, a home in Shenandoah, a family and a career as one of
KMA's major radio homemakers were inexorably intertwined in the life
of Edith Hansen.

"Edith began her broadcasting experience on a Norfolk, Nebraska, station WJAG on December 31, 1940. In the spring of 1942, she and her husband and two sons moved to Shenandoah. On June 1st of that year she
began 'The Edith Hansen Kitchen Club' on KMA, replacing Jessie Young
who had left the station to move to Philadelphia.

"Life was difficult during those lean war years and Edith worked diligently to find and share the best ways to cope with the many problems
that surfaced in her own life and in the lives of her listeners . . .

"Little did Edith realize when she started her public career how much
sorrow she would share with her listeners. Eldest son Donald joined the
Marines at age 18. He was in the Iwo Jima campaign where he was
wounded and reported missing in action. When he was located and
eventually returned to the United States, Don was a paraplegic. His in-
juries eventually caused his death. Edith's husband Aage carried the
effects of World War I all his life and he died in 1948 in the Veterans
Hospital in Lincoln, Nebraska.

"Circumstances, mostly related to the war and its effects on her family, took Edith out of Shenandoah several times, but each time she returned. Eventually, along with fellow broadcaster Martha Bohlsen, Edith

KMA Broadcasting

Edith Hansen in her Shenandoah kitchen

became a part of the Tidy House syndicated radio network and was heard over 90 stations across the country."

While her son Don was recuperating in a hospital in California, Edith often boxed up treats to send to him and the other young men in his ward.

Serviceman's Special Candy

2 cups granulated sugar
1 cup cream (can use
    half-and-half)
1 tablespoon butter
1½ squares (1 ounce each) bitter
    chocolate

1 teaspoon vanilla
1 pound marshmallows
1 cup nuts, chopped
3 cups graham cracker crumbs

In a large saucepan combine sugar, cream, butter, chocolate, and vanilla. Cook to soft-ball stage (234 degrees). Remove from fire and beat in remaining ingredients. Spoon into a buttered 9 × 13-inch pan. Press firmly, then cut into squares. This candy is excellent for mailing and can be left uncut for easier packaging. Makes about 70 pieces.

ADELLA SHOEMAKER

"'Happy day to you,' was the cheerful sign-off signature of Adella Shoemaker during her days as a radio homemaker. 'Cookbook Time' was one title for Adella's broadcast, but she also used the term 'Kitchen Klinik' during the time when using K's instead of C's seemed to be one way to attract attention . . .

"In 1952, four years after coming to KMA, Adella became director of women's activities for the Georgie Porgie breakfast cereal company and her program was syndicated.

"A list of Adella's favorite recipes would invariably include Soda Cracker Pie, Crystal Pickles and French Chocolate Silk Pie. A funny story was told recently about the Soda Cracker Pie. A radio listener gave a 1984 bride a copy of the recipe. The young woman read the ingredients of the recipe, laughingly declared it was a great joke to suggest she put soda crackers into a dessert, and threw the recipe away!

KMA Broadcasting

Adella Shoemaker

"The friend who had given the recipe to the newlywed made up the light, delicious pie and presented it as a gift to the bride with a duplicate copy of the recipe."

Soda Cracker Pie

3 egg whites
1 cup granulated sugar
14 soda crackers, rolled very fine
¼ teaspoon baking powder
½ cup broken pecans
1 teaspoon vanilla

2 or 3 peeled, thinly sliced fresh peaches, or
well-drained canned
1 cup whipping cream, stiffly whipped and
sweetened to taste

Preheat oven to 325 degrees. Beat egg whites stiff; gradually beat in sugar. Add soda crackers, baking powder, and pecans. Flavor with vanilla. Fill a 9-inch buttered pie plate with this mixture. Bake for 30 minutes in pre-heated oven. Cool. Top with a layer of thinly sliced peaches. Blanket with a layer of whipped cream (it will take 1 cup) and store in refrigerator overnight. The pie is much improved by storing, so don't be afraid to follow these directions. Makes 6 to 8 servings.

Adella passed on this helpful household hint to her readers.

Mildew Remover

Soak garments stained with mildew in 2 quarts water, ½ cup liquid bleach, and ½ cup vinegar. Wash after stain is completely removed in hot, soapy water.

WARREN NIELSON

"Men have also been radio homemakers. . . . Through the years he was on KMA, Warren Nielson hosted an amazing variety of programs including 'Kiddie Korner,' 'Party Line,' and 'Sportsman.' On the 'Party Line' people called in to ask Warren all kinds of questions—how to blow soap bubbles, trace down strange noises in the night, what to do with old hens, how to find the owner of 20 stray hogs, the best way to make snickerdoodles and how a person can unzip the back zipper in a dress when she is all alone, things like that. On the 'Sportsman' program, Warren featured stories of hunting and fishing and then gave the readers recipes for preparing wild game."

Warren's Cozy Rabbit

6 to 8 slices bacon
2 rabbits, cut into serving pieces

CURRANT JELLY SAUCE:
2 tablespoons butter

3 tablespoons all-purpose flour
1 cup water or stock
Salt and pepper to taste
⅓ cup currant jelly
2 tablespoons sherry

Preheat oven to 350 degrees. Fry bacon. Reserve cooked bacon and use the fat to brown the rabbits. Place the browned meat in a baking pan and arrange bacon on top.

For the sauce, melt the butter, stir in flour, and brown together. Add water or stock gradually, simmer gently, and stir until smooth. Add salt and pepper. Melt currant jelly in the sauce and add sherry. Pour the sauce over the meat. Bake in preheated oven until meat is tender, about 1 hour. If bunny has tough muscles, this is sure to tenderize them. Makes 4 to 6 servings.

EVELYN BIRKBY

"In the fall of 1949, the publisher of the *Shenandoah Evening Sentinel* advertised for a farm woman to write a weekly newspaper column. I applied, I was accepted, and I began a weekly column called 'Up a Country Lane.' My column was read by Doris Murphy, women's director for KMA. Ever alert for women she felt had something of value to offer radio listeners, Doris asked me to try broadcasting.

"KMA decided that 'Down a Country Lane' sounded more poetic than 'Up' so they gave my program that title. The lilting tune 'Swingin' Down the Lane' was the theme music."

Evelyn's Gourmet Chicken

1 8-ounce can crescent rolls (you can make your own yeast dough if desired)
1 5-ounce can boned chicken
1 8-ounce package cream cheese
⅓ cup (2 ounces) chopped water chestnuts

1 tablespoon lemon juice
Pinch of sage or poultry seasoning
Salt and pepper to taste
¼ teaspoon chicken bouillon granules
Melted butter and dry bread crumbs (optional)

Preheat oven to 375 degrees. Roll out dough *very* thin. Combine remaining ingredients. Spoon a portion of this chicken mixture onto each section of thin dough. Fold dough over filling to make little pillows. Place on a baking sheet and bake in preheated oven 12 to 15 minutes, or until golden brown, top and bottom. Makes 8 main-dish pastries (4 servings).

For an extra touch for company, roll each pillow in melted butter and then in fine bread crumbs before baking. These can be made a day or two ahead of time and then, just before baking, rolled in melted butter and bread crumbs and baked as directed. For hors d'oeuvres, make them very small and dainty. These are delicious!

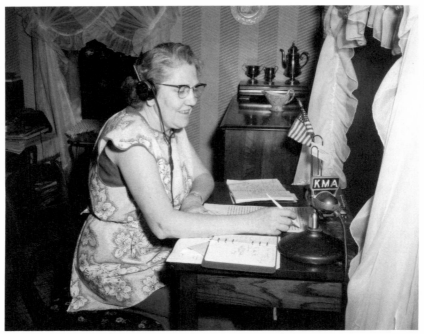

KMA Broadcasting

Florence Falk broadcasting from her home

FLORENCE FALK

"The year 1949 brought a devastating tornado to the Falk farm near Essex, Iowa. After the disaster, Florence appeared on both Adella Shoemaker's and Bernice Currier's broadcasts; listeners responded favorably. In August of 1952, when Adella began her syndicated broadcasts, Florence was asked to audition for the position of homemaker . . .

"Florence started on the air in August after doing a number of introductory broadcasts with Adella. By September, she was actually broadcasting from her farm home some eight miles north and east of Shenandoah. Her program was called 'The Farmer's Wife.' . . .

"She shared every detail of her life on the farm with listeners: her husband, Byron, whom she always called 'The Farmer' on her broadcasts, their two children Karenann and Bruce, five border collies who, in sequence, were named Tippy (Tippy I, Tippy II, etc.), and the Old Red Rooster, whose shape and sounds became the trademark of her program . . .

"The famous early KMA Cookie Teas provided a showplace for the radio homemakers. . . . Florence always included sugar cookies, staying up for hours before the festival to put little decorations onto each cookie. . . . Her rosettes, pecan tassies and snickerdoodles became traditions at the teas . . ."

The Farmer's Wife's Snickerdoodles

1 cup soft shortening
1½ cups granulated sugar
2 eggs
2¾ cups flour
2 teaspoons cream of tartar
1 teaspoon baking soda

½ teaspoon salt
2 tablespoons granulated sugar
mixed with 2 teaspoons
cinnamon
Finely chopped pecans or large
pecan halves (optional)

In a mixing bowl, cream shortening, sugar, and eggs. Sift together flour, cream of tartar, baking soda, and salt and add to creamed mixture. Chill dough for 1 hour (this is important because the dough handles much better when chilled). Preheat oven to 400 degrees. Roll dough into balls the size of walnuts (do not flatten) and then roll them in the sugar and cinnamon mixture. Place on a cookie sheet about 2 inches apart. Bake in preheated oven about 12 to 15 minutes or until nicely browned. Makes 3 to 3½ dozen.

These cookies may be made into smaller balls and rolled in finely chopped pecans for a fancy cookie. They may also be topped with a large pecan half before baking.

BILLIE OAKLEY

"Both KMA and KFNF were holding big, annual jubilees that included contests for musicians. In the summer of 1932, just before her junior year in high school, Billie traveled to Shenandoah, entered a singing contest at station KFNF, and won. She stayed in Shenandoah the rest of the summer and sang at the station for $15 a week . . .

"Later, when she first sang on KMA, Billie remembers the homemakers bringing cookies to the station to share with the musicians. . . . Billie realized she was not really a singer. It was time she developed the kind of radio program where she could utilize talking, her primary talent. Radio homemaking, she decided, was what she wanted to do.

". . . She began moderating 'The Party Line,' a program commonly known as the talk-back-to-Billie show. . . . Unfortunately, the subjects on the Party Line became overly controversial. 'Running the show as a peacemaker was giving me ulcers and the station fits,' Billie remembers. So it was taken off the air.

"Up until her retirement in February 1987, 'The Billie Oakley Show' included a half-hour segment for listeners who would like to call in. They were still welcome to express their opinions though most callers preferred to discuss recipes rather than solve the problems of the world.

"'It's a lot easier on my stomach and KMA has fewer fits,' Billie comments.

"The Indian Cake has, in a way, become Billie's good luck charm. The original recipe came from a 4-H girl to whom Billie had given a home permanent. The girl decided to bake her favorite cake and give it to Billie as a thank-you gift.

"This has become the cake which Billie has made through the years to take as a gift to welcome a new baby, to say her own thank-you to a friend, to comfort a family that has had sorrow or to take to a covered-dish dinner. 'I have many memories tied up in that small cake,' Billie says.

"When Billie began her homemaker broadcasts in 1963, the first recipe she gave was the Indian Cake."

Indian Cake

½ cup shortening or 1 stick
   margarine
2 cups granulated sugar
2 eggs
½ cup cocoa
½ cup cold, strong coffee
2 cups all-purpose flour

1 teaspoon baking soda
1 teaspoon salt
1 teaspoon vanilla
½ teaspoon burnt sugar flavoring
   (optional)
1 cup boiling-hot water

Preheat oven to 350 degrees. In a mixing bowl, cream together shortening and sugar. Add remaining ingredients, except boiling-hot water, in order given and mix until smoothly blended. Carefully blend in the hot water. Pour batter into a greased and floured 9 × 13-inch pan. Bake in preheated oven approximately 30 minutes or until cake tester inserted in middle comes out clean. Cool and frost. Makes 9 to 12 servings.

Indian Cake Frosting

1 cup granulated sugar
⅓ cup water
⅓ teaspoon cream of tartar

2 egg whites
Vanilla and/or almond flavoring
  to taste

In a heavy pan mix together the sugar, water, and cream of tartar. Bring to a boil. Cook until syrup forms a hard ball in cold water. Stiffly beat the egg whites. Drizzle boiling hot syrup onto the egg whites while you continue to beat at a medium high speed. Flavor with vanilla or your favorite flavoring (I prefer vanilla and almond). For a lovely color, substitute maraschino cherry juice for water.

ITALIAN COAL MINERS

When Mary Batteni Sertich was growing up in southern Iowa, having overnight guests rarely meant a visit from an out-of-town relative or friend of the family's. Rather, it meant she, her parents, and five siblings would have to squeeze into their squat four-room house a little tighter to make room for complete strangers, as many as four at a time.

Like many other wives of Italian coal miners in Iowa, Mrs. Sertich's mother supplemented her husband's meager salary by feeding, clothing, and providing a place to sleep for teenage newcomers to America. Room, board, and all other services were provided at a cost of two or three dollars per person. Some of the boarders stayed a few nights, others stayed years. "Mama always treated the boarders as if they were her own children," Mrs. Sertich said.

Though the boarders were usually strangers to the family at first, it usually didn't take long before a kindred bond developed between them. Only a few years earlier, Mrs. Sertich's parents had left their own home and family in the mountains of northern Italy for a flimsy wooden company house in a coal camp on a barren Iowa prairie. The boxlike structures, lined up uniformly like rows of corn, were painted gray or brick-red. They were small, run-down, and poorly constructed, with leaky roofs, loose window sills, and warped doors. In the winter the pumps froze, and in the summer the wells often dried up. Steam water frequently had to be brought up from the mines for washing clothes.

All the women strictly adhered to the old-country tradition of maintaining their domestic roles in the home as wives and mothers. Yet in many instances they brought in almost as much money as their husbands. Besides taking in boarders, they often sold dairy products or garden vegetables or performed services for other mining families. For a few extra dollars some would pick up chunks of coal that fell from the loading chute along the railroad tracks.

For first-generation Italian-American women like Mrs. Sertich's mother, the work day began around 4:00 A.M., tending the large gardens and fruit trees, canning fruits and vegetables, milking the cows, making butter and cheese, baking bread and pastries for the men's lunches, rolling out pasta for evening meals.

Nothing ever went to waste in these Italian-American households. "We had a big garden; that was a must," Mrs. Sertich remembered. "My father was the butcher in the community; he slaughtered mostly pork and chicken and a little beef. My mother always saved the feet of the chickens and made a delicious broth with them. She'd use the heads, too, if Dad didn't eat them first!" The women made salami, blood sausage, and head cheese, which could be kept for extended periods of time. Once a year the men made wine with the grapes from their vineyards.

Breakfasts were simple. "Lots of times we'd just have big bowls of coffee and milk with crackers and cheese," Mrs. Sertich said. But other meals were considerably more substantial. "Sometimes the boarders would go out hunting and bring back game for Mama to cook. It might be a rabbit or squirrel; other times, it would be some sparrows, or a skunk."

Flora Betta, a first-generation Italian-American, noted that "people today think they have come up with something new with this thing they call 'quiche.' Well, we had quiches all our lives! Frittatas, we called them. Mama would crack some eggs into that old black skillet with some onions and zucchini, or maybe spinach or asparagus. She might stick in a few slices of bread, and mix in a little hamburger or cheese, if we had it. She'd cook it over a real slow fire 'til it set, then she'd flip it onto a plate. And we'd have a nice, beautiful pie—only with no crust."

And of course there was always homemade pasta. "My mother would use a long rolling pin, sort of like a broomstick only a little wider, to make her pasta for ravioli," Mrs. Sertich recalled. "After she'd roll out a real thin layer of dough, she'd put little spoonfuls of filling on top. Then she'd cut them into squares, and give each one of us little kids a fork to seal them shut."

For Mrs. Sertich, the daily cooking chores she was responsible for included packing substantial lunches for her father and the boarders and later for her husband, John. Usually lunch consisted of two big sandwiches, filled with either ham and cheese or salami, and canned fruit. "Johnny used to say canned fruit tasted good down in the mines. We did lots of canning then since there was no refrigeration."

Cooking was only one of the duties Mrs. Sertich learned as a young child. Another was cleaning house, which required as many helping hands as possible, especially since "we had no running water, no electricity, and we had to wash all the men's 'pit' pants by hand," she explained. "They were always filthy black with coal dust."

Without proper plumbing facilities, bathing, an activity which per-

mitted little modesty, was particularly cumbersome for the miners and
their families. Even so, Mrs. Sertich's mother was strict with the boarders when it came to personal hygiene. When the men returned from the
mines, the women would drag out washtubs and fill them with warm
water. "One boarder—his name was Frank—used to tell my mother he
couldn't take baths, or else he would rust," Mrs. Sertich said, laughing.
"But she told him, 'You will if you plan to sleep in my house!'"

In the early days especially entertainment was almost nonexistent.
The tiny coal-mining town of Granger offered no outside activities, and
there was no transportation to a larger city. But community ties were
strong, especially since many of the town's occupants were from the
same villages in Italy. "Every now and then we'd have a picnic, or visit
relations," Mrs. Sertich said. "We'd play bocci ball. Sometimes for fun
the kids would see how far they could roll a wheel of real hard cheese
down the street before it fell over." Weddings were particularly festive
occasions. "We always had a dance in somebody's house after we left
the church," Mrs. Sertich recalled. "And everyone would dance all night.
I remember going to a wedding when I was eight or nine years old; that
was the first time I'd ever stayed up 'til midnight."

By the 1940s, most of Iowa's coal-mining operations had shut down.
The coal-mining families had moved to the closest incorporated town,
where the men commuted by automobile to work. But in several small
southern Iowa towns like Granger you can still spot such names as
Biondi, Cerrato, and Brugioni on the mailboxes as you drive through the
peaceful middle-class neighborhoods. The yards are neatly manicured,
blooming with flowers and shrubs—a far cry from those of the drab
mining camps.

There's more time for socializing these days, and most residents take
full advantage of it. Many participate in activities connected with the
Italian Lodge and the Catholic church in Granger. Every summer a number of residents take part in the Italian festival celebrated in Des Moines.
And they particularly enjoy getting together with friends and relatives to
share the culinary delicacies passed on to them by their parents and
grandparents.

"Every now and then, a group of friends and relatives will go up to
Chester Park and make polenta (cornmeal mush) and tomato sauce over
an open fire," John Sertich said. "That's really a community treat." Mrs.
Betta added that she sometimes invites company over for "Bagna Cauda."
"Everybody takes some cabbage leaves and bread and dips them in a
sauce made with garlic, anchovy, and butter. It stinks, but it's good!"

At Christmastime, Mrs. Betta plans a big feast for a house full of relatives. Though the main course—pork roast and mashed potatoes—is

all-American, there are always heaping side dishes of tortellini ("just like ravioli, except it's shaped like little hats") to go with it. Dessert for a special occasion would likely be torta di riso, a sweet rice pie topped with almonds. But all year round, both the Bettas' and Sertiches' cookie jars are likely to be filled with contuccis, a tender, anise-flavored cookie with almonds.

Here are some of the family favorites.

Spinach Ravioli

¼ cup (½ stick) butter
½ medium onion, chopped
1 clove garlic, minced
1 10-ounce package chopped spinach, thawed, drained, and squeezed dry
1 3-ounce package cream cheese

½ carton (1 cup) dry ricotta cheese (or drained in a sieve)
⅓ cup grated Parmesan cheese
2 eggs, slightly beaten
¾ cup soft bread crumbs
Salt, pepper, and nutmeg to taste
Pasta dough (recipe follows)

In a skillet over medium heat, sauté the onion and garlic in butter until tender. Add spinach and sauté until tender. Turn heat down to low and stir in cream cheese, ricotta, and Parmesan until they melt. Mix in eggs, bread crumbs, and seasonings. Set aside.

On a floured surface, roll out one of the balls of pasta dough from the center outward with a long, thin rolling pin or a floured broom handle until dough is very thin (or put through a pasta maker according to manufacturer's directions). Place teaspoons of filling in rows several inches apart. Roll out the other ball and place on top. Cut into squares and seal edges by pressing them with a fork. Boil in a large pot of boiling water about 10 minutes, or until tender. Serve with a sauce made of melted butter, cream, a dash of garlic, and "quite a bit of Parmesan cheese." Or serve with tomato sauce (recipe follows). Makes 6 to 8 main-course servings.

Pasta Dough

3 cups all-purpose flour
4 large eggs
1 tablespoon oil

1 tablespoon water
½ teaspoon salt

Make a well in the flour. Break eggs into the well. Add oil, water, and salt. Beat the mixture in the well, then mix all ingredients together until smooth. Place dough on floured surface and knead with heel of hand, giving it a quarter turn and folding it over with each push. Let rest, covered, 10 minutes. Knead again until the dough is smooth and elastic. Divide the dough into two balls and let them rest in a plastic bag about 30 minutes. Roll out according to above recipe. Makes enough pasta for 3½ to 4 dozen ravioli.

Tomato Sauce

1 or 2 cloves garlic, minced
1 large onion, chopped
1 cup chopped celery
2 tablespoons oil or butter
1 medium carrot, grated
3 to 4 tablespoons chopped
　parsley
1 teaspoon salt

¼ teaspoon crumbled rosemary
⅛ teaspoon pepper
1½ pounds beef cubes
12 large fresh tomatoes, peeled,
　seeded, and chopped (or 8 cups
　canned tomatoes, seeded and
　chopped)

In a Dutch oven over medium heat, brown the garlic, onion, and celery in oil or butter. Add the carrot, parsley, and seasonings. Add meat and brown. Add tomatoes and enough water to half cover the meat (if using canned tomatoes, add the juice from the can and additional water if necessary). Cook over low heat, partially covered, about 2 hours, stirring occasionally. Remove meat and serve separately or save for another meal. Makes 6 to 8 servings.

Zucchini Frittata

¼ cup (½ stick) butter
½ large onion, chopped
1 garlic clove, minced
1 medium zucchini, thinly sliced

Salt and pepper to taste
½ cup grated Parmesan (or
　cheddar) cheese (optional)
6 eggs, beaten

In an 8-to-10-inch skillet, melt butter over low heat. Sauté onion, garlic, and zucchini until tender. Add salt, pepper, and cheese, if desired, to eggs. Pour over vegetables. Allow mixture to set. Loosen frittata with spatula. Place a plate on top of the skillet and flip frittata onto the plate. Slip frittata back into skillet for a few minutes until cooked underneath. Makes 4 servings.

This unusual dessert was a surprise hit with tasters. It features a meltingly rich, cookielike crust and a dense, almond-scented filling with a pleasantly chewy texture that reminded one taster of coconut.

Torta di Riso (Rice Pie)

CRUST:

1 cup (2 sticks) butter   ½ teaspoon granulated sugar
2 cups all-purpose flour
1 egg yolk, mixed with enough
   milk to equal ½ cup

FILLING:

1¼ cups milk   1 tablespoon almond extract
1 cup water   4 eggs, separated
Dash salt   1 to 1¼ cups granulated sugar
1 cup long-grain white rice

TOPPING:

5 to 6 ounces almonds   ¼ cup granulated sugar

To make the crust, cut butter into flour with a pastry blender or two knives until mixture resembles coarse crumbs. Add remaining ingredients and toss lightly with fork. Do not overmix. Pat out in two 9-inch pie plates.

In a 2- or 3-quart saucepan, bring the milk, water, and salt to a boil, watching carefully so that mixture does not boil over. Add rice, reduce heat, and simmer, tightly covered, until rice is tender, 15 to 20 minutes. Cool, then stir in almond extract. Beat egg yolks with sugar until light and lemon colored and mix into rice. Beat egg whites until stiff and fold into rice mixture.

Preheat oven to 400 degrees. For the topping, grind the almonds with sugar in a blender. Sprinkle over top of pie. Bake in a preheated oven 15 to 20 minutes, or until knife inserted in center comes out clean. Cool before slicing. Makes 12 servings.

Contucci Cookies

1 cup (2 sticks) butter
2¼ cups granulated sugar
6 eggs
1 teaspoon lemon extract

2 teaspoons anise extract
8 cups all-purpose flour
6 teaspoons baking powder
*1 pound chopped almonds (or
    walnuts)*

In a large mixing bowl, cream together butter and sugar until fluffy. Beat in eggs and flavorings. Sift together flour and baking powder and add to creamed mixture. Add nuts and stir until you have a stiff dough. Chill several hours. Preheat oven to 300 degrees. Shape pieces of dough into log forms about 1½ inches in diameter. Slice into cookies about ¼ inch thick and bake on cookie sheet for 20 to 25 minutes, or until lightly browned around the edges. Makes about 160 2-inch cookies. (Recipe may easily be cut in half.)

REMEMBERING BUXTON

The town of Buxton may be gone from the map but not forgotten. Dorothy Collier and other former residents still fondly remember the bustling coal-mining community as "the black man's utopia of Iowa." Founded by the Consolidation Coal Company in 1900, Buxton had one distinct feature which set it apart from Iowa's other coal-mining towns: well over half its population was black. And it possessed another characteristic rarely found anywhere else in the country during that era: it was virtually free of discrimination.

"I had a lot of beautiful experiences growin' up in Buxton," said Mrs. Collier, who now lives in a cozy little house in Des Moines filled with greenery and family photographs. "My mind's a-goin' down and there's a lot I can't remember. But then, what do you expect from a lady who's seventy—or is it seventy-five?" As she flipped through the pages of her bulging photo album, however, those memories started coming back to her.

Mrs. Collier's father came to Buxton from Muchakinock after the coal mines there played out. He was recruited by Ben Buxton, the mining company supervisor who practically "owned the town," she said. "He was a lovely man. He paid everyone equally; there was never any discrimination or segregation."

Not only did the blacks and whites of Buxton work together, they attended school together, played together, lived in the same neighborhoods. "We did have both a white and colored Methodist church," Mrs. Collier added. "But we could attend either service we wanted." Although most of the black men who moved to Buxton started out working in the mines, many later attained white-collar positions in town as doctors, lawyers, druggists, and sales clerks. Mrs. Collier's father, George Neal, became a tailor, always spruced up for work in a handsome three-piece suit, starched white shirt, bow tie, and gold pocket watch attached to his vest. "Never in my life did I see my father go into town when he wasn't wearing his bow tie," she said. Her mother's wardrobe was equally lavish: fine lace gowns with high Victorian collars, dainty evening slippers for balls, fancy touring hats held firmly over her coiffured bouffant by sheer scarves tied under the chin. "They were a dressin' bunch in Buxton, I tell you," Mrs. Collier said wistfully.

The company houses Ben Buxton provided for his workers were much more comfortable than the miners' homes in other coal camps in the state. All were painted dark red, had five or six rooms, and were maintained well by the coal company. Mrs. Collier remembered that in the home she shared with her parents and brother "there was wall-to-wall carpet tacked down to the floors. In the living room there was a pretty green davenport, a couple of rockers, and a lamp with one of those Tiffany shades."

The cupboards were always well stocked in the Neals' household. "We didn't have an icebox, but we had a smokehouse where we used to preserve all our meats: bacon, smoked hams, pork chops, roasts." They also had a large garden, some chickens, and a few fruit trees. She and her brother, she recalled, often gathered berries for her mother to use for making jellies.

Breakfasts were typically hefty back then, especially when her father worked in the mines. "Toast and coffee and an egg or two just wasn't enough to keep the coal miners until lunch," she said. "We nearly always had fried chops or liver, with hot biscuits and maybe corn bread."

If her mother was able to get to the fish market, for a change they would have "salt mackerel soaked in water overnight, then cooked with a little water, some butter and some egg slices on top." The children were strictly disciplined in manners, particularly at the dinner table. "Mama made us all napkins out of flour sacks, and she taught us real early how to use our silverware proper. Of course, we always had to wash our hands and faces and brush our hair before we sat down at the table. If we had a lady over for dinner, like our school teacher, my brother would always pull her chair out for her."

Before they could begin passing the piping-hot platters and bowls around the table there was a blessing. "Sometimes I didn't think those prayers would ever end, especially when I was real hungry and the smell of all that good food made me even hungrier," she laughed. "One time I whispered to my uncle, 'Could you please not pray so long?' But Papa heard me and I got a spanking for that."

One of her favorite dinners, she recalled, began with an appetizer of hog's head cheese on crackers, followed by a main course of chicken or salmon croquettes, with black-eyed peas and mustard greens with turnip tops on the side. And even if belts had to be loosened a notch or two, everyone somehow managed to find room for one of her mother's delectable desserts. "Sometimes she'd make one-egg cake," Mrs. Collier

Neal family portrait from Mrs. Dorothy Collier's album

remembered. "It was real simple, but a delicious cake. Usually she'd serve it with a custard sauce. And she made lots of pies: lemon or apple or berry." If the fruit trees weren't so abundant, Mrs. Neal might make an Irish potato pie that "tasted a lot like a custard, with nutmeg." Or else she'd make a vinegar pie, a cider-flavored custard pie which made a surprisingly tasty stand-in for apple pie.

There was plenty of holiday spirit in Buxton at Christmastime. "I never saw the Christmas tree 'til Christmas morning. Then I'd come downstairs and it would be all lit up with little candles clipped on its branches." That afternoon, the family would sit down to a feast of stuffed goose, cranberries, and all the trimmings, a tradition Mrs. Collier carried on long after she moved from Buxton. "But for some reason, it just never tasted as good as it did back then."

Little Dorothy rarely spent much time helping her mother cook or doing any other household chores, for that matter. "Us kids did nothing but play and play, all day long," she said. "We did have to carry our little buckets down to the railroad tracks to pick up coal now and then. But mostly, we just played ball, flew kites, climbed trees, went berry picking."

She especially looked forward to going into town on shopping sprees with her mother. "Mama and I would walk down the cinder road and rent the surrey, the kind that had a purple canopy with fringe around it," she recalled. "It was sort of like the taxi in those days." After trying on clothes at the Monroe Mercantile Company, they'd stop in for lunch at a little sandwich shop on the square. While her mother went to the hairdresser, Dorothy was allowed to treat herself to an ice cream sundae at the soda fountain.

Buxton never lacked for entertainment. At one time it had a large YMCA which boasted a star basketball team, a swimming pool, tennis courts, pool rooms, roller skating facilities, weekly musical concerts put on by the town band, minstrel shows, and speeches by such notables as George Washington Carver. The liveliest time of year was during baseball season. Mrs. Collier's father played second base and shortstop for the Buxton Wonders, the pride of the community. Regarded as "professional" by hometown fans, the players traveled throughout the state and played host to teams from such cities as Chicago, Kansas City, and St. Paul.

There was much socializing among the women. "Of course they had their federated clubs, where they'd get together and do things like can and sew," she said. "Whenever they'd come over for quilting and refreshments, Mama would give me a needle and thread to poke through the quilt, too."

Mrs. Collier loved to go to school, which she remembered as having lots of "spelling bees, recitation, and singing. I always liked to sing, even though I never could carry a tune." One thing she could do, however, was play the organ her mother had bought for her. When she was older, she played for her church choir.

Mrs. Collier was nine years old when the coal mines folded and her family moved away to Cedar Rapids. "It's just like a pasture now," she said, a little sadly. "After we left Buxton, life just never was the same."

Several years ago she and a group of other former Buxton residents formed the Buxton Club to try to preserve as much of their hometown's history as they could. Among the vestiges which haven't completely faded away are the recipes for some of the dishes most enjoyed by its citizens. Mrs. Collier could still remember the ingredients for some of her mother's creations. "Sometimes Mama cooked from what she already knew. But her favorite cookbook was the *White House Cookbook,* a big white cookbook with a picture of the capitol on the front that had tips for curin' arthritis and getting rid of bedbugs."

Company Salmon Croquettes

2 cups mashed potatoes   *2 beaten eggs*
2 cups flaked salmon   *Salt and pepper to taste*
1 tablespoon grated onion   *¾ cup cracker crumbs*
1 tablespoon mayonnaise, or   *Oil for deep-fat frying*
  mayonnaise-type salad dressing   *1 cup medium white sauce*
  ("Mother's was homemade. . .")   *(optional)*

In a large bowl, mix together potatoes, salmon, onion, mayonnaise, 1 beaten egg, salt, and pepper. Cover and chill several hours. Pull off small handfuls of mixture and shape into cones. Dip in remaining beaten egg, then roll in cracker crumbs. Fry in hot (375-degree) oil until golden brown. Top with white sauce if desired. Makes 15 to 18 croquettes.

Mustard Greens with Turnip Tops

1 pound pork hocks or bacon, cut   *2 pounds chopped turnip tops,*
  into squares   *leaves only (use less if very*
3 pounds fresh mustard greens   *strong)*
                                       ½ cup chopped onion
                                       Salt and pepper to taste

In a large kettle with just enough water to cover, simmer meat for 45 minutes to 1 hour. Wash greens, leaf by leaf. Add greens, turnip tops, onion, and seasonings to kettle and simmer for 1 hour. Makes 8 to 10 servings.

Vinegar Pie

3 egg yolks
1 cup brown sugar, level (not packed)
¼ cup granulated sugar
3 tablespoons cornstarch
¼ teaspoon salt
¼ cup cider vinegar
2 cups boiling water

1 tablespoon butter
1 9-inch pie shell

MERINGUE:
3 egg whites
3 tablespoons sugar
Few drops lemon extract

Preheat oven to 400 degrees. In the top of a double boiler, beat egg yolks until thick, then add brown sugar, white sugar, cornstarch, salt, and vinegar. Add boiling water, stirring constantly. Cook over simmering water until thick and smooth. Add butter just before removing from stove. Meanwhile, bake shell (pricked with a fork first) at 400 degrees for three minutes. Remove crust; reduce oven to 325 degrees.

In a mixing bowl, beat egg whites with sugar (one tablespoon at a time) and lemon extract until stiff, but not dry, peaks form. Pour custard into shell, then cover with meringue. Bake until both crust and meringue are brown, about 25 minutes. Makes one 9-inch pie.

This recipe was adapted from the *White House Cookbook* by Janet Halliday (Follet Publishing Co., Chicago, 1964).

No one (not even me) volunteered to test this next recipe, so try it at your own risk.

Head Cheese

Boil the forehead, ears, feet, and nice scraps trimmed from the hams of a fresh pig until the meat will almost drop from the bones. Then separate the meat from the bones, place it in a large chopping bowl, and season with pepper, salt, sage, and summer savory. Chop it rather coarsely; put it back in the same kettle it was boiled in, with just enough of the liquid in which it was boiled to prevent its burning; then warm it thoroughly, mixing it well together. Now pour it into a strong muslin bag, press the bag between two flat surfaces with a heavy weight on top, then chill. When cold and solid it can be cut in slices. Good cold or warmed up in vinegar.

Adapted from the *White House Cookbook* by Hugo Zieman and Mrs. F. L. Gillette (Saulfield Publishing Co., New York, 1914).

One-Egg Cake

½ cup granulated sugar
1 tablespoon butter
1 egg
½ cup milk

1 heaping cup all-purpose flour
1 teaspoon baking powder
1 teaspoon vanilla
¼ teaspoon salt

Preheat oven to 375 degrees. In a mixing bowl, cream sugar, butter, and egg. Beat until very light. Add milk, flour, baking powder, vanilla, and salt. Beat well, then pour into a greased 8-inch pan. Bake 25 minutes. Use as shortcake for strawberries and other fruit or serve with custard sauce. Makes 4 to 6 servings.

Adapted from the *White House Cookbook* by Janet Halliday.

THE CLOISTERED LIFE

The Trappistine nuns of Our Lady of the Mississippi Abbey enter the cloistered life not only to fortify their souls and spirits. "Because we are incarnational, we believe in strengthening the body as well," explained Sister Rosemary, one of about twenty sisters who make up this unique spiritual community near Dubuque. The hardy, rosy-cheeked woman, whose austere black habit and stockings were set off by her gaily printed apron and bright red sneakers, had just returned to the kitchen toting a large cardboard box of freshly picked strawberries from the field to be used for the shortcake she was making for the midday meal.

The Trappistine nuns are one of eighteen congregations of men and women who serve the archdiocese of Dubuque, the oldest city in the state. Dubuque has such a substantial Catholic population that it's been nicknamed Iowa's "Little Rome." What sets this particular congregation apart from the other nuns who live secluded from society, they say, is their emphasis on community rather than solitude. They go into town for food and supplies as infrequently as possible and instead rely on the fruits and vegetables from their own orchards and gardens for the meals they share together. They support themselves by selling the corn, oats, wheat, alfalfa, hay, and soybeans grown on the 150 acres they cultivate themselves. They're best known, however, for their other source of income: the Trappistine Creamy Caramels they make in the candy house down the dirt road apiece from the abbey.

Our Lady of the Mississippi Abbey was founded in 1964 after the Trappist monks of Dubuque's New Malleray Abbey invited thirteen members of a Trappistine monastery in Massachusetts to establish a new foundation. The basis for both monasteries grew from the Rule written during the sixth century by an obscure monk named Saint Benedict which laid down a strict daily routine of communal prayer, private meditation, spiritual reading, and manual labor.

"But we're really a Cistercian order, an offshoot of the Benedictine Rule," Mother Gail, the monastery's abbess, explained. Though the Cistercians of the twelfth century modified Benedict's Rule to better suit

Sister Rosemary with freshly picked strawberries

their needs, they still lived by the fundamentals established in the beginning: poverty, manual work, and detachment from worldly concerns. Each sister must play a role in keeping the community thriving within that framework, whether it's plowing a vegetable patch, baling hay, making candy, mending clothes, doing maintenance work, or cooking. Sister Rosemary, who entered the monastery thirty years ago at the age of nineteen, assumes the responsibility of preparing three primarily vegetarian meals a day with the help of a novice cook. "I just love to cook," she said, beaming. "Knowing that we grew most of the foods ourselves makes it even more rewarding." The reason they don't eat meat, she said, is "mainly for economic reasons; it is a luxury we choose to sacrifice. And it is said that meat stimulates passion."

All meals are served in a sparsely furnished dining room with three narrow wooden tables surrounded by benches. At each place setting is a plain china cup and saucer and a vase containing a single fresh flower. "We use a lot of energy, so we eat a good bit, especially at noon," she said. "We get our protein from soybeans prepared in a variety of different ways. We also eat a lot of natural peanut butter, potatoes with cream cheese, tuna salad with eggs." For breakfast and supper she provides lighter offerings such as granola, applesauce, cinnamon toast, scrambled eggs, and plenty of whole-grain bread made with freshly ground wheat from their fields.

Dinner is a special treat for the nuns on occasions such as Christmas, Easter, Thanksgiving, and the Assumption Feast Day. The main entrée is usually a rich soybean casserole baked with cheese and herbs which is topped with seasoned bread crumbs that give it a flavor reminiscent of turkey dressing. Often they have a grated carrot salad on the side, whole wheat bread and butter, and "we always try to have a really nice dessert like pistachio nut cake. That's everyone's favorite."

Soybean Casserole

2 cups soybeans	1 teaspoon soy sauce
1 cup diced celery	Salt and pepper to taste
1 large onion, diced	1 teaspoon kelp (optional)
1/2 cup (1 stick) margarine	1 cup shredded sharp cheese
1 13-ounce can evaporated milk	1 cup crushed and seasoned dry
1 teaspoon Worcestershire sauce	bread crumbs

Wash and pick over soybeans. Cover with 8 cups water and let soak overnight. Remove any that float or are moldy. Drain, place in a large pot, and cover with water. Bring to a slow boil, reduce heat, and simmer until tender, about 1 to 1½ hours.

Preheat oven to 375 degrees. In a large skillet over medium heat, sauté celery and onion in margarine until tender. Stir in milk, Worcestershire sauce, soy sauce, salt and pepper, kelp, and cooked soybeans. Pour half of mixture into greased 2-quart casserole dish. Sprinkle with ½ cup cheese. Pour other half of mixture on top; sprinkle with remaining cheese. Top with seasoned bread crumbs. Bake in preheated oven for 45 minutes. Makes 4 to 6 servings.

Asparagus Quiche

1 9-inch unbaked pie shell,
   pricked with fork
4 eggs
1 cup heavy cream
½ cup milk
1 cup sharp cheese, grated
1 onion, thinly sliced and sautéed
   in butter

½ teaspoon nutmeg
½ teaspoon sage
½ teaspoon pepper
2 teaspoons salt
1 cup raw asparagus, trimmed of
   woody bottoms and cut up

Preheat oven to 450 degrees. Partially bake pie shell for 7 minutes. Remove from oven and reduce heat to 350 degrees. In a large bowl, lightly beat eggs. Stir in cream, milk, cheese, onion, nutmeg, sage, pepper, and salt. Line bottom of pie crust with asparagus. Pour in egg mixture. Bake about 45 minutes, or until set. Makes 4 to 6 servings.

Trappistine Wheat Bread

"I sometimes substitute ingredients, using sour milk instead of water. Also, I may add various leftovers, such as oatmeal, cream of wheat, mashed potatoes, etc."—Sister Rosemary

2 tablespoons yeast
1/3 cup warm water
3 cups hot water
4 cups whole wheat flour
1/3 cup molasses
1/3 cup vegetable oil

1 tablespoon salt
3 tablespoons carob powder
  (optional)
1/4 cup soy flour
Additional whole wheat flour (1 1/2
  to 4 cups)

In a small bowl, dissolve yeast in warm water and let stand until bubbly. In a large mixing bowl, combine hot water, whole wheat flour, molasses, vegetable oil, salt, carob, and soy flour. Beat for 2 to 3 minutes. If it splatters too much, add more flour. Add yeast mixture and 1 1/2 cups more flour. Mix thoroughly. Continue adding flour until dough does not stick to sides of bowl. Turn out onto floured surface; knead 8 to 10 minutes. Place in greased bowl, turn once, cover, and let rise in warm place until doubled in bulk. Punch down, cover, and let rise again until doubled in bulk. Punch down again, divide, and shape into 3 loaves and place into greased and floured loaf pans. Let rise until increased in bulk by about one-third. Preheat oven to 350 degrees. Bake 40 to 45 minutes, or until hollow sounding when tapped on bottom. Makes 3 loaves.

Pistachio Nut Cake

2 1/4 cups all-purpose flour
1 1/2 cups granulated sugar
3 teaspoons baking powder
1 teaspoon salt
1 3 3/8-ounce package pistachio
  pudding mix
1/2 cup margarine, melted
1/2 cup cooking oil
1 cup yogurt

1 teaspoon vanilla
4 eggs, slightly beaten
1/2 cup milk

NUT FILLING:
1/2 cup granulated sugar
1/2 cup finely chopped nuts
1 teaspoon cinnamon

Preheat oven to 350 degrees. Grease and flour two 9-inch round cake pans; set aside. In a large bowl, mix flour, sugar, baking powder, salt, and pudding mix. Add melted margarine, cooking oil, yogurt, vanilla, eggs, and milk. Stir until thoroughly combined. Pour two-thirds of the batter into the prepared pans. Make the nut filling by combining sugar, nuts, and cinnamon. Sprinkle filling on top of batter. (It's best if filling does not touch sides of pan.) Pour rest of batter over filling. Bake for 50 minutes.

Cake is very heavy and will not have much spring, even when finished. *Do not overbake.* When cool, frost with your favorite white frosting or the butter frosting recipe which follows. Makes 10 to 12 servings.

Butter Frosting

¼ cup (½ stick) margarine
2 cups confectioner's sugar
1 egg

1 teaspoon vanilla
Milk to thin, if necessary

In a mixing bowl, beat together all ingredients until smooth. Makes enough frosting for one 9-inch cake.

COFFEE BREAKS,
SWEDISH-STYLE

There's a standing invitation for coffee in the predominantly Swedish community of Stanton.

In the heart of this tidy little village, the "World's Largest Coffeepot," reputed to hold 640,000 cups of coffee, can be spotted for miles around. Actually, it's a water tower equipped with a handle and a spout and painted white with bright stenciled designs to resemble a Swedish coffeepot. The tower was originally decorated as a tribute to the town's most famous native daughter and guest of honor at its 1970 centennial celebration: Virginia Christine. Most television viewers know her better as "Mrs. Olson," the kindly Swedish lady on Folger's coffee commercials who taught many a newlywed the secret of making a good cup of coffee.

The giant coffeepot also represents the friendly hospitality Stanton residents readily extend to neighbors and visitors alike. A pot of freshly brewed coffee, accompanied by a few Swedish treats, is the only excuse this community needs for a get-together. It's the staple of every social gathering, whether it's a meeting of a civic group, the literary society, or one of the numerous "neighborhood clubs," which go by names like the Worthwhile Club, the Happy Hour, the Friendly Neighbor Club. And it's the main attraction every afternoon at the local senior citizens' hall, where the men gather to play a game of pool or cards and the women frequently bring along their stitchery.

"But mainly we just like to visit with each other and drink coffee," Ino Anderson, an active Stanton senior citizen, said. "Swedes have always been known to be big coffee drinkers," Alta Shogren, the town librarian, added. "The farmers always drank a lot of it during a hard day in the fields. And it's a good way for neighbors to socialize."

Stanton is primarily a farming community, with a population that's close to 90 percent Swedish. Its founding father was the Reverend B. M. Halland, a young Swedish pastor from Burlington, Iowa, in search of a

place for his fellow countrymen to settle. In 1870, he ran an advertise-
ment in a Swedish magazine, offering sections of land in his proposed
southwest Iowa community for six to eleven dollars an acre, restricted
only to "nondrinking, God-fearing Swedes." Shortly thereafter he organized the Mamrelund Lutheran Church. The bell still tolls in its tall,
sparkling white steeple today, often the only sound interrupting the
peace of a Saturday or Sunday afternoon.

Throughout the community there are other signs of its Swedish heritage as well. In front of the white-washed homes, which earned for
the town the pseudonym "Little White City," are little red wooden
horses imported from Sweden bearing the homeowners' names. Family-
operated shops such as Troll House offer Swedish imports and foods.

A number of Swedish traditions are still faithfully observed. Since
1896, the local men's chorus has gathered on a street corner the last
night of April to sing "Skona Maj, Valkommen," or "Beautiful May, Welcome." Afterward, families invite the singers into their homes for coffee
and Scandinavian refreshments. But the biggest celebration is the Festival of Lights, observed on the weekend closest to December 13, the
official beginning of the Christmas season. That date marks the death
around A.D. 300 of Santa Lucia, the young girl who gave up her sight
rather than marry a wealthy suitor who wanted her to renounce her
Christian faith. Each year the eldest daughter of each household in Stanton is eligible to represent the town as Santa Lucia, provided she serves
her family coffee and hot, freshly baked Santa Lucia buns in bed. Her
mother notifies the festival committee once this task has been com-
pleted, and citizens then cast their votes at the library. That evening,
Santa Lucia, wearing a white gown and red sash to symbolize her purity
and blood from the heart given for Christ, is crowned with a wreath of
lighted candles. She carries a copper coffee pot symbolizing that she
was a guardian of the poor, and two younger girls dressed as Swedish
dolls carry her creamer and sugar bowl. Two small boys play the parts
of household gnomes of good spirits. After the coronation, Santa Lucia
and her attendants serve coffee and cookies to all, followed by Swedish
dancing.

At home, many Swedish cooks such as Janis Peterson like to serve an
old-country Swedish dinner: "We always have lutefisk—dried codfish
that's creamed and served over boiled potatoes," she said. "And we have
dopp i gryta. Each person is given a rye bun to dip in a rich beef broth
that's served in a big bowl in the middle of the table. For dessert we like
to have ostakaka, a very delicious pudding served with a sauce made of
lingonberries, which are like cranberries only much tinier." That pudding is so popular in the community that it's served at other times of the

year, when lingonberries aren't available, with a grape-flavored krem sauce instead. During my visit to the senior citizens' hall one afternoon I had an opportunity to sample not only ostakaka but also an array of Swedish pastries, breads, and cookies served with plenty of hot, fresh coffee. A lot of trouble for one guest? "Why, heavens no!" exclaimed Mrs. Anderson. "It's a real treat to show a guest some of our hospitality. That's what we want Stanton to be remembered for."

Swedish Rye Bread

¾ cup granulated sugar
3½ cups hot water
¼ cup lard
¼ cup bacon grease
¼ cup molasses
½ cup brown sugar

3½ teaspoons salt
3 packages dry yeast
2 cups rye flour
About 8½ cups all-purpose flour

Melt white sugar in a heavy skillet until brown. Add hot water, lard, bacon grease, molasses, brown sugar, and salt. Mix yeast with rye flour and add to above mixture when lukewarm. Add 3 cups flour and beat with mixer until smooth. Add remaining flour and knead until smooth. Put in a bowl, cover, set in a warm place, and let rise until double. Punch down; let rise again. Form into 4 loaves; cover and let rise again. Preheat oven to 375 degrees. Bake bread in preheated oven 15 minutes; reduce heat to 325 degrees and bake 30 minutes longer. Makes 4 loaves.

MRS. JAMES LINDEN

Sometimes referred to as "Swedish cheesecake," this almond-scented custard is thickened with rennet much like cottage cheese.

Ostakaka

1 gallon plus 2 cups milk
1 cup all-purpose flour
½ rennet tablet
4 tablespoons lukewarm water
1 cup heavy cream

2 eggs plus 1 egg yolk
1 cup granulated sugar
1 teaspoon vanilla
½ teaspoon almond flavoring
½ teaspoon salt

In a 6-to-8-quart saucepan, heat 1 gallon of the milk to 100 to 105 degrees, or slightly warmer than lukewarm. Combine the 2 cups milk with the flour and add to warm milk. Dissolve rennet in lukewarm water; add to mixture. Let stand until whey forms, about 30 minutes to 1 hour, tilting the pan so you can tell if it's getting solid. When settled, gently cut through the mixture both ways. Drain off the loose whey as it forms. You should have about half a gallon of liquid (it varies, and sometimes there will be a little more). You don't want it too solid or your finished product will be too dry. Stir gently.

Preheat oven to 400 degrees. Beat eggs; add cream, sugar, flavorings, and salt. When well mixed, stir gently into the pudding mixture. Place in a 9 × 13-inch pan. Bake 10 minutes in preheated oven; reduce heat to 350 degrees and bake 45 minutes to 1 hour longer, or until center is raised. Serve with lingonberries, strawberries, or krem (recipe follows). Makes 10 to 12 servings.

MRS. HAROLD C. ANDERSON

Krem Sauce for Ostakaka

*1 12-ounce can grape juice
   concentrate
1 12-ounce can water*

*2 tablespoons cornstarch
3 tablespoons granulated sugar*

In saucepan, stir all ingredients until smooth. Bring to a boil; cook and stir until thickened and clear. Serve warm or cold. Makes 3 cups.

ESTHER LARSON

Spritz Cookies

*1 cup (2 sticks) butter or
   margarine
1/2 cup granulated sugar
3/4 cup powdered sugar
2 egg yolks*

*1/2 teaspoon vanilla
1 teaspoon almond flavoring
2 1/2 cups all-purpose flour
1/2 teaspoon cream of tartar*

Ino Anderson and Maurine Holmstead serving Swedish treats at the Stanton Senior Citizens' Community Center

Preheat oven to 350 degrees. In a mixing bowl, cream together butter and sugars. Beat in egg yolks, then add remaining ingredients. Put dough through a cookie press. Bake on ungreased cookie sheet in preheated oven 10 to 12 minutes. Makes 5 dozen cookies.

MYRTLE LEVINE

Mandal Skorper
(Esther's Swedish Rusks)

½ cup (1 stick) butter or
   margarine
½ cup granulated sugar
1 beaten egg
2 tablespoons milk

½ teaspoon vanilla
½ teaspoon almond flavoring
1¾ cups all-purpose flour
1½ teaspoons baking powder

Preheat oven to 350 degrees. In a mixing bowl, cream butter or margarine and sugar until light and fluffy. Beat in egg, milk, and flavorings. Combine flour and baking powder; add to creamed mixture. Bake in a well-greased 9 × 5-inch bread pan 25 to 30 minutes. While hot, turn out on bread board immediately and cut into thin slices. Spread slices on cookie sheet and return to hot oven. Turn off heat and leave rusks in oven until cold. Makes about 2 to 2½ dozen rusks.

MRS. GLENN LARSON

AN AMISH SABBATH

It was a warm and breezy Sunday morning, not a cloud in the sky, and May, all hitched up and ready for church, was standing patiently beside the small iron fence in front of the rambling white farmhouse. From the porch, above the clink-clink of dishes being washed, I could hear the voice of a young woman singing a hymn softly in German. I tapped on the door. The singing stopped. The door opened and I was greeted by an elfin figure with a fuzzy, silver-white beard that came to a stiff point halfway down his homemade cotton shirt. His face, with its twinkling blue eyes, apple blossom cheeks, and warm smile, put me immediately at ease. He extended a firm handshake and invited me in.

There was no electricity inside, only kerosene and gas lamps. No family portraits were hanging on the walls—just a small picture of Jesus and some framed needlepoint passages of Scripture. With the exception of the hand-sewn cushions for the rockers and sofas, most of the furnishings had probably been around since Mr. Beachy's father-in-law built the house in 1923.

At the rear of the spacious kitchen was a table filled with gallon-size jars of freshly made jams, jellies, and preserves. "Yesterday we canned forty quarts of rhubarb, strawberries, and mulberries," Mr. Beachy's wife, Susan, explained. She stretched out her blue-stained palms and chuckled. "Mulberries are certainly tasty, but my, how they do color the hands!"

The lives of Glen and Susan Beachy, who were both born and raised in Kalona's Amish-Mennonite settlement, follow a pattern not much different from that of anyone living in the community today—or a century ago, for that matter. Descendants of early sixteenth-century Mennonites, the Amish were among the first white settlers in Iowa, having arrived from Pennsylvania in the 1840s. For three centuries the Old Order Amish have clung to the basic religious tenets set forth by the Swiss Anabaptists, who formed during the Protestant Reformation in Switzerland. They still practice adult baptism, refuse to bear arms or take an oath, believe in agrarian superiority, and remain as isolated from modern society as they can. They are friendly with the members of their religion's more liberal offshoots, the Mennonites and the Beachy Amish, who drive cars, have electricity and mingle freely with the rest of the community. But they are adamant in their refusal to conform.

The community is organized into church districts comprised of about fifteen to twenty farm families, each with its own minister and all under the leadership of a bishop. Church services are held every other Sunday in the home or barn of a member of each district to discuss both religious and civic matters, in addition to worshipping and socializing. On alternate Sundays, they congregate in a barn or perhaps a welding or carpentry shop for Sunday school, Beachy said.

When the kitchen was tidy, the Beachys' daughters Ruth and Mary donned heavy black bonnets identical to their mother's, bade farewell, and joined their brothers, who were waiting outside with the buggies. Mr. Beachy retrieved his wide-brimmed felt hat from the nail on the wall and the rest of us headed out the door.

Mrs. Beachy climbed into the wooden coach and I followed behind her. "You'll have to ride in my lap so we can all fit in," she warned me, noting the narrow space provided by the felt seat. Somewhat startled, I scooted cautiously onto her knee. She smiled. "Just sit back and relax. You won't hurt me." Her husband squeezed in beside us and latched the door. Grasping the reins in one hand and the leather and nylon whip in the other, he gave the chocolate-colored horse a swat on the hip and we were on our way. "Ol' May's been with us quite awhile—got her in May of '59," Mr. Beachy said. "I s'pose she's about ready to retire, but she gets us where we need to go."

Along the way, the Beachys pointed out their four married children's homes, the one-room schoolhouse they all attended through the eighth grade, the home where their partially deaf son, Timothy, receives special instruction, a welding shop, and a harness shop which also repairs broken-down buggies.

As May guided the rickety wagon around a sharp corner, I steadied my position on Mrs. Beachy's lap as I felt my body sway heavily to one side. Through a haze of dust up ahead we could see a trail of other buggies, all headed in the same direction. A few minutes later we arrived at the home of Elmer Helmuth. "Whoa," Mr. Beachy commanded. He hitched the horse to a tree and we all hopped out. Mr. Beachy headed toward the back of the barn to join the other men, and I tagged along behind Mrs. Beachy to a tool shed where the women, many with small children and infants, had gathered. All of them, from toddlers to great-grandmothers, wore high-necked, ankle-length dresses, pinafores held together with straight pins, and prayer caps which covered their tightly coiled braids. The older women wore heavy black stockings and shoes; many of the children were barefoot. Several of the older children carried small suit-cases, "probably filled with diapers and such for their younger brothers and sisters," Mrs. Beachy whispered to me.

The women entered the barn single file, filling the benches on one side. Then the men filled the opposite side, each tossing his hat in a pile beside the front door as he entered. The three men who would be con-ducting the services took their places on a bench facing the other men. Chatter ceased as the congregation opened their black hymnals. A man's voice set the pitch for the first syllable of the verse and then the others joined in, accompanied only by the sparrows chirping noisily from the rafters.

The service—all three hours of it—was in German. After nearly an hour and a half of singing, an elderly, white-haired minister stood before the crowd and began his sermon: solemn, heartfelt, and heavily punctu-ated with hand gestures. Many of the mothers laid handkerchiefs in their laps as pillows for their children. Some infants snoozed on a mattress behind the women's pews. A row of young boys rested their heads against a stall, eyes closed and mouths agape. Even some of the adults' heads were drooping before the service was over.

At 12:30, while the last chorus of the closing hymn was sung, the younger members of the congregation and I were directed outside, while the older ones remained longer to discuss some private business matters. Meanwhile, Mrs. Helmuth and her daughters finished preparing a light lunch for everyone. After the meeting, the men carried the benches into the home and set them around long, oilcloth-covered tables—one in the living room for the women, the other in the dining room for the men. Each place was set with a knife, fork, and a cup of spearmint tea on a tiny white saucer—no napkins, no plates. In the middle of the table were large platters filled with thick slices of white and wheat homemade bread, jars of home-canned sour pickles and beets, strawberry pre-serves, and plastic containers filled with peanut butter thinned with corn syrup or lumps of butter. After a silent prayer, the diners helped themselves to the offerings and the room filled with light-hearted chat-ter, about the rainstorm that had caused their freshly bailed hay to turn sour, the new baby born to their neighbors, the upcoming "sewing" to make clothes for the needy.

When they'd finished eating and the small container of toothpicks had circled the table at least once, the women dispersed into other areas of the home to make room for the second shift. After an hour or so of visiting, the Beachys and I piled into the buggy and headed home, where we found Ruth and Mary chatting on the front porch swing.

They spoke candidly about their life as a self-sustaining farm family and how much of it revolves around food. Breakfast is usually ready at "around five or five-thirty—time for us to milk the cow and get all the other choring done," said Ruth, the eldest of the nine Beachy children. In the summertime, they often have cold bread and milk soup with seasonal fruits to go along with eggs, cooked oatmeal, or granola. "And in the winter we keep quite a kettleful of cornmeal mush cooked with milk, or maybe fried mush with molasses," she added. Except for Sundays, when the work day is easier, noontime is "dinner," a hearty meal consisting of home-butchered meats, poultry, or some thick cheese slices, lots of fresh vegetables, a dessert, fruit, and "always homemade bread or corn bread. We eat fish if we like, or chicken fixed in a variety of ways—either baked whole or dipped in egg, rolled in cracker crumbs and baked," Mrs. Beachy said. Meat dishes are usually stretched with potatoes or pasta. "We eat a lot of hash—potatoes and peas and meat all mixed up together," Ruth said. Their evening meal is lighter, often much like breakfast. One of their favorites, Ruth said, is "corn bread with tomato gravy; we make it with juice from the tomatoes we can."

Grocery lists are kept to a minimum. "We buy our salt, flour, baking powder, spices, and different kinds of teas," Mrs. Beachy said. "Some of the women still churn their own butter, but we buy ours ready-made. We try to supply most everything else ourselves." Virtually all the fruits and vegetables are raised in their own gardens and orchards. They butcher their meats, stuff sausages, and bake all their bread. What produce and meats aren't eaten fresh are frozen in lockers at the local cheese shop, they said.

Sundays provide a welcome relaxing break in the workload for Amish families, especially the young people. In the evenings, Ruth and Mary told me, they often get together for "Sunday night sings." "We usually make a big casserole of some kind, like yummasetti: hamburger, noodles, vegetables, and canned soups, if we have them. If we don't, we mix in a white sauce, or some leftover gravy instead," Ruth said. There's socializing after the singing, and "if a boy and girl happen to take a liking to one another, they may decide to go out on a date," Mr. Beachy explained, noting that it was such an occasion which set the stage for his and his wife's courtship.

Yet, even during the week, one rarely hears a grumble about "choring."

Jo Futrell

In fact, work and play are often synonymous. "When we were small, we used to make a game out of our chores," eighteen-year-old Mary remembered. "We'd write down the chores on little slips of paper, and then drop them in a hat to see who would do what." Ruth said her family particularly looked forward to "work days." About once a month, the entire family, including married brothers and sisters, gather together to help each other with chores, both inside the homes and out. "We usually make it an all-day affair," she said. "On the last work day we had, all the girls picked strawberries in the forenoon. In the afternoon, Mary and I stripped a piece of furniture while Mom canned strawberries. Then we baked bread and patched some clothes, while the men built a fence." One of the main community social events, they added, is the "frolic," for which neighbors all pitch in to help a family build a new barn or perhaps repair a house that's been damaged by fire or storm.

Most of the big get-togethers which aren't centered on work are focused on a joyful occasion, such as a wedding or the welcoming of a new baby. "A girl who lives down the road a piece just got married a few weeks ago," Ruth recalled. "It was on a Wednesday, in the forenoon. They had a service in their barn. Afterward we had ham and cheese casserole, cheese and celery, tapioca pudding, and fruit in her parents' home. Then they served the cake that the bride had made herself. It was in the shape of an open book with a Bible verse written on top, and it was decorated with real roses."

As the sun began to go down, Mrs. Beachy turned to me. "Wouldn't you stay and have some supper with us?" she asked. Reluctantly, I declined, explaining that I needed to get back before dark. Mary and Ruth slipped into the kitchen while the Beachys and I chatted a while longer.

"I guess you must wonder why we live like this," Mr. Beachy said. "Sure, people stare at us when we go to public places, but we feel we have nothing to be ashamed of. And besides, we hardly ever go in places where people might be likely to put us down—like a saloon, for instance. A saloon doesn't belong to a Christian, anyway.

"We think it's better for the family to live without the convenience of cars and such, otherwise it would be too easy for the kids to up and leave. In our community, parents are less likely to be pushed off in an old folks' home. Our attitude is that since our parents took care of us when we were young, it's our duty to care for them when they're old.

"If it was good enough for our forefathers to live this way, it's good enough for us."

When Mary and Ruth returned, they handed me a snack for the road: a huge sandwich of canned meat and lettuce leaves on thick slices of buttered wheat bread, some slices of home-dried, seasoned beef, and a small bag of dried fruit. And as another memento of my visit, they shared with me some of their favorite recipes—some from their recipe file, some from the cardboard cookbook compiled by the schoolchildren as a gift to their mothers, and some, as Mrs. Beachy put it, pointing to her temple, "from what we have up here in our heads."

Pumpkin Chiffon Pie
with Peanut Crust

CRUST:
½ cup (1 stick) butter
1⅔ cups all-purpose flour
½ cup finely chopped peanuts or
    other nuts
Pinch of salt
3 to 4 tablespoons water

FILLING:
2 cups canned pumpkin
3 egg yolks

¼ cup granulated sugar
½ cup milk
½ teaspoon salt
1 tablespoon cinnamon
1 package unflavored gelatin
¼ cup cold water
3 egg whites
¼ cup granulated sugar
1 pint whipping cream, whipped

For the crust, preheat oven to 400 degrees. With a pastry blender or two knives, cut the butter into the flour, nuts, and salt until mixture resembles coarse crumbs. Add water, 1 tablespoon at a time, tossing lightly with a fork. Gather dough into a ball. Roll dough out thinly and fit into a deep-dish 9-inch pie pan. Prick crust; bake in preheated oven until lightly browned, 10 to 12 minutes.

For the filling, thoroughly whisk together pumpkin, egg yolks, sugar, milk, salt, and cinnamon in a saucepan. Cook over medium heat until thickened, about 10 to 15 minutes. Dissolve gelatin in cold water. Remove pumpkin mixture from heat and add the dissolved gelatin. Let cool. In a mixing bowl, beat egg whites, gradually adding sugar. Continue beating until stiff peaks form. Fold beaten egg whites into pumpkin mixture. Pour into cooled crust. Chill. Top with whipped cream before serving. Makes 1 9-inch pie.

Amish Granola

9 cups quick-cooking oatmeal
1 cup wheat germ
1 cup flaked coconut
½ cup chopped nuts
1 cup raisins (optional)
½ cup brown sugar

½ cup water
½ cup cooking oil or melted
    margarine
½ teaspoon salt
1½ teaspoons vanilla
1 teaspoon maple flavoring

Preheat oven to 200 degrees. In a large bowl, mix together oatmeal, wheat germ, coconut, nuts, and raisins. In another bowl, mix together brown sugar, water, oil or margarine, salt, vanilla, and maple flavoring. Pour over dry mixture. Spread into 2 9 × 13-inch pans and bake in preheated oven for 90 minutes, stirring and reversing the pans every 10 minutes. Store in airtight container. Makes about 13 cups.

Yummasetti

2 tablespoons butter
1 large onion, chopped
3 pounds ground beef
1 1-pound package spaghetti
   noodles, cooked
1 pint peas, slightly cooked

2 10¾-ounce cans mushroom
   soup
1 10¾-ounce can cream of celery
   soup
1 cup sour cream
½ loaf buttered bread, toasted
   and made into crumbs

Preheat oven to 350 degrees. In a large skillet, melt butter. Sauté onion in butter till soft. Add ground beef and cook until meat is no longer pink. Drain off excess fat. Put all ingredients except the bread crumbs into a large bowl and mix. Pour into roaster, top with bread crumbs, and bake in preheated oven for 45 minutes. Makes 12 to 16 servings.

Tomato Gravy

1 cup tomato juice
½ cup water or milk

3 tablespoons flour, diluted in ⅓
   cup water
2 to 3 tablespoons cream

In a saucepan over medium heat, heat tomato juice; dilute with water or milk. Thicken with flour/water mixture. Add cream and season to taste before serving over hot corn bread. Makes 2 cups.

Mary's Lollipops

"Whenever I bake bread, I roll the leftover scraps into small balls and put them in a pan. I cover them and let them rise in a warm place. Then I sprinkle them with brown sugar and pour cream on top. I bake them in the oven (375 degrees) till they're done (about 30 minutes), and then serve them warm with fresh strawberries or some other fresh fruit."

These cookies remind me of what a soft, homemade version of Oreos might taste like. Instead of the supersweet filling called for here, I like to put ice cream between the two chocolate wafers and then pop them into the freezer for homemade ice cream sandwiches. But that happens to be my personal preference, not the Amish folks'.

Whoppie Pies

COOKIES:
1/2 cup lard or shortening
1 cup granulated sugar
1 egg, well beaten
1 teaspoon vanilla
2 cups all-purpose flour
1/2 cup cocoa
1 teaspoon salt
1/2 cup sour milk or buttermilk

1 teaspoon baking soda
2/3 cup hot water

FILLING:
1 egg white
2 cups powdered sugar, divided
1 teaspoon vanilla
1 1/2 tablespoons milk
3 tablespoons Crisco

Preheat oven to 350 degrees. In a mixing bowl, cream lard or shortening and sugar. Add egg and vanilla. Sift together flour, cocoa, and salt. Add alternately to creamed mixture with sour milk or buttermilk. Dissolve soda in hot water and add to mixture. Beat well. Drop by teaspoons onto greased cookie sheets. Bake in preheated oven 8 minutes. Cool cookies on wire rack.

   To prepare filling, beat egg white until frothy. Gradually beat in 1 cup of the powdered sugar and vanilla until thick and glossy. Beat in milk and Crisco; gradually beat in remaining cup of powdered sugar until mixture is of fluffy spreading consistency. Spread filling in between two cookies. Makes about 40 filled cookies.

Graham Cracker Fluff

1 package unflavored gelatin
⅓ cup cold water
½ cup granulated sugar
¾ cup milk
2 egg yolks
1 teaspoon vanilla
2 egg whites, stiffly beaten

1 cup heavy cream, whipped
3 tablespoons butter
3 tablespoons brown sugar
6 whole graham crackers, crushed fine
Fresh strawberries or blueberries (optional)

In a small bowl, dissolve gelatin in cold water. In a medium saucepan, mix together sugar, milk, and egg yolks. Cook over medium heat, stirring constantly until mixture has boiled for 1 minute. Remove from stove and add dissolved gelatin and vanilla. Set in a cool place until the mixture begins to thicken. Then gently fold in the stiffly beaten egg whites and whipped cream.

In a medium skillet, melt together the butter and brown sugar; mix with the crushed graham crackers. Line the bottom of an 8-inch square or round pan with half the crumbs; pour in gelatin mixture and sprinkle remaining crumbs on top. Chill until ready to serve. Serve with fresh berries, if desired. Makes 6 servings.

A GRANGE POTLUCK

It isn't impossible to find entertainment off the family farm in communities like Killduff, Iowa, with populations too negligible to record on a map. You just have to know where to look.

Delwin Cross is one Killduff farmer who can point you in the right direction. The insignia of a sheaf of wheat attached to his shirt pocket attests to his reliability. It's the symbol of the Grange, a family-oriented fraternal organization formed in 1867 to improve the deplorable agricultural and economic conditions faced by farmers. Mr. Cross, a former state Grange master, had been active in the organization for more than fifty years. In addition to lobbying for legislation to help farmers at its national headquarters in Washington, the Grange serves an equally important function: providing a social outlet for farm families who live miles from their nearest neighbors.

Although there are some 500,000 Grangers nationwide, memberships have dropped in many areas with increasing urbanization. But the Grange is still alive and well in the largely agrarian Iowa counties of Jasper, Poweshiek, Delaware, and Muscatine. Both men and women attend monthly meetings followed by "social hours" at their local Grange halls, sometimes in an old schoolhouse, sometimes in an abandoned country church. Junior Grangers between the ages of five and fourteen conduct their own secret meetings under the supervision of an adult. Sometimes members of different Grange units will converge for a potluck supper, as was the case this particular evening, when some forty or fifty Grangers piled into a public assembly room in Newton, the home of Iowa's first active Grange and the nation's second. At this meeting of the regional, or Pomona, Grange, they came to share the home-baked casseroles in their hefty picnic baskets, ideas for fund-raising projects, and reminiscences of life as a Granger.

The Grange means something extra special to Lucille and Delwin Cross. "Why, the Grange was the start of mine and Del's romance," said Mrs. Cross with a schoolgirlish giggle. "We joined the same night, but heaven knows I never thought I'd go with him!" It wasn't until they were both assigned to pick out a gift of appreciation for their club's pianist that the couple detected a mutual spark. It's been burning brightly ever since.

Few have witnessed as many changes in the organization as Adolph Altemeier of Grinnell, who said he'd been an active Grange member since 1925—"except for a few years when we were raising our babies. We started out as kind of a protest against the railroad; they were gouging the farmers so badly," he said. "We still believe in good sound government and a good sound economy, with special emphasis on a fair price for the farmer. But we're really more social now than anything else. Sort of makes life more interesting."

Even in between meetings there are numerous activities to keep the Grangers' calendars full: picnics, family talent shows, grocery showers for soon-to-be newlyweds. They raise money for charity by sponsoring cake walks or auctioning off box suppers prepared by the women Grange members. The highest bidder receives the supper for two, which he must share with the cook. "At our last box supper, one bidder paid eleven dollars for the box his wife fixed because he was too shy to eat with any of the other ladies," Marilyn Keenan of Grinnell noted, laughing.

The proceeds may be used for a national Grange project, such as providing songbooks in sign language for the deaf. Or it may be used to "help a community member who's sick or in distress," added state women's chairperson Bayonne Birkenholz of Sugar Grove Grange. They once raised six hundred dollars to build a deck for a blind woman living out in the country in a trailer by herself "who never got a chance to get outside," recalled one member.

The Grange women, who sponsor one of the largest sewing contests in the country, often pool their talents by making stuffed toys for charity. "We just get together in somebody's basement and have a fun time of it," Mrs. Birkenholz said. "The Grange is basically people caring about people," added Ellis Harlan of Kellogg. "Living way out on a farm can be lonely sometimes. But in the Grange, farmers get to know other farmers and learn how to express themselves." That self-expression may take the form of a patchwork quilt made for an outgoing Grange master, a proposal to help farmers get a better price on their crops, or a home-cooked dish that seems to appear—and disappear—at nearly every Grange function.

Marilyn Keenan of Grinnell, a member of Victor Grange, shared these potluck favorites.

Rhubarb Bread

1½ cups brown sugar
⅔ cup oil
1 egg, lightly beaten
1 teaspoon salt
1 cup sour milk or buttermilk

1 teaspoon vanilla
1½ cups diced rhubarb
2½ cups all-purpose flour
1 teaspoon baking soda
½ cup chopped nuts

Preheat oven to 350 degrees. In a large bowl, combine all ingredients in the order given. Pour into 2 greased and floured 8½ × 4½-inch loaf pans. Bake in preheated oven for 60 to 70 minutes, or until a toothpick inserted in the middle comes out clean. Makes 2 loaves.

Fruit, marshmallows, and strawberry-flavored Jell-O—all the makings for a Midwestern fruit salad. But wait until after dinner to serve it. Rather than turned out of a pretty mold, these ingredients are layered atop a melt-in-your-mouth cookielike pie crust, a combination that inevitably pleases Junior and Senior Grangers alike.

Strawberry "Salad"

1 cup all-purpose flour
¼ cup brown sugar
½ cup chopped pecans
½ cup (1 stick) margarine
1 pound marshmallows
¼ cup milk

1 3-ounce package strawberry-
   flavored Jell-O
1 10-ounce box frozen
   strawberries, thawed
Whipped topping

Preheat oven to 350 degrees. For crust, mix together flour, brown sugar, and pecans. Cut in margarine until the mixture resembles coarse crumbs. Pat down in a 9 × 13-inch pan. Bake 10 to 15 minutes.

In a saucepan, melt marshmallows in milk, stirring constantly. Spread on crust and let cool. Prepare Jell-O according to package instructions and add strawberries. Cool and pour on top of marshmallow layer. Chill until firm and spread with whipped topping. Makes 10 to 12 servings.

Everyone's Favorite Rice Pudding

1 quart milk
⅔ cup Minute rice
1 tablespoon butter
⅔ cup granulated sugar

2 eggs, lightly beaten
2 teaspoons vanilla
¾ teaspoon salt
Cinnamon

In a 2-quart saucepan over low heat, combine milk, rice, butter, and sugar and cook for 10 minutes. Preheat oven to 325 degrees. Cool rice mixture and add eggs, vanilla, and salt. Pour into a buttered 1½-to-2-quart baking dish. Place dish in a shallow pan of water. Sprinkle pudding with cinnamon. Bake in preheated oven for 1 hour and 15 minutes, or until knife inserted in middle comes out clean. Makes 6 to 8 servings.

These three recipes were contributed by Iowa Grange members to the *National Grange Bicentennial Year Cookbook* (1616 H St. N.W., Washington, D.C. 20006). This unusual but tasty salad contributed by Theresa Beason of the Sonora Grange would be appropriate not only for a pot-luck but for a light luncheon dish served atop lettuce leaves or as a spread for crackers.

Corned Beef Salad

1 3-ounce package
  lemon-flavored Jell-O
1½ cups boiling water
1 cup mayonnaise-type salad
  dressing
1 green pepper, chopped

1 onion, chopped
¼ cup chopped olives
1 cup diced celery
2 teaspoons vinegar
3 hard-boiled eggs, diced
1 cup chopped corned beef

Dissolve Jell-O in boiling water; let chill until partially congealed. Combine salad dressing and remaining ingredients; add to Jell-O. Mix well. Pour into a lightly oiled 1-quart mold. Chill until firm. Unmold onto a platter lined with lettuce leaves. Makes 4 to 6 main-dish servings.

Denise Smith of Sonora Grange offers this tasty version of "blondies." Chocolate or peanut butter chips, incidentally, could be used in place of the butterscotch chips if you're so inclined.

Banana Brownies

⅔ cup shortening
1 1-pound box brown sugar
2 eggs, slightly beaten
2 large ripe bananas, mashed
3½ cups all-purpose flour
1 tablespoon baking powder
1 teaspoon salt
1 teaspoon vanilla

1 cup chopped nuts
1 6-ounce package butterscotch
  chips

GLAZE:
2 tablespoons mashed bananas
1½ teaspoons lemon juice
2 to 2½ cups powdered sugar

Preheat oven to 350 degrees. In a mixing bowl, cream shortening and brown sugar; blend in eggs and bananas. Stir together flour, baking powder, and salt; gradually add to creamed mixture. Stir in vanilla, nuts, and butterscotch chips. Spoon into greased 10 × 15-inch baking pan. Bake in preheated oven 30 to 40 minutes, or until toothpick inserted in center comes out clean. Meanwhile, mix all glaze ingredients. Remove brownies from oven and immediately spread with glaze. Cut into squares while warm. Makes 25 2 × 3-inch bars.

Enez Birkett of West Liberty shares this super-simple, tasty, and eye-appealing stew.

Easy Baked Stew

1½ pounds stew beef
4 carrots, sliced
3 to 4 stalks celery, chopped
1 cup chopped tomatoes, or
  tomato juice

1 green pepper, chopped
1 medium onion, chopped
⅓ cup quick-cooking tapioca
Salt and pepper to taste
1 teaspoon dried basil

Preheat oven to 300 degrees. Mix all ingredients in a large casserole; cover. Bake in preheated oven for 3½ to 4 hours. Makes 6 to 8 servings.

Fruit Slush

1 6-ounce can frozen orange juice
  concentrate
1 6-ounce can frozen pink
  lemonade concentrate
2 10-ounce packages frozen
  raspberries

1 15¼-ounce can crushed
  pineapple
16 ounces 7-Up
1 cup granulated sugar
2 large, very ripe bananas,
  mashed

Thaw frozen ingredients. Combine all ingredients in a 3-quart mixing bowl; mix well. Freeze until firm. Thaw for 30 minutes. Stir until slushy. Spoon into glasses. Makes 2½ quarts or 20 servings.

Watch out, these rolls are addictive!

Refrigerator All-Bran Rolls

1 cup boiling water
1 cup All-Bran cereal
¾ cup granulated sugar
2 teaspoons salt
1 cup lard

2 packages dry yeast
1 cup lukewarm water
2 eggs, beaten
6½ cups all-purpose flour

Pour boiling water over the All-Bran, sugar, salt, and lard in a bowl; mix well. Cool. Dissolve yeast in lukewarm water. Add dissolved yeast, eggs, and flour to bran mixture; mix well. Do not knead. Chill, covered, in refrigerator overnight. Shape into rolls and place in greased baking pans. Let rise until doubled in bulk. Preheat oven to 425 degrees. Bake for 15 to 20 minutes or until golden brown. Makes about 3 dozen rolls.

MRS. HERBERT BIRKENHOLZ

A CHRISTMAS HOMECOMING

Tony Braun will never forget his Christmas homecoming of 1981. His family won't let him.

That was the year he made the mistake he and his eleven brothers and sisters try to avoid every holiday: arriving home late after the rest of the family has gone to bed. All thirty-two of them.

Not only was every bed in the house occupied by brothers and sisters, nieces and nephews, but so were all four couches, every sleeping bag, and even Dad's Lazy-Boy recliner. He tiptoed down the hall to the closet for a blanket and pillow. It was empty.

Undaunted, he walked downstairs to the game room, set down his suitcase, wedged himself between two slumbering bodies, and closed his eyes, without even taking off his coat.

Boy, it felt great to be home!

Christmastime at Leo and Rosemary Braun's home, which sits in the middle of a cornfield between Granville and Remsen in northwest Iowa, is three or four days of droopy eyes, stiff necks, and constant racket. They wouldn't have it any other way. "Every Christmas, our house is practically bursting at the seams; it's just wonderful!" exclaimed Diane, mother of two. It's a special kind of joy perhaps only a Braun can fully appreciate. "Whenever we get real excited, especially when we haven't seen each other in a long time, about five of us will all start talking at once," laughed her older sister Alice. "Sometimes the brothers-in-law will go outside and sit in their cars for hours, just for some peace and quiet." Her husband, Ron, however, knew what he was getting into before acquiring his army of in-laws. Besides promising to love, honor, and cherish his wife, he also agreed to spend every Christmas with her family.

"Our Christmases are wild, but having all the kids here together makes it all worthwhile," said Rosemary Braun, the petite, energetic mother of twelve. The house seems pretty empty to her these days, now that all the kids are grown. Come Christmas Eve, however, the Braun nest is overflowing once again. "Newlyweds and couples with tiny babies are given first choice of the double beds," Jeanine explained. "Every other place in the house to sleep is first come, first served."

A prime-rib feast with all the trimmings is served that evening around the old kitchen table surrounded by benches. After the dishes are done, the family move downstairs for homemade cookies, candy, slices of holiday breads, and punch while they exchange Christmas gifts. "At Thanksgiving we draw names," Jeanine said. "We try to set a five-dollar limit. And all of us chip in whatever we can to get something for Mummy and Dad—usually something real practical, like new sides for their fishing boat, or faucets and sinks for the bathrooms."

Later that evening comes an equally long-standing Braun tradition: the Christmas play. "A few of the girls will plan the program; Jeanine really does a great job in that department," Mrs. Braun said. Each year Jeanine, a former home economics teacher who minored in drama at Iowa State, composes a new script. "Our plays used to be a lot more elaborate when we were younger," she explained. "We'd make costumes out of sheets or anything else we could find. One year Lea got really creative and decided we should have a puppet show with puppets we'd made out of paper cups." Alice, a secretary, mimeographs programs for each family member at her office. They open with a poem and Bible reading, and a musical intermission is provided by the "Braun Ensemble." "A bunch of us played in the band in high school," Mary noted. "You should have heard how 'Silent Night' and 'The Little Drummer Boy' sounded, with Peter on the tuba, me on the French horn, Tony on the trombone, Lenore on the drums, and Pat on the recorder."

After the little ones are tucked away in bed, the family leave extra early for midnight Mass to try to find three pews so they can all sit together. Afterward they have a huge breakfast of bacon, eggs, and Mum's homemade cinnamon rolls, which "just never seem to taste the same when we try to make them ourselves," lamented Terry, a homemaker and cook in a nursing home.

"It's just terrible; we come home for vacation and we don't get a moment's worth of rest," said Jeanine in feigned disgust. "No matter how late we stay up, we're always up at the crack of dawn, 'cause nobody wants to miss out on any conversations."

Christmas Day is more relaxing, with lunch at home and often a family reunion at St. Mary's High School gym in nearby Alton. "One night before everybody leaves, all of us will usually go bowling together," Jeanine said. "We have to make reservations ahead of time, since we need at least three lanes. The Alton bowling alley only has four."

Rosemary begins preparing for her Christmas company months ahead of time, stocking her three refrigerators and two extra-large freezers with vegetable casseroles, homemade bread and rolls, baked ham, and the fudge "all the kids just love." Her children bring along their own specialties: Lea's pasta salad, Carol's peach salad, Georgia's Christmas breads. A few days prior to Christmas Eve the kitchen turns into a cookie factory, with brothers and sisters whipping up tray after tray of date cookies, caramel turtle cookies, and Aunt Emma's sugar cookies, rolled out and cut in various Christmas shapes and sprinkled with colorful decorations.

"I would just hate to spend Christmas Eve slaving over a hot stove," said Mrs. Braun, who can well remember a time when she had little choice in the matter. "When the kids were small, the cooking and cleaning seemed endless," she recalled. Her days began at 4:00 A.M., scrubbing the hardwood floors of the old farmhouse they used to live in. A substantial breakfast was always waiting for her family when they awoke. She baked fourteen loaves of bread a week, rendered lard and soap, tended a huge garden, and performed all other domestic chores. And somewhere in between she found time to feed and clothe her expanding family while trying to instill in them the values she and her husband felt were essential: honesty, kindness, education, and a strong Christian faith.

All the Braun children learned to accept responsibility early in life. Their eldest son, Mike, had to forgo sports and extracurricular activities at school to help his father on the farm. Georgia, now with three children of her own, took on the duties of caring for the younger siblings, which included bathing them in groups of four or five in the old wringer wash tub. During harvest, they all worked as their father's field hands, walking beans, detasseling corn, "pulling up acres and acres of weeds." "I always had the top of the terrace," Tony grimaced. "That was the worst, because it was all thistles."

"Yeah, but you got to keep the dogs and cats," Alice retorted playfully. "We used to eat all of my pets."

Alice replaced Mike as chief farm hand when he left for Vietnam, which involved taking on the responsibilities of milking the cow and tending the livestock. "I always adopted the runts," she remembered. "I had a hog named Flower and a steer named Valentine. I even had names for our ducks and geese. I could identify every one of them— even when they were in the sink without their feathers."

All the girls helped their mother can and freeze the year's supply of fruits and vegetables: seventy-five quarts of green beans, fifty quarts of whole tomatoes, one hundred quarts of sweet corn, one hundred pounds of potatoes, and all the produce from six huge beds of strawberries and raspberries. During their childhood each was allowed one family vacation to the Black Hills of South Dakota. "Mum and Dad took us in shifts; every five years, four of us got to go," Terry said.

One memorable trip they all got to take was to Des Moines in 1979 to visit Terrace Hill. The invitation was extended by Governor and Mrs. Robert Ray after the governor received a letter from Alice. "I told him that eleven out of twelve of us had earned our way through college or had gone to technical school and that Pat was planning to go to college when he gets out of high school," Alice said. "Dad has always stressed the importance of higher education, and I felt our family deserved some kind of recognition."

Mrs. Braun said she and her husband were "proud of our children— every one of them."

"Ours is a very close-knit family," she said. "All the kids love to come home and are always anxious to see one another. Someday neither Leo nor I will be here, but I hope they'll try to keep the family get-togethers, especially at Christmastime."

CHRISTMAS DINNER WITH THE BRAUNS

Prime Rib au Jus   Baked Ham
Holiday Potato Casserole*   Sweet Potatoes with Apples
Asparagus with Cheese Sauce
Carol's Peach Salad*   Lea's Sweet and Sour Mostacioli Salad*
Seven-Layer Salad*
Mummy's Dinner Rolls
Georgia's Cranberry Nut Bread*   Applesauce Bread
Pumpkin Loaf
Butter Pecan Turtle Cookies*   Mum's Fudge*
Aunt Emma's Sugar Cookies*
Jeanine's Christmas Punch*

Holiday Potato Casserole

4 pounds potatoes, boiled in skins
  until tender
1 cup chopped onion
1/4 cup (1/2 stick) butter
1 10¾-ounce can condensed
  cream of celery soup

1 pint sour cream
1½ cups shredded cheddar cheese
½ cup cornflakes, crushed
3 tablespoons melted butter
Chopped fresh parsley and
  pimiento strips for garnish

Remove skins from potatoes, then shred potatoes into a bowl. In a large skillet, sauté onion in butter until tender. Remove from heat. Stir in soup and sour cream. Pour over potatoes, add cheese, and mix well. Turn into a 9 × 13-inch pan. Cover and refrigerate overnight. Before serving, preheat oven to 350 degrees. Sprinkle casserole with cornflakes; drizzle with melted butter. Bake in preheated oven for 1 hour. Garnish with parsley and pimiento. Makes 12 servings.

Although "salads" such as this are often served in Iowa, many people may find this awfully rich and sweet for a side dish. But it also makes a wonderful, ice cream–like dessert.

Carol's Peach Salad

1 21-ounce can peach pie filling
1 8¼-ounce can crushed
  pineapple
1 14-ounce can Eagle Brand
  condensed milk

¼ cup lemon juice
1 teaspoon vanilla
1 cup whipping cream, whipped,
  or 1 8-ounce container whipped
  topping

In a large bowl, stir together all ingredients. Freeze in a 9 × 13-inch pan and cut into squares. Makes 12 servings.

Lea's Sweet and Sour Mostacioli Salad

1 pound mostacioli noodles,
  cooked according to package
  directions
1 large cucumber, peeled and
  thinly sliced
1 green pepper, cut into bite-size
  pieces
1 onion, diced

DRESSING:
1½ cups sugar
1 teaspoon black pepper
1 teaspoon Accent (optional)
1 teaspoon salt
1 clove garlic, minced
1 2-ounce jar chopped pimiento,
  drained
2 tablespoons prepared mustard
1½ cups vinegar

In a large bowl, combine noodles, cucumber, green pepper, and onion. In another bowl, combine all dressing ingredients in order given. Pour over salad ingredients. Seal tightly; chill overnight. Makes 12 to 16 servings.

Seven-Layer Salad

First layer: 1 head lettuce, torn into bite-size pieces
Second layer: 1 cup finely diced celery
Third layer: 1 cup thinly sliced onions
Fourth layer: 1 10-ounce package frozen peas, partially thawed
Fifth layer: 2 cups mayonnaise
Sixth layer: ½ pound bacon, fried crisp and crumbled
Seventh layer: 4 to 6 ounces grated cheddar or Swiss cheese

In a large salad bowl or 11 × 16-inch pan (preferably a clear one, so you can see the layers), layer ingredients in order given. Cover and refrigerate 24 hours. Makes 12 to 16 servings.

Georgia's Cranberry Bread

2 cups all-purpose flour
1 cup granulated sugar
1½ teaspoons baking powder
1 teaspoon salt
½ teaspoon baking soda
¼ cup (½ stick) butter or
* margarine*

1 egg, lightly beaten
1 teaspoon grated orange peel
¾ cup orange juice
1½ cups raisins, chopped
1½ cups fresh or frozen
* cranberries, chopped*

Preheat oven to 350 degrees. In a large bowl, sift together flour, sugar, baking powder, salt, and baking soda. Cut in butter or margarine until mixture is crumbly. Add egg, orange juice, and orange peel all at once. Stir just until mixture is evenly moistened. Fold in raisins and cranberries. Spoon into greased 9 × 5-inch loaf pan. Bake in preheated oven for 60 to 70 minutes, or until cake tester inserted in middle comes out clean. Remove from pan and cool on wire rack. Makes 1 large loaf.

Butter Pecan Turtle Cookies

CRUST:
2 cups all-purpose flour
1 cup brown sugar, firmly packed
½ cup (1 stick) softened butter
1 cup pecan halves

CARAMEL LAYER:
½ cup brown sugar, firmly packed
⅔ cup butter
1 cup milk chocolate chips

Preheat oven to 350 degrees. In a mixing bowl, combine flour, brown sugar, and butter. Mix at medium speed, scraping sides of bowl often until well mixed. Pat firmly into 9 × 13 × 2-inch pan. Sprinkle pecans evenly over unbaked crust.

In a heavy 1-quart saucepan, combine brown sugar and butter. Cook over medium heat, stirring constantly, until mixture turns to caramel. Do not boil. Pour mixture evenly over pecans and crust. Bake 15 minutes, until crust is light golden and caramel layer is bubbly. Remove from oven and immediately sprinkle with chips. Allow chips to melt slightly (2 to 3 minutes), then swirl them with a knife, leaving some whole, for a marbled effect. Cool completely. Cut into 3 to 4 dozen bars.

Mum's Fudge

½ cup (1 stick) margarine
1 13-ounce can evaporated milk
4 cups granulated sugar
1 teaspoon vanilla

1 12-ounce package chocolate chips
30 large marshmallows
Chopped nuts (optional)

In a heavy pan, combine margarine, evaporated milk, and sugar. Cook to soft-ball stage (234 degrees), stirring constantly. Remove from heat. Stir in vanilla, chocolate chips, marshmallows, and nuts. Stir until chips and marshmallows are melted. Pour into a 9 × 13-inch pan. Cut into 2 to 3 dozen squares.

Aunt Emma's Sugar Cookies

1 cup shortening
2 cups granulated sugar
2 eggs
1 cup sour cream
1 teaspoon baking soda

1 teaspoon vanilla
1/4 teaspoon lemon extract
  (optional)
4 cups all-purpose flour

In a large bowl, cream shortening, gradually adding sugar, until fluffy. Beat in eggs, sour cream, baking soda, vanilla, and lemon extract. Gradually add flour. Wrap dough in waxed paper and chill. Preheat oven to 375 degrees. Roll out dough. Cut into shapes and decorate as desired. Bake 8 to 10 minutes. Makes 4 to 5 dozen cookies.

Jeanine's Christmas Punch

1 3-ounce package
  cherry-flavored Jell-O
1 12-ounce can frozen orange
  juice
1 quart cranberry juice

1 6-ounce can frozen lemonade
1 46-ounce can pineapple juice
1 quart ginger ale

Dissolve Jell-O according to package directions. Dilute orange juice according to directions. Combine all ingredients except ginger ale. Refrigerate; add ginger ale just before serving. Makes 1 gallon.

A GRADUATION PIG ROAST

Not long after Jim Korslund learned the art of roasting a pig, he began providing the main attraction for all sorts of excuses for an Iowa get-together, from dormitory beer busts to wedding receptions. But the pig roast he was preparing for this particular occasion was of special significance to him.

He was the guest of honor.

The Eagle Grove native could think of no better way to celebrate his graduation from Iowa State University than by throwing himself the kind of party that helped him earn his way through school.

In a place where lean, corn-fed pork is the pride of the state, it's no wonder that this sensational version of the outdoor barbecue is one of Iowa's favorite forms of warm-weather entertainment. That's why Jim's older brother Doug decided to specialize in pig roasts when he opened his small barbecue business in Ames while working on his master's degree in agricultural engineering. Jim followed in his brother's footsteps, not only by choosing the same major but by learning the tricks of the pig-roasting trade as well. "It's an easy, cheap way to feed a lot of people with food that just about everyone will like," said Jim, who'd been running the business almost single-handedly ever since his brother graduated. "We've never even had to put an ad in the paper."

The two brothers conducted their first pig roast on the family hog farm in Humboldt County after their father bought a roaster. When Doug went off to school he constructed a makeshift roaster of his own out of an old fuel oil tank, set it on wheels, and began transporting his services wherever a pig roast was ordered. He and Jim have provided single hogs with all the trimmings for family reunion picnics, high school graduations, and even enough pork to feed multitudes of fair-goers at the Iowa State Fair.

The methods of pig roasting vary. Some people prefer a showy presentation by roasting the pig whole on a spit with an apple in its mouth.

Others prefer to bury it in a pit. Like other pig roasters, the Korslunds think their procedure works best.

On the day of his graduation party, Jim began his ritual early as usual, shortly before 7:00 A.M. The 240-pound hog from his parents' farm which was slaughtered and cut up by a local butcher a few days earlier was laid out on a rack made of steel bars and heavy chains wired together with coat hangers. After seasoning the pieces generously with salt and pepper and wrapping them with foil, he covered them with another rack, placed them over the smoldering coals, and closed the lid. For most of the day, he said, he'd "just watch the fire, drink some beer, and start the beans," flipping the racks every forty-five minutes or so for even cooking. Later in the afternoon he would inject the pieces with 60 cc hypodermic needles filled with homemade barbecue sauce, then return them to the fire until his guests were ready to eat.

Underneath the shelter at Emma McCarthy Lee Park in Ames, friends and relatives had set up the picnic tables with the trappings essential to a successful pig roast: potato salad, baked beans, carrot sticks kept crisp in ice water, chocolate chip cookies, and homemade brownies. "And of course you want to make sure there's never a shortage of beer," Jim added with a grin.

With paper plates and napkins in hand, the guests formed a long line while Jim and his dad filled sesame seed buns with the piping hot pork, dripping in savory juices. "I figure since I've been in school here I owe quite a few people parties and dinners," Jim said. "This way I can pay them all back at the same time."

Today Jim works as an engineer for Haggar Slacks in Dallas. His brother Doug runs a French restaurant in Chicago. Jim says he's thrown a few "partial" pig roasts in Texas, using parts of the pig and slathering them with his sauce. "But nothing like the ones we used to do in Ames," he said. "People in Texas just don't eat pork the way they do in Iowa. As a matter of fact, the last big pig roast I went to was given by a friend of mine in Eagle Grove last year, a week after I got married."

Jim Korslund's Barbecue Sauce

1 pound (4 sticks) butter
½ gallon Open Pit Original
  Barbecue Sauce
36 ounces Open Pit Smoky
  Barbecue Sauce

1 32-ounce bottle Italian salad
  dressing, strained
1 32-ounce bottle lemon juice

Jim Korslund

In a large saucepan melt butter, then pour in barbecue sauces and dressing. Clean out bottles with lemon juice and add to mixture. Stir over low heat. Inject sauce in meat with 60 cc hypodermic needles while sauce is warm. Wrap meat in foil and place over coals until ready to serve. Makes enough sauce for one hog.

This long-standing family favorite, shared by Jim's aunt, Jan Korslund, makes an ideal side dish to the main attraction.

Old-Fashioned Potato Salad

For each person to be served, use:
1 small potato, peeled, cooked,
*   diced, and cooled*
1 tablespoon diced red onion

Cooked salad dressing (recipe
*   follows)*
1 hard-cooked egg, cooled
Paprika

In a large bowl, mix diced potato and red onion. Add cooked dressing until mixture is covered generously. Slice egg; retain enough egg slices to cover top of salad and mix remaining slices with potato mixture. Add more dressing if needed. Garnish with egg slices and sprinkle with paprika. Chill for several hours, if possible, for flavors to mellow.

Cooked Salad Dressing

¾ cup granulated sugar
2 tablespoons all-purpose flour
2 teaspoons dry mustard
1½ teaspoons salt

5 whole eggs or 9 egg yolks,
*   beaten*
1 cup water
1 cup vinegar
2 tablespoons butter

In a bowl, mix together sugar, flour, mustard, and salt. In a saucepan, beat together the eggs, water, and vinegar. Stir in flour/sugar mixture. Cook over moderate heat, stirring, until mixture starts to bubble around edge. Remove from heat, add butter, and stir. Cool; refrigerate. Makes 3 cups of dressing.

Part Two

IOWA SPECIALTIES

SWEET CORN

It has been said that sweet corn ears, fixed properly, should always be "run from the garden row to the kettle boiling for them before the shock of being picked has a chance to make them nervous or revengefully tough." Maybe that's why the hot, buttered corn on the cob served with the beef burgers and lemonade at the sixty-second annual Gladbrook Corn Carnival tasted exceptionally tender and milky-sweet. The sixty-dozen ears didn't have much of a chance to get "nervous," and neither did the Tama County Beef Producers and Cowbelles, who sponsored the dinner for seven hundred. Only a few hours earlier, the meal's feature attraction arrived, husks and all. But Paul Koester, the friendly young beef producer coordinating the event, had everything under control.

"Anybody who wants to help us shuck some corn, we sure can use you," he called out to some bystanders. Within a few minutes a handful of recruits were perched around the sides of the dusty green pick-up. With sleeves rolled up they peeled off the snug wrappings, cornsilks and all, with a few swift yanks. Almost miraculously (at least from a novice husker's point of view), every ear was ready for the boiling pot by 7:30 P.M., right on schedule.

These huskers were clearly no amateurs. But then, what would you expect from the largest corn-producing state in the nation? Corn production in Iowa has quadrupled since 1929 from 400 million bushels to about 1.7 billion bushels annually. To put that in perspective, industry spokespeople point out that one bushel of corn will provide twenty-three people with enough food, energy, and protein for a day's nutritional requirement.

The citizens of Gladbrook honor their state's number one cash crop early in July each year with a parade, a few carnival rides, exhibits and drawings put on by local merchants, and fare ranging from hamburgers and hot dogs to Indian fry bread. The carnival frequently arrives before the corn does, especially if, as the old saying goes, the corn isn't "knee-high by the Fourth of July." So why not postpone the carnival until they

can be sure the guests of honor will be present? "If we did that, every-body'd be too busy harvesting to come to the carnival," Koester replied with a shrug.

Gladbrook is only one community which outwardly expresses its pride for the state's top resource. Elkader, West Point, and West Union also host sweet corn festivals during harvest season. And the Old-Fashioned Husking Bee at Living History Farms attracts hordes of brawny contenders to test their stamina each fall. In the town of What Cheer, a woman uses an old Indian recipe to make corncob jellies and syrups which may be mail-ordered or purchased in tourist spots all over the state.

Iowa's abundant corn yields are attributable not only to its fertile soil but to the work of Adair County native Henry A. Wallace, secretary of agriculture and vice-president under Franklin Roosevelt. As a young Iowa State College graduate, Wallace developed a hybrid seed corn through genetic experiments and in 1926 his family and some associates started the Hi-Bred Corn Company in Johnston, Iowa, to market it. The company currently produces about a third of the nation's seed corn. The techniques of inbreeding and crossbreeding developed by Wallace and his colleagues now make it possible to develop strains of corn for practically any type of soil.

Field corn, characterized by a dented kernel, is the main constituent of the diets of Iowa's top-quality cattle and hogs. In addition to both yellow and white sweet corn, "a lot of farmers around here are growing a variety called 'honey and cream,' which has both white and yellow kernels," said Bill Brandt of Dysart, who raises corn and beef. Brandt, who was in charge of boiling the corn at the Gladbrook Corn Carnival this year, says that regardless of the color of its kernel, corn should always "be picked before it gets too ripe; there's more sugar in it that way." Many Iowans who also raise beef find ways of combining the two, including Brandt, who says he always makes his one-dish corn and beef bake whenever his grandchildren come for a visit.

Here is Brandt's recipe, along with other local corn favorites from Gladbrook and around the state.

Bill Brandt's
One-Dish Corn and Beef Bake

1½ pounds ground beef
1 medium onion, chopped
1 10½-ounce can condensed
   tomato soup
½ teaspoon salt
¼ teaspoon pepper

2 cups fresh or frozen corn, or 1
   16-ounce can whole-kernel
   corn, drained
1 8-ounce package enriched
   refrigerator biscuits

Preheat oven to 425 degrees. Brown ground beef and onion in a frying pan, stirring occasionally. Stir in soup, salt, pepper, and corn. Bring to a boil and then pour into a 1½-quart round casserole dish. Separate biscuits and arrange on top of corn mixture. Bake in preheated oven for 15 to 20 minutes, or until biscuits are lightly browned. Makes 4 to 6 servings.

Scalloped Corn

2 cups cooked corn (fresh, frozen,   1 teaspoon granulated sugar
    or canned)   2 tablespoons melted butter
1 cup milk   ½ cup soda crackers, crushed
3 eggs   ½ to 1 cup crushed cornflakes,
½ teaspoon salt   divided
¼ teaspoon pepper

Preheat oven to 350 degrees. Combine thoroughly all ingredients except
cornflakes. Place half of the mixture in a buttered 1-quart baking dish.
Sprinkle cornflakes on top. Put in rest of corn mixture, then remaining
crushed cornflakes. Bake 20 to 30 minutes. Makes 4 servings.

BERNEDA V. THEDE

Here's a tangy accompaniment to fried chicken, hamburgers, or pork
chops.

Corn Relish

1 10-ounce package frozen,   2 tablespoons finely chopped
    whole-kernel corn   green pepper
½ cup granulated sugar   2 tablespoons chopped pimiento
1 tablespoon cornstarch   1 tablespoon chopped onion
½ cup vinegar   1 teaspoon ground turmeric
⅓ cup cold water   ½ teaspoon dry mustard
2 tablespoons finely chopped
    celery

Cook corn according to package directions; drain. In a saucepan, combine sugar and cornstarch; stir in vinegar and cold water. Add corn, celery, green pepper, pimiento, onion, turmeric, and dry mustard. Cook,
stirring constantly, until thickened and bubbly; cook and stir 3 to 4 minutes longer. Cover and chill thoroughly. Makes 2 cups.

ALMA GILCHRIST

Here's an interesting experiment to try with your leftover corncobs. Its
subtle corn flavor makes for a delicious alternative topping for pancakes
and waffles.

Corncob Syrup

12 cobs red field corn (or sweet *4 quarts water*
 corn if field corn is not   *1½ cups light brown sugar*
 available)   *2½ cups granulated sugar*

Remove kernels from cobs. Break cobs and place them in a large kettle. Cover with 4 quarts water. Boil for 30 minutes. Drain, reserving liquid, then add sugars to liquid. Bring to boil and simmer until desired consistency. Makes 2 to 3 cups of syrup.

LIVING HISTORY FARMS

This unusual condiment is based upon several recipes from Iowa cookbooks. Try it on toast or hot biscuits.

Corncob Jelly

6 or 8 sweet corncobs (kernels *4 cups granulated sugar*
 removed)   *Few drops yellow food color*
Water to cover   *(optional)*
1 1¾-ounce box Sure Jell

In a large kettle, boil sweet corncobs for 10 to 15 minutes in water to cover. Strain liquid; measure 3 cups liquid back into the same pan. Add Sure Jell and bring to a rolling boil. Add sugar; bring to a boil again and boil for 1 minute. Stir in food coloring. Pour into hot, sterilized glasses and seal with paraffin. Fills 5 6-ounce glasses.

The next two recipes are adapted from *Recipes from Iowa . . . with Love* by Peg Hein and Kathryn Cramer (New Boundary Designs, Inc., Chanhassen, Minn., 1982).

Skillet Sweet Corn

"Cream corn right off the cob."

6 ears corn
6 tablespoons butter
½ cup light cream

½ teaspoon salt
½ teaspoon granulated sugar
Ground pepper to taste

Husk corn and remove silks. Slice off kernels with a long sharp knife or electric knife. Using the back of a dinner knife, scrape the milky substance from the cob into the corn. Heat butter in a skillet, add corn and milky substance, and cook and stir 3 to 4 minutes or until desired tenderness. Add cream and seasonings. Stir over low heat for 2 to 3 minutes. Makes 4 servings.

Cream of Corn Soup

2 slices bacon, finely diced
2 tablespoons finely chopped
    onion
2 cups frozen or fresh corn
2 tablespoons butter
2 tablespoons all-purpose flour

2 cups milk
1 teaspoon salt
1/4 teaspoon pepper
2 cups light cream

In a medium saucepan, fry bacon until crisp. Add onion and sauté over medium heat until soft. Add corn to bacon and onion and cook until corn begins to brown. Add butter, stir until melted, and then add flour. Cook for 3 minutes. Add milk, salt, and pepper and cook until thickened. Add cream and heat thoroughly. Makes 4 to 6 servings.

From the Mamrelund Lutheran Church cookbook, contributed by Mrs. Lester R. Anderson, Mary Hanson, and Mrs. Lyle Wickstrom.

Spectacular Frozen Corn

35 to 40 (depending on size) fresh
    sweet corn ears
1/2 to 1 pound butter or top brand
    margarine

1 pint half-and-half
1 teaspoon butter flavoring
    (optional)

Husk, silk, and wash corn. Cut 18 cups of corn from the cobs and place in a heavy roaster. Add butter and half-and-half and butter flavoring, if desired. Place in a 300- to a 325-degree oven. Cook 1 hour, stirring occasionally. Remove from oven. Cool down by dividing into two pans and place them in a sink with ice water. When cool, package and freeze as quickly as possible. To serve, heat through and season to taste. Makes 35 to 40 servings.

By far the most popular way to take advantage of Iowa's number one cash crop is in its purest form. Eleanor Cook Thomas of Cedar Rapids, a former student of Grant Wood's, shared her technique in the *American Gothic Cookbook* (Penfield Press, 215 Brown St., Iowa City, Iowa 52240).

Corn on the Cob, Iowa-Style

1 tablespoon sugar   *Enough corn on the cob for each person*

Use a large pan with a cover. Fill half full with water; add sugar. Add corn, cover, and boil for exactly 5 minutes. Remove corn and place immediately on a towel on a plate and wrap completely. Serve at once. Keep pan of water hot and bring to a boil again each time a round is cooked. Do not remove the pan from the heat until everyone has had enough corn. The corn is served first, and nothing else is served until everyone has had enough.

Joyce Dennison of Mount Pleasant gets credit for this whole-meal version of scalloped corn, which makes a great potluck supper dish as well as a brunch entrée. It's featured in the *Midwest Old Threshers Cookbook,* published by the Midwest Old Threshers Association (Midwest Old Threshers, Route 1, Threshers Road, Mount Pleasant, Iowa 52641). Each year since 1950, the group has sponsored the Midwest Old Threshers Reunion, one of the Midwest's top farm events and the nation's largest steam festival. Featured are steam engines, antique tractors, gas engines, vintage cars, horsedrawn vehicles, and artisans at work demonstrating early-day crafts such as caning, carving, and soap making. Not surprisingly, corn on the cob is an essential constituent of the Old Threshers dinners served by church groups along with other delicacies of the era: fried chicken, hordes of vegetables, relishes, cakes, pies, and ice cream.

Golden Corned Beef Casserole

½ cup (1 stick) margarine
2 green peppers, chopped
2 large onions, chopped
2 12-ounce chunks of corned beef
2 16-ounce cans cream-style corn

1½ cups crushed crackers
1½ teaspoons salt
½ teaspoon pepper
1 tablespoon minced parsley
2 cups milk
5 beaten eggs

Preheat oven to 375 degrees. In a large skillet, melt the margarine. Add peppers and onions and sauté until tender. Transfer to a large bowl and add corned beef. Stir in remaining ingredients. Pour into an oiled 3-quart casserole or 9 × 13-inch dish. Bake until set, 45 minutes to 1 hour. Makes 8 to 10 servings.

POPCORN

Hollywood can't take all the credit for the success of the movie industry. Sac County, Iowa, has also made a valuable contribution. It's a leading producer not of Oscar-winning films but of the long-standing hit of the concession stands: popcorn.

The popular snack food has been grown in the area ever since the Indians discovered it centuries ago, but it wasn't until 1888 that a local Odebolt farmer tried growing a few acres of it commercially. As the other farmers watched their neighbor's crop grow and flourish, they began making experimental plantings of their own.

By the turn of the century, Odebolt was said to have bought, housed, and shipped more popcorn than anywhere else in the world. Although that claim no longer holds true, there's no question that popcorn is still the pride crop of Sac County. Up until the last decade or so it boasted of ten popcorn companies, several of which have since been bought out by larger firms. "And that's in a county of only about 15,000 people," pointed out James Stock, president of the Stock Popcorn Company in Lake View and vice-president of the National Popcorn Association. An ex-Marine captain who grew up with a perpetually blistered thumb from shucking fresh ears of popcorn on the family farm, Stock decided to make the crunchy kernels his livelihood in 1969 when he took over the Armstrong Popcorn Company, which had been established nearly half a century earlier.

Nowadays he distributes popcorn grown in Iowa, Nebraska, Minnesota, and South Dakota throughout the United States and Canada. Though he sells to some theaters and large packers, most of his product is packaged in miniature burlap sacks under the Little Chief Popcorn label and sold through fund-raising drives. "Recently we've begun putting it in white cotton bags with a drawstring and allowing the [fund-raising] group to design their own bags," he said. "We like to personalize the trade as much as we can."

In the field the ears of popcorn, both white and yellow, look much like miniature versions of sweet corn. Once harvested, they're delivered to the bin site where they're put into cribs to dry naturally for six to nine months or field-shelled and then force-dried in mechanical driers. Although it's not always feasible, Stock greatly prefers to let the cobs dry naturally. "They tend to yield a higher-quality kernel."

Before each batch is ready for market, a sample of the kernels is put through a machine to measure its moisture content and expansion. "We heat a pan with a temperature control to 480 degrees, then put in half a cup of oil. When the pan is hot, we add 250 grams of kernels. As it pops, it fills a calibrated tube. Then we get a kernel count for 10 grams."

Each kernel should expand to about forty times its original size; the bigger it gets, the better, Stock says. There are numerous varieties of popcorn in existence, each with its own specific purpose, he added. "Most of the popcorn you get at the movies is light and flaky and real tender; that's what people like to experience in the theater." From a profit standpoint, theater owners prefer the larger yellow kernels, because they "fill the bag up quicker." Some people, including himself, favor the taste of the white popcorn, which tends to be "smaller and more tender." Larger, tougher kernels are needed to withstand the caramel coating of Cracker Jacks. Years back, candy manufacturers found other imaginative uses for the kernel. One firm is said to have purchased it in "carload lots" so that it could be popped and ground into a soft flour for making soft chocolate candies.

Stock also sells kernels appropriate for microwaving, and lately he's been investigating the possibility of supplying the products for yet another new popcorn marketing scheme: popcorn on the cob, sold in a jar. The idea, he said, is to "give people the experience of shelling popcorn themselves. A lot of city kids have no idea where popcorn comes from. And if the corn is allowed to dry naturally, it should pop to a higher expansion than the corn that sits in corn cribs."

At home, Stock and his family have tried numerous ways of making use of the kernel with varying degrees of success. "I once tried to make corn bread with it, but it really didn't come out too good," he recalled with a chuckle. "Maybe I should have ground the corn finer. I'm hooked on just the buttered and salted popcorn myself."

Other folks around the Lake View area have produced more successful experiments with their town's leading product, as evidenced by these entries which appeared in their centennial cookbook. Ai Walrod, son of one of the Lake View rural pioneers, concocted this unusual taffylike treat at Christmastime. According to his daughter Shirley, "Any other time of the year almost became Christmas when he mixed up another batch."

Ai's Popcorn Candy

3 cups granulated sugar
3 cups Karo syrup
½ cup (1 stick) butter

10 to 12 cups salted, ground
    popcorn (6 quarts popped)

In a 6-to-8-quart saucepan over medium heat, combine sugar, syrup, and butter. Cook to soft-ball stage (234 degrees). Remove from heat and stir in all the salted, ground popcorn you can. Spread in a buttered 9 × 13-inch pan. Let set. Cut into small squares. Makes about 70 pieces.

Marshmallow Popcorn Balls

6 tablespoons butter or margarine   3 tablespoons (half of a 3-ounce
3 cups minature marshmallows   box) any flavor Jell-O
                                       3 quarts unsalted popped corn

In a medium saucepan, melt butter or margarine over low heat. Add
marshmallows; stir until melted. Stir in Jell-O. Pour over popcorn, mixing
well. With buttered hands, form into balls. Makes 12 medium (3-inch) or
18 small (2-inch) balls.

Bango Popcorn Balls

2 cups granulated sugar   1 tablespoon butter
1 cup dark corn syrup   ½ teaspoon baking soda
½ teaspoon cream of tartar   6 quarts popcorn

In a large saucepan, cook sugar, corn syrup, cream of tartar, and butter
to hard crack stage (290 degrees). Remove from fire, add baking soda,
and pour over popcorn. Transfer to an enamel dishpan. Grease hands
and form into balls. Nuts and coloring may be added. Makes about 24
3-inch balls.

ANABEL SMIDT

Karo Crazy Crunch

"A good treat at Christmastime."

2 quarts popped corn   1 cup (2 sticks) margarine
1⅓ cups pecans   ½ cup Karo syrup
⅔ cup almonds   1 teaspoon vanilla
1⅓ cups granulated sugar

Mix popped corn and nuts together. In a medium saucepan, combine
sugar, margarine, and syrup. Bring to a boil over medium heat, stirring
constantly. Continue boiling, stirring occasionally, for 10 to 15 minutes

or until mixture turns a light caramel color. Remove from heat; add vanilla. Pour over popped corn and nuts; coat well. Spread onto cookie sheet to dry. Break apart. Makes about 3 quarts.

JERI SCHULTE

Oven Caramel Corn

1 cup (2 sticks) margarine
2 cups brown sugar
½ cup Karo syrup
1 teaspoon salt

1 tablespoon vanilla
½ teaspoon baking soda
5 quarts popped popcorn

Preheat oven to 250 degrees. In a medium saucepan over medium heat, combine margarine, brown sugar, syrup, and salt; bring to a boil, stirring constantly. Boil for 5 minutes. Add vanilla and baking soda. Pour over popped popcorn. Stir well. Spread in roaster in preheated oven for 1 hour. Stir every 15 minutes. Store in airtight containers. Makes 5 quarts.

BARB BUNDT, ALVERA RUCHTI, FRAN SCHMIDT, LUCILE STOELK, MARY TJADEN

THE IOWA CHOP

Folks everywhere immediately associate sourdough bread with San Francisco, cream cheese with Philadelphia, lobster with Maine, and a budget-buster of a beef strip with New York. And more and more they're beginning to recognize another area's claim to fame: the state of Iowa and its Iowa chop.

The Iowa chop is no ordinary chop, as any Iowan can testify. Perhaps no one knows the difference better than the John Wall family, one of Johnson County's most active pork-producing families. "To be a true Iowa chop, it's got to be a lean, center-cut loin or rib chop that's an inch and a fourth to an inch and a half thick," Wall explained. When company comes for dinner at the Walls' cozy home off the bumpy rural route near Solon, it's a good bet that the main course will be this succulent, home-raised delicacy, especially if the guests are from out of state.

"I don't think I've ever served an Iowa chop to anybody that hasn't liked it," Mary Ellen Wall claimed. When the weather's warm, she or her husband may grill the chops outdoors in a spicy barbecue sauce or a beer marinade. Or if the forecast isn't so favorable, she may bake them in the oven with seasonings and a little butter or with a savory stuffing.

The concept of the Iowa chop was developed several decades ago, Wall said, "but it wasn't until around '75 or '76 that the pork producers began a nationwide campaign to try to promote it. I guess every state wants to have something they're especially known for. Since Iowa produces 25 percent of the nation's pork, the chop seemed like a logical choice." He and his wife cited several reasons why it took so long for the Iowa chop to reach the marketplace.

"In the old days, people never cut them that thick because they were worried about trichina, a parasite found in uncooked pork," Mrs. Wall said. The quality of pork, however, has improved to such an extent that trichinosis in this country today is rarely heard of. As an extra precaution, the pork producers advise cooking the chops to 160 degrees, the ideal temperature for pork.

Besides being safer to eat, the pork Wall eats today has only about half the fat of the pork he grew up on, he said. A three-ounce serving of lean pork today contains less than two hundred calories and is loaded with protein, iron, thiamine, and other nutrients.

The entire Wall family educates not only their dinner guests on the product but the general public as well. For Wall that means riding in parades, sponsoring or promoting Iowa chop feasts at state and county fairs, and talking to consumers in supermarkets throughout the country. As a member of the Porkettes, the women's auxiliary to the Pork Producers, Mrs. Wall participates in school and community demonstrations and programs featuring Iowa chops as well as other pork products. Such activities have earned for her the Bell Ringer Award, presented to the Porkette whom the Pork Producers believe has contributed the most to the industry, for both the county and the state.

Both their son Tom, an Iowa State graduate who now farms with his dad, and daughter Mary, a former Pork Queen, have collected enough ribbons and trophies for their 4-H pork projects to fill a trophy case. The family's contributions to the community, particularly in the area of pork, also haven't gone unrecognized. Several years ago they were presented Johnson County's Farm Family of the Year award. And it probably came as a surprise to no one when in 1980 recording star and television entertainer Kenny Rogers picked the Walls to feature as a typical Iowa farm family on a fifteen-minute segment of his television show "Kenny Rogers' America." Hanging on the wall in the living room above the trophy case is a framed photograph of the silver-bearded entertainer at the dining room table with the Walls eating a hearty breakfast of pancakes, kolaches, and, of course, fresh pork sausages, all prepared by Mrs. Wall. Had he stayed for supper, he might have gotten a taste of the stuffed Iowa chops her family raves about. Here's Mrs. Wall's recipe, along with some other delectable ways Iowans have devised for preparing their local specialty.

Mary Ellen Wall's
Stuffed Iowa Chops

1 tablespoon butter
¼ cup chopped celery
¼ cup chopped onion
2 cups coarse bread crumbs
1 egg, beaten
¼ teaspoon salt
½ teaspoon sage

½ cup chicken giblets, ground or
  chopped (optional)
Enough milk or chicken broth to
  moisten dressing
4 Iowa chops, 1¼ to 1½ inches
  thick, with pockets cut

Preheat oven to 325 degrees. In a small skillet, melt butter. Add celery and onion and sauté until tender. Mix with bread crumbs, egg, salt, sage, and giblets and moisten with milk or broth. Fill pockets of chops and fasten together with toothpicks. Sear chops in a hot skillet with a little fat, then place them in a baking dish. (Remaining dressing can be added around the sides of the chops.) Bake 1 hour covered, then 20 minutes uncovered. Makes 4 servings.

Porkettes' Chops à l'Orange

*4 Iowa chops, 1¼ to 1½ inches
    thick
Fat for frying
Salt and pepper
⅔ cup long grain rice
1 cup water
1 cup orange juice*

*½ cup chopped apple
¼ cup raisins
2 tablespoons brown or
    granulated sugar
½ teaspoon ground cinnamon
½ teaspoon salt
Thin orange slices (optional)*

Preheat oven to 350 degrees. In a large skillet (preferably ovenproof), brown chops in hot fat. Season with salt and pepper. Remove chops and set aside, reserving drippings. In the same skillet, cook rice in reserved drippings until golden, stirring constantly. Stir in water and orange juice; bring to a boil. Reduce heat; stir in apple, raisins, sugar, cinnamon, and salt. If your pan is not ovenproof, turn mixture into a 9 × 9 × 2-inch baking pan. Arrange chops atop rice mixture. Cover with foil and bake in preheated oven for 40 minutes. Remove cover; arrange orange slices on top if desired. Bake, uncovered, 10 minutes longer or until chops are tender. Makes 4 servings.

Corn-Stuffed Chops

*4 pork rib chops, cut 1½ inches
    thick (about 3 pounds total)
3 tablespoons butter or margarine
½ cup fresh, frozen, or drained
    canned corn
½ cup chopped celery
½ cup chopped mushrooms
¼ cup chopped green or red
    pepper*

*¼ cup sliced green onions or
    shallots
2 cups herb-seasoned stuffing
½ cup hot water
1 beaten egg
2 tablespoons fresh, snipped
    parsley
Salt and pepper to taste*

Grilling chops at the Iowa State Fair

Trim fat from pork chops. With a sharp knife, cut an opening in the rib side of each chop. Insert the knife into each opening and cut a pocket without cutting through to the other side of the chop. Set chops aside.

In a large skillet, melt butter or margarine. Add corn, celery, mushrooms, green or red pepper, and green onions or shallots and cook over medium heat about 5 minutes, stirring occasionally, until vegetables are tender. Add herb-seasoned stuffing, hot water, egg, and parsley; toss gently. Spoon about ½ cup stuffing mixture into each chop. Placed stuffed chops on rack in broiler pan. Broil 4 to 5 inches from heat for 10 to 12 minutes on each side, or until cooked through. Season chops to taste with salt and pepper. Makes 4 servings.

Marinated Iowa Chops

4 Iowa chops, 1¼ to 1½ inches   *½ cup olive oil*
   thick   *⅛ teaspoon pepper*
¼ cup soy sauce   *¼ teaspoon dried basil*
¼ teaspoon thyme   *¼ cup vinegar*
¼ cup chopped onion

Place chops in a nonaluminum baking dish. In a bowl, stir together remaining ingredients. Pour over chops; cover and let marinate, refrigerated, at least 2 hours or overnight. Cook over medium to low gas grill for
30 to 45 minutes, or until cooked through. Makes 4 servings.

KATHY TABKE

Cracker-Coated Iowa Chops

2 egg whites   *1 cup finely crushed saltine*
2 Iowa chops, 1¼ to 1½ inches   *crackers*
   thick   *½ cup (1 stick) margarine*
                             1 teaspoon seasoned salt

Gently whip egg whites with a fork. *Do not beat.* Dip chops in egg whites,
then roll in cracker crumbs. Repeat. Melt margarine and seasoned salt in
a heavy skillet over medium heat. Fry chops slowly until golden brown,
about 20 minutes on each side. Makes 2 servings.

BEP NOTEBOOM

MAYTAG BLUE CHEESE

Don't bother searching every cheese market in Europe for the world's finest blue cheese. Try your own back door—here in Iowa!

Perhaps no other cheese in the country has done more to erase the stigma attached to the term "American cheese" than the blue-veined products produced at the Maytag Dairy Farm in Newton, Iowa. In taste tests among blue cheese varieties from all over the world, renowned food authorities, including the late James Beard, have rated Maytag blue above all its European competitors: Italy's gorgonzola, Britain's Stilton, Denmark's blue, and even France's prized Roquefort made from sheep's milk. Its producers attribute that superior rating to the personal touch that goes into every wheel of cheese. "We're probably the smallest blue cheese makers in the United States, and that's probably why we're the best," remarked one of the workers.

The farm is located scarcely a mile away from the modern, sprawling plant which houses the Maytag washing machine industry, a sharp contrast to the pastoral countryside where herds of black and white Holstein-Friesian cattle graze. E. H. Maytag, son of the washing machine mogul, heard about the high-quality milk produced by the cattle back in the 1920s and decided to raise them as a hobby. After his death in 1940, his son Frederick and Mel Campbell, the herd manager who later became vice-president of the company, set out to find a unique product to make use of the milk. During their quest they learned of a new process for making American blue cheese formulated by Dr. Verner Nielsen and a team of dairy scientists at Iowa State University's food technology department. Nielsen had learned the process by observing it firsthand in Denmark and then shared those secrets with his students.

Maytag Dairy Farms worked out an agreement with Iowa State which would allow them to use the university's patented process, and one of the dairy's creamery men was sent to the campus to learn the technique. Some were a little skeptical the first time they tasted the creamy but strangely pungent new cheese, including Mel's nine-year-old son Donn. "I remember thinking to myself, 'Gee, that tastes sorta funny, but I sup-

pose I'll try it again,'" recalled the younger Campbell, who now sits behind the president's desk at the dairy farms' main office. Its taste gradually became accepted as more and more curious customers decided to
sample it a second or third time. Soon its popularity began growing by
"leaps and bounds, not just in Iowa but in other parts of the country as
well," Campbell said.

Each year a handful of cheesemakers at the plant produce about a
quarter of a million pounds of the blue cheese not much differently from
the way the first vat was made more than forty years ago. The cottage
cheese–like curds coagulated from fresh Holstein milk are still stirred
by hand with Paul Bunyan–size wooden forks until they're "firm like
Jell-O," one of the cheesemakers explained. After being drained and
placed in stainless steel hoops, the cheese is inoculated with the mold
from whole wheat bread crusts to give it its distinctive racy flavor. The
wheels are then dipped one at a time in hot wax and placed on wooden
slats in a manmade "cave" for six months, about twice as long as most
blue cheese varieties. Once the aging process is complete, the wax is
removed and the outer surface is scraped. Some of the wheels are
wrapped as they are in foil; others are cut into wedges with the cheese
cutters made from parts of old wooden washing machines. Along with
the blue cheese, the farms also produce a raw-milk cheddar cheese and
an Edam cheese. Campbell's wife, Linda, sister Lois, and other family
members, with the help of a home economist, devise and test many of
the recipes using Maytag products which appear in pamphlets and
booklets sent out to mail-order customers. (To request a free catalog,
write Maytag Dairy Farms, RR1, Box 806, Newton, Iowa 50208, or call
1-800-247-2458, or, in Iowa, 1-800-BLU-CHES.) A number of those recipes
are sent in by the customers themselves. Here are just a few of the
Campbells' all-time favorites using Maytag blue.

Donn's Delight Salad Dressing

½ cup mayonnaise
2 ounces Maytag blue cheese
3 tablespoons light cream
1 teaspoon granulated sugar
1 teaspoon parsley flakes
2 teaspoons lemon juice
2 teaspoons vinegar

1 teaspoon grated onion
½ teaspoon Worcestershire sauce
½ teaspoon prepared horseradish
¼ teaspoon garlic salt
Dash of freshly ground pepper

Add mayonnaise to room temperature blue cheese; blend thoroughly until smooth. Add remaining ingredients; mix well. Cover and chill. Makes 1 cup salad dressing.

Blue Velvet Mousse

2 egg yolks
¼ cup light cream
1 envelope (1 tablespoon)
   unflavored gelatin
¼ cup cold water

8 ounces Maytag blue cheese,
   pressed through a sieve
2 egg whites, stiffly beaten
1 cup whipping cream, whipped
Chopped parsley for garnish

In a saucepan, combine egg yolks and cream; stir constantly over low heat till mixture thickens slightly and coats a metal spoon. Remove from heat immediately. Soften gelatin in cold water; dissolve over hot water. Add to egg yolk mixture. Stir in blue cheese. Gently fold in egg whites and whipped cream. Pour into lightly oiled 1-quart mold. Chill several hours, or till firm. Unmold on serving plate and garnish with parsley. Serve with assorted crackers and melba toast. Makes about 20 appetizer servings.

Burgers Sophisticate

1 pound ground chuck
4 tablespoons crumbled Maytag
   blue cheese
Dash of garlic salt
Dash of pepper
¼ cup burgundy wine

2 tablespoons water
1 teaspoon Worcestershire sauce
Blue cheese croutons (recipe
   follows)

Divide ground chuck into eighths. Place 4 portions between layers of waxed paper. With a rolling pin, roll thin patties about 4 inches in diameter. Sprinkle each pattie with 1 tablespoon blue cheese. Roll remaining ground beef into thin patties. Place atop blue cheese; seal edges. Brown burgers quickly on both sides; pour off grease. Reduce heat. Sprinkle lightly with garlic salt and pepper. Add wine, water, and Worcestershire

sauce. Cover and cook slowly 10 to 15 minutes. Remove burgers to warm serving plate; spoon sauce over them. Top with croutons. Makes 4 servings.

Blue Cheese Croutons

In a saucepan, combine 1 ounce (about 3 tablespoons) Maytag blue cheese and 3 tablespoons butter. Stir over low heat until melted and blended. With pastry brush, brush mixture onto 6 slices of white bread. Cut each slice of bread in 5 strips one way, then across 5 times to make cubes. Spread cubes on baking sheet. Heat in very slow (225-degree) oven 2 hours till very crisp and dry. Cool; store in a jar. Makes 1 quart.

Lois Cox's Stuffed Mushrooms

1 pound fresh mushrooms
¼ cup (½ stick) butter
3 green onions, cut up, tops and
  all
½ cup finely grated bread crumbs
3 tablespoons crumbled Maytag
  blue cheese

1 tablespoon minced parsley,
  fresh if possible
1 tablespoon lemon juice
½ teaspoon salt
Paprika

Preheat oven to 450 degrees. Remove stems from mushrooms, chop, and sauté in butter with onions. Add crumbs, cheese, parsley, lemon juice, and salt. Mix all together and stuff into mushroom caps; place caps into a shallow baking pan. Sprinkle with paprika and bake 8 minutes in pre-heated oven until slightly brown. Serve hot. Makes 6 to 8 appetizer servings.

This recipe, developed by Maytag president Donn Campbell, was first served at a Taste of Iowa food show in Davenport and later at a governor's conference in Des Moines.

Blue Satin Soup

4 tablespoons butter
¼ cup finely minced green onion
¼ cup finely minced green pepper
¼ cup finely minced celery
½ cup all-purpose flour
1 14-ounce can chicken broth

4 ounces Maytag blue cheese
1 cup light cream
1 cup milk
2 ounces dry sherry
Freshly ground pepper
Sour cream, chives, and croutons
    for garnish

In a heavy saucepan, melt butter; add vegetables and sauté very slowly until soft but not brown. Add flour and cook, stirring constantly, over low heat a few minutes until flour is cooked but not brown. Add warm chicken broth, stirring constantly to prevent lumps, and simmer 2 minutes. Add blue cheese and stir until smooth. Add cream and milk and heat to serving temperature (do not boil). Add sherry and pepper to taste and serve garnished with sour cream, chives, and croutons. Makes 6 to 8 appetizer or 3 to 4 main-course servings.

Blue Cheese–Artichoke Salad

⅓ cup olive oil or salad oil
2 tablespoons red wine vinegar
4 tablespoons lemon juice, or 6
    tablespoons white wine vinegar
1½ teaspoons salt
¼ teaspoon pepper
1 teaspoon granulated sugar
2½ to 3 quarts salad greens (head
    lettuce, leaf lettuce, and
    parsley), washed, dried, chilled,
    and broken into bite-size pieces

1 6-ounce jar marinated artichoke
    hearts, drained and cut into
    bite-size pieces
1 8-ounce can water chestnuts,
    sliced
2 tablespoons chopped sweet red
    pepper or pimiento
¼ cup Maytag blue cheese

Mix oil, red wine vinegar, lemon juice, salt, pepper, and sugar. Place salad greens, artichoke hearts, water chestnuts, sweet red pepper or pimiento, and blue cheese in a large bowl. Toss with dressing. Makes 8 to 10 servings.

This easy but elegant dish is the concoction of Donn Campbell's son-in-law.

Tom Cunningham's
Shrimp Fettuccine

*4 ounces Maytag blue cheese,
   room temperature*
*8 ounces cream cheese, room
   temperature*
⅓ cup dry white wine
2 tablespoons half-and-half
*¼ cup parsley, very finely
   chopped*

*4 scallions, finely chopped (tops,
   too)*
1 clove garlic, minced
*Freshly ground pepper (we like
   lots)*
*1 pound cooked, shelled, and
   deveined shrimp*
8 ounces fettuccine

Preheat oven to 375 degrees. Bring a large pot of salted water to a boil. Combine room temperature cheeses with wine and half-and-half in a 2-quart casserole. Add parsley, scallions, garlic, pepper, and shrimp and bake in preheated oven until heated through, about 20 minutes. Meanwhile, cook fettuccine in boiling water al dente. Toss cooked fettuccine with shrimp/cheese mixture. Makes 4 servings.

APPLES AND CIDER

Not many Iowans these days have access to their own orchard for apple picking and cider making, yet they can still fight the bitterness of a brisk winter day with a mug of steaming cider as rich and sweet as the juices that once flowed from their grandparents' hand-cranked presses. Jerald Deal, a man who says he's "always felt at home up in a tree," makes enough cider to satisfy hundreds of fans of "true" cider within at least a fifty-mile radius of his orchard near Jefferson.

Interestingly enough, it was in Peru, Iowa, that the best-known apple of all—the Red Delicious—came to be. It sprang up by itself from a wild seedling in the orchard of a Quaker named Jesse Hiatt outside his regular rows. Twice he cut it down, but when the sturdy little tree grew back a third time larger than ever he decided to let it live. Ten years later it bore a strawberry-colored apple streaked with dark red. Hiatt took one bite and proclaimed it "the best apple in the world." For years he took samples of his apple, which he called the Hawkeye, everywhere he went. In 1893 he sent four of his Hawkeyes to a fruit show in Louisiana, Missouri, sponsored by Stark Nurseries. The apple won first prize. C. M. Stark was so impressed he renamed it the Red Delicious apple and bought the propagating rights. Today it's the world's most popular apple variety and is grown on every continent.

Iowa is still fertile territory for apple growing, as the Deals can attest. Jerald's grandfather Frank Deal planted the first tree on the family orchard in 1917, "back when just about everybody around here had at least a few apple trees in their back yard," Jerald said. "Making cider was more of a hobby to him than anything else. Grandpa—he really enjoyed that sort of thing." From that tiny grove grew a forty-three acre orchard flourishing with dozens of apple varieties which are prominently displayed on long wooden tables inside the barn. Along with the familiar Red and Golden Delicious, Winesaps, McIntoshes, and Jonathans, there are also some lesser-known varieties: Red Birds, Jo Annes, King Davids, Snyder O'Connells.

"The Snow apple is a novelty that's fun to show the kids," said Jerald's wife, Cindy, who gave up schoolteaching to sack apples, jug cider, and act as tour guide for busloads of schoolchildren on field trips to the Deal orchards. "The flesh of most apples is slightly yellow, but the Snows are pure white." Jerald's father, Forrest, an expert at grafting apple plants, is responsible for many of those offbeat varieties. Jerald assists in just about all other aspects of the operation, whether it's "making sure the bees are doing their job" transferring pollen from the tiny spring blossoms or giving the trees "flat tops" so the highest apple can be reached during harvest.

A few years ago Deal replaced the old hand-cranked contraption his grandfather used for making cider more than half a century ago with a modern hydraulic press, increasing a day's production of one hundred gallons seven- or eightfold. Handfuls of apples from a water trough are sent up a chute to a hammer mill comprised of "lots of tiny knives that cut the apples into small pieces," he explained. Those pieces are then pressed between wooden slats covered with cheesecloth, which must be wrung out by hand between batches. No preservatives are added or heat treatment applied, and Jerald admits that "our filtering system isn't nearly as refined as other orchards." And he's quick to warn that if it's not drunk or frozen within a couple of weeks, "it'll start to get a little kick to it and turn to vinegar."

But Deal makes no apologies. "Some people don't think preservatives change the flavor, but to us, the taste of processed cider just doesn't compare to fresh. That's what our customers expect from us, and we've never seen any reason to give them anything different."

Before the cloudy, amber juice was pumped into the four hundred–gallon holding tank for jugging on this particular day, Deal took a swig from a paper cup. He frowned. "Gotta add more Johnnies, Leon," he yelled to his assistant over the raucous machinery. "To get the degree of tartness and sweetness you want, you've got to have just the right blend of varieties," he said. That "recipe" varies, depending on which apples are in season. "The ones that are harvested first tend to be more bland and mushy than the later ones; better for cooking," Cindy added. Her mother-in-law, Edna, has another method for determining which apples to recommend to her customers. "Every time we harvest a new recipe, I make an apple pie with it," she said. "Or if we're tired of pie, maybe muffins or apple crisp, or fried apples in butter." Here are some Deal specialties.

Apples from the Deal orchards

Pink Apple Pie

*Pastry for a 9-inch double-crust
   pie*
*5 to 6 cups tart cooking apples,
   cored, peeled, and sliced*
*¼ to ½ cup honey (depending on
   sweetness of apples)*

*2 dozen red hot cinnamon
   candies*
½ cup granulated sugar
2 tablespoons flour
½ teaspoon cinnamon
Dash of salt
2 tablespoons butter
Granulated sugar (optional)

Preheat oven to 400 degrees. Line a 9-inch pie pan with bottom crust. Fill with apples, heaping them up slightly in the middle. Drizzle honey over the apples; dot with red hot candies. Combine sugar, flour, cinnamon, and salt and sprinkle over apples. Dot with butter. Make slits in top crust and place over apples; crimp edges together. Sprinkle crust with granulated sugar, if desired. Bake in preheated oven for 30 minutes; turn oven heat down to 350 degrees and bake 20 minutes longer. Makes 1 9-inch pie.

Wassail Punch

2 quarts apple cider
1/2 cup brown sugar
1 6-ounce can frozen orange juice
   concentrate

1/4 teaspoon nutmeg
3 sticks cinnamon
1/4 teaspoon whole cloves
1/4 teaspoon whole allspice

In a large pan, combine cider, brown sugar, orange juice concentrate, and nutmeg. Place cinnamon sticks, cloves, and allspice in a cheesecloth bag and add to liquid. Simmer for 20 minutes. Serve warm. Makes about 2 quarts.

Cindy's Apple Crunch Muffins

1/4 cup shortening
1/2 cup granulated sugar
1 egg
1 1/2 cups all-purpose flour
1/2 teaspoon salt
3 teaspoons baking powder
1/2 teaspoon cinnamon

1/2 cup milk
1 cup chopped apples

TOPPING:
1/3 cup brown sugar
1/3 cup chopped nuts
1/2 teaspoon cinnamon

Preheat oven to 375 degrees. In a mixing bowl, cream shortening and sugar until fluffy. Beat in egg. Sift together flour, salt, baking powder, and cinnamon. Add alternately to creamed mixture with milk. Fold in apples. Spoon into 12 greased muffin tins. Mix together topping ingredients and sprinkle over muffins. Bake about 20 minutes, or until toothpick inserted in middle comes out clean. Makes 1 dozen muffins.

Edna's Fresh Apple Cake

4 cups chopped tart apples
2 cups granulated sugar
2 eggs
½ cup vegetable oil
1 teaspoon vanilla
2 cups all-purpose flour

2 teaspoons baking soda
2 teaspoons cinnamon
½ teaspoon salt
Whipped cream or your favorite
   frosting (optional)

Preheat oven to 350 degrees. In a large bowl, combine apples and sugar; let stand 30 minutes. In another bowl, beat together eggs, vegetable oil, and vanilla. Sift together flour, baking soda, cinnamon, and salt. Thoroughly combine all three mixtures. Pour into a greased and floured 9 × 13-inch pan. Bake in preheated oven 50 to 60 minutes, or until knife inserted in middle comes out clean. Serve warm or cold with whipped cream or your favorite frosting. Makes 10 to 12 servings.

These chewy, chocolaty cookies make wonderful and (reasonably) wholesome after-school snacks for children, but adults love them, too!

Edna's No-Bake
Apple-Oatmeal Cookies

½ cup (1 stick) butter or
   margarine
2 cups granulated sugar
3 tablespoons cocoa
Dash of salt

1 cup grated tart apples
1 teaspoon vanilla
3 cups quick-cooking oatmeal
Powdered sugar

In a medium saucepan, melt butter and add sugar, cocoa, salt, and apples. Bring to a rolling boil and boil 1½ to 2 minutes. Remove from heat and add vanilla and oatmeal. Stir well. Drop by teaspoons onto waxed paper. If desired, flatten with fork. When cool, roll in powdered sugar. May be frozen or refrigerated. Makes about 4½ dozen cookies.

TURKEYS

For Story City native Janet Hermanson, Thanksgiving Day has always been "a great big organized potluck." It's often a toss-up, she says, deciding who among the thirty or forty relatives will bring the home-made cranberry sauce, scalloped corn with oysters, mashed potatoes, or pumpkin pie—"with real whipped cream, of course." As for the turkey, however, there's no need for discussion. That's unequivocably Janet's specialty. Years of helping her mother prepare the family's favorite sage-spiced bread stuffing enhances her qualifications for grooming the star of the Thanksgiving feast. And being married to the vice-president of the National Turkey Federation doesn't hurt, either. "We've got our image to maintain," she says, exchanging an amused glance across the kitchen table with her husband, Pete.

Some 200,000 turkeys brood in modern, mechanized facilities behind the Hermansons' tidy red brick home on the outskirts of this Scandina-vian-settled town. It's the same farm which marked the final destination for Mrs. Hermanson's great-grandparents, who arrived in Story City from Denmark more than 110 years ago. For years, the Hermanson clan relied solely on corn, soybeans, and cattle for their mainstay. Then in the 1940s, they added a flock of 15,000 turkeys to the operation. They decided to investigate the nutritional and economical advantages of turkeys not long after some farmers in nearby Ellsworth began raising them.

Today Iowa ranks among the ten top turkey-producing states in the nation, with turkey-processing plants in Ellsworth, West Liberty, Post-ville, and Storm Lake. "Hamilton County used to be one of the heaviest turkey-raising areas in the country," Hermanson pointed out. "There used to be lots of farmers growing a few turkeys; now there are fewer farmers growing lots of turkeys."

As the turkey supply grew, so did the need for hired help and con-trolled conditions. Although he still makes regular trips to the long nar-row sheds to observe his flocks, Hermanson's days are now occupied more with paperwork than manual labor. But the turkey business hasn't always been a white-collar job. "When I was a boy, most of our Thanksgiving turkeys were home-dressed and home-delivered," he recalled. For him that meant spending extra-long hours plucking feathers with half a dozen or so other workers, assuring customers fresh fowl on the dinner table come Thursday noon.

But work was far from finished even after the last turkey was delivered. Holiday or not, the Hermanson boys still had to mount their horses to deliver milk from their dairy to other Story City residents. "We especially dreaded snowstorms; that always meant extra work with the livestock." But the hungry farmers always received their just reward with the elaborate spread assembled by the mothers, sisters, aunts, and cousins who'd been toiling diligently in the kitchen since daybreak. "My mother used to spend nearly half the day buttering and basting that 22-pound bird every half-hour in an open pan until it was real pretty and brown," he recalled.

Modern cooking methods have greatly minimized the time Janet must spend in the kitchen on Thanksgiving morning, just as advanced technology has relieved much of the farm workload from her husband. She now simply pops her self-basting turkey in the oven and forgets about it "till the meat's falling off the bone." And rather than stuffing the turkey she usually prepares the dressing in a pan beside the bird. "From a safety standpoint, it's much better to fix it that way. And if you baste it with the drippings, it has just as much flavor."

Not surprisingly, turkey isn't just reserved for special occasions in the Hermanson household. Janet is just as likely to use it in a hearty casserole for a church picnic, a summer salad for a ladies' luncheon, or a hearty barbecue sandwich for a 4-H outing. "Whenever I have leftover turkey, I like to grind it with soda crackers and other ingredients and use it as a spread for sandwiches to feed the workers," she added.

Here are some of the family's favorites.

Old-Fashioned
Sage-Bread Dressing

Turkey giblets and neck
½ cup fat, melted (or use salad oil)
1 cup chopped celery
½ cup chopped onion

¾ loaf (approximately 2 quarts) dry bread, cubed
2 teaspoons dried sage
Giblet broth
Salt and pepper to taste

In a small saucepan filled with water, simmer giblets and neck 2 hours, until tender. Chop giblets and meat from neck; reserve broth. In a skillet over medium heat, heat fat. Add celery and onion and sauté until tender. In a large bowl, combine bread cubes with sautéed onions and celery, sage, chopped meat, and enough giblet broth to moisten. Season to taste with salt and pepper. If desired, stuff turkey just before putting in oven. Do not stuff it the night before! Stuffing can also be baked in a separate dish and basted with turkey drippings. Makes enough dressing for a 15-pound turkey.

Swiss Turkey Quiche

1 9-inch unbaked pastry shell
4 ounces shredded Swiss cheese
2 tablespoons flour
1 tablespoon chicken-flavored
  bouillon crystals
2 cups cubed cooked turkey
1 cup milk

3 eggs, well beaten
¼ cup chopped onion
2 tablespoons chopped green
  pepper
2 tablespoons chopped pimiento
Canned French-fried onions
  (optional)

Preheat oven to 425 degrees. Bake pastry shell 8 minutes; remove from oven. Reduce oven temperature to 350 degrees. In a medium bowl, toss cheese with flour and bouillon; add remaining ingredients, except French-fried onions. Mix well. Pour into prepared shell. Bake 40 to 45 minutes or until set, topping with French-fried onions during the last 5 minutes. Let stand 10 minutes before serving. Makes 4 to 6 servings.

Janet Hermanson's
Turkey-Fruit Salad

4 cups diced cooked turkey,
  chilled
1 cup thinly sliced celery
1 cup halved green grapes
1 13½-ounce can pineapple
  chunks, drained, with ¼ cup
  juice reserved

1 cup shell macaroni, cooked and
  cooled
½ cup sliced almonds
1 cup mayonnaise-type salad
  dressing

In a large bowl, toss together turkey, celery, grapes, pineapple chunks, macaroni, and almonds. In a small bowl, blend together salad dressing and pineapple juice and add to other ingredients. Mix together and chill thoroughly. Makes 6 servings.

Turkey Sandwich Spread

"There's no real formula for this recipe, but I do like to go long on the celery. Grind leftover (about 6 to 8 cups) cooked turkey, sweet pickles, onions, and celery. 'Clean' the grinder by putting through half a dozen soda crackers into turkey mixture. Add turkey broth and mayonnaise until it has a spreading consistency."

Turkey–Wild Rice Salad

⅔ cup mayonnaise
⅓ cup milk
2 tablespoons lemon juice
¼ teaspoon dried tarragon
3 cups cubed cooked turkey
3 cups cooked wild rice
⅓ cup finely sliced green onion

1 8-ounce jar sliced water
  chestnuts, drained
½ teaspoon salt
⅛ teaspoon pepper
1 cup halved seedless green
  grapes
1 cup salted cashews
Clusters of grapes for garnish

In a small bowl, blend mayonnaise, milk, lemon juice, and tarragon; set aside. In a large bowl, combine turkey, wild rice, green onion, water chestnuts, salt, and pepper. Stir in mayonnaise mixture and refrigerate, covered, for 2 to 3 hours. Just before serving, fold in grapes and cashews. Garnish with clusters of grapes. Makes 8 servings.

Turkey–Wild Rice Casserole

1 cup raw wild rice
3 cups water
3 heaping teaspoons chicken-
*   flavored bouillon crystals*
4 tablespoons butter
5 tablespoons flour
1½ cups turkey or chicken broth

1½ cups evaporated milk
1 teaspoon salt or to taste
2 cups diced cooked turkey
¾ cup sliced mushrooms
¼ cup chopped pimiento
⅓ cup chopped green pepper
½ cup sliced almonds

Preheat oven to 350 degrees. Rinse wild rice thoroughly and place in a 2-quart Pyrex dish with cover. Add water and bouillon crystals, cover, and bake in preheated oven for 1½ hours. Check rice after 1 hour. Add more water if necessary, fluff rice, and continue baking until tender. (Cooked wild rice may be wrapped airtight and frozen for later use.)

In a skillet over medium-low heat, melt butter; add flour and blend. Cook, stirring constantly, about 2 minutes. Add broth and milk, raise heat to medium, and cook until thick, stirring constantly. Season with salt. Combine cooked rice, turkey, mushrooms, pimiento, and green pepper. Pour into a 6 × 10-inch baking dish or a 1½-quart casserole. Pour sauce over all. Top with sliced almonds. Cover and bake in preheated oven for 50 to 60 minutes. This is excellent with a cranberry salad. Makes 6 servings.

These grilled turkey tenderloins have been served at the Iowa State Fair on hot dog buns. However, Mrs. Hermanson points out that they're also delicious served as an entrée for a family meal.

Marinated Turkey Tenderloins

¼ cup soy sauce
¼ cup vegetable oil
¼ cup white wine
2 tablespoons lemon juice
⅛ teaspoon black pepper

1 small clove garlic, crushed
1 tablespoon grated onion
⅛ teaspoon ground ginger
2 to 4 pounds turkey tenderloins,
*   split (also labeled scallopine)*

In a large, nonaluminum container, combine all ingredients. Cover and marinate, refrigerated, 24 hours, turning occasionally. Preheat grill. Remove tenderloins from marinade; grill 3 to 4 minutes per side, or just until turkey loses its pink color. Do not overcook. Makes 8 to 16 servings.

WILD GAME

R etirement doesn't keep Johnny Pezzetti from working for his supper. The proof is in the entrées that grace the Pezzetti supper table at least two or three times a week: fried rabbit or pheasant, squirrel stew, catfish, or, for a special treat, coon that's been soaked overnight in brine.

Most every morning at 7:00 A.M. sharp, the stocky, overall-clad Saylorville resident hops in his four-wheel-drive pick-up and heads for untamed Iowa territory, areas he knows as well as if they were marked by luminous street signs. In the fall he hunts squirrel, rabbit, and pheasant. "I used to hunt deer and geese and quail, too; ohhh, are they good to eat! But I'm just gettin' too old for that," said Pezzetti, who's now in his seventies.

He stays busy in the winter setting out his traps for foxes, raccoons, and coyote, provided the snow isn't too deep, and then sells the furs and hides for a little extra income, he said. In warmer weather he's most likely to be found perched on his favorite river bank at Big Creek, reeling in catfish, quailbacks, walleyes, northerns, buffalo, crappies, bullheads. "I remember when we was kids driving 150 miles in our model-T Ford to the Skunk River in Oskaloosa, spending three or four days doin' nothing but fishing. Man oh man, did we catch a lot of fish in our time!"

The son of an Italian immigrant who settled in the southern Iowa community of Melcher to mine coal, Pezzetti began tagging along on hunting and fishing expeditions with some of the older boys in the area when he was about ten. "My three brothers and sister and I—we all hunted. But my Dad never even owned a gun." When Pezzetti was fourteen he took some odd jobs for farmers and bought himself a little single-shot rifle "to start with." A few years later he advanced to a 12-gauge Winchester— the same gun he uses today—with the money he'd saved from his paycheck for digging coal.

He slipped down to his basement, then returned a few moments later with the shotgun, displaying it as affectionately as a child showing off a beloved pet. "She's an old timer, I'll tell ya. I got her for $17.70; now she's probably worth about $400. Haven't really taken too good care of her, but then when you use a gun this much, it's hard to keep her lookin' pretty for very long."

Pezzetti does most of his hunting and trapping alone, unless one of his three sons accompanies him. When his last hunting dog, Pitch, passed away, he never bothered to find a replacement. But with an innate bloodhound sense like Pezzetti's, who needs one? "These foxes and coyotes—they like a big, huge field to roam around in, like alfalfa or hay," he said. "You'll find coons around running water, especially big creeks."

These days, he said, he can sell a coon skin for $40 and a fox hide for $55. That's a far cry from the days when he was lucky to get a dollar for one coon and only two dollars from the Story County courthouse for a pair of fox ears. "There was a bounty back then on foxes," he recollected. "The hides were so thick, they weren't worth a thing."

Trapping involves more preliminary preparation than hunting or fishing, Pezzetti explained. "You gotta boil your traps and dye 'em real black, and you don't ever want to touch them with your hands, 'cause the animals can smell it."

While working in the coal mines and then at the Des Moines Firestone plant after the mine shut down in 1945, Pezzetti had much less time to devote to his outdoor hobbies, although he and his sons did occasionally go out to hunt a few squirrels or rabbits before dark, he said.

"I've been retired eleven years now, and I ain't complainin' a bit," he readily admitted. "I go out hunting or trapping or fishing every darn day till noon; that's when I come back and take my little nap. Then I drive to Des Moines to play shuffleboard till dinnertime. Awaiting him most evenings is some of his catch, dipped in seasoned flour and fried like chicken, stewed in a spicy sauce or roasted, with a big helping of rice or fried potatoes and vegetables. "My wife, Ann—she's a Croatian girl, but she learned how to cook Italian-style from my mother, you know, with lots of garlic and stuff. She makes this squirrel stew that's just about the best thing you ever tasted, I ain't kiddin'!"

Squirrel Stew

Crisco
2 squirrels, cleaned and cut up
½ medium onion, chopped

1 clove garlic, chopped
2 cups canned tomatoes
Salt and pepper to taste

In a heavy skillet, melt Crisco until smoking. Brown squirrels on both sides; place in a kettle. Add more Crisco to skillet, if necessary, and sauté onion and garlic over medium heat until tender. Add to kettle. Pour tomatoes over squirrel and add salt and pepper. Put lid on kettle and simmer until done, about 1½ hours. Makes 2 to 3 servings.

In contrast to the simple game dishes prepared by the Pezzettis, younger generations of the family are as adventurous in their kitchens as they are in the fields. Pezzetti's third cousin, Nick Roelofs, an organic chemist from Des Moines who got some of his first hunting lessons from Pezzetti, has different ideas about what to do with his catch. Here are two results from his productive hunts.

Pheasant Paprikash

6 tablespoons vegetable oil, divided (more, if necessary)
2 young pheasants, about 2 pounds each, cleaned and disjointed
3 tablespoons butter
2 medium onions, finely chopped

4 to 6 tablespoons sweet Hungarian paprika
10 dashes black pepper
1 teaspoon salt
4 cups seasoned stock (chicken or pheasant)
2 tablespoons flour
2 cups sour cream
Cooked rice or noodles

In a heavy skillet over medium-high heat, heat 3 tablespoons oil. Add pheasant, a few pieces at a time, and brown on all sides. Add more oil if necessary. Remove to a platter. In a heavy pot, melt butter and 3 tablespoons oil. Add onions with paprika to pot and sauté until the onions are glossy and red. Add black pepper, salt, and stock. Bring to a boil and add pheasant. Simmer, covered, until tender, about 1 hour. Remove pheasant pieces to platter; keep warm. Combine flour and sour cream. Stir slowly into pot until thickened and smooth, about 5 minutes, over low heat. (For a thicker sauce, blend a little more flour with just enough water to make a paste, add to mixture, and cook a few minutes longer.) Serve over rice or noodles. Makes 4 to 6 servings.

Venison Marsala

Lean venison roast (about 4
  pounds, boned, rolled, and
  tied)
1 tablespoon lemon juice
1 quart water
½ teaspoon salt
½ cup beef kidney suet or butter
1 cup Marsala wine, room
  temperature

1 clove garlic, minced
½ teaspoon each dried oregano,
  thyme, and basil
1 carrot, split lengthwise
8 ounces noodles
2 chopped garlic cloves
½ cup olive oil

Soak roast in lemon juice, water, and salt in refrigerator overnight. Preheat oven to 350 degrees. In a food processor or blender, process suet or butter, wine, garlic, and seasonings. Place roast with carrot in a shallow baking pan and cover with wine mixture. Bake, covered, in preheated oven about 30 minutes per pound, or until internal temperature reaches 170 degrees. Let roast stand for 20 minutes. Meanwhile, cook noodles al dente in boiling water. In a small pan, sauté garlic cloves in olive oil until tender. Remove from heat and mash with fork. Toss with noodles. Slice roast into medallions and arrange on separate serving dish. Pour a trail of sauce down the center of the medallions. Serve remainder with noodles. Makes 6 to 8 servings.

HONEY

You won't find a single head of cattle on Bob and Shirley Vande Hoef's ranch in northwest Iowa. But that doesn't mean this family isn't contributing to one of Iowa's important agricultural industries.

Each year, the Vande Hoefs produce about 100,000 pounds of honey at the Busy Bee Ranch behind their home in Newkirk, a town Mrs. Vande Hoef claims "might have a population of eighty, if you stretch it." What started out as a hobby some thirty years ago is now the major source of income for the Vande Hoefs. Inspired by his grandfather, who was also a beekeeper, Bob got a couple of hives shortly after he was married while working as a hired hand on his father's farm.

For his first batch of honey, he recalled, he carried a couple of frames down to the basement and cut the wax off with an electric knife. Nowadays, a sophisticated aluminum extractor decaps about fifty frames at a time in an old barn perfumed with a sweet, waxy aroma which also houses huge barrels of honey and white wooden hives piled high to the ceiling.

For years the couple sent their excess honey to the Sioux Honey Association in nearby Sioux City, which markets more than half the nation's commercially packed honey under the labels Sue Bee and Aunt Sue. More recently, they've been distributing almost all their honey for commercial use, except for a small portion they bottle themselves for their own family and friends.

About one thousand of Bob Vande Hoef's hives are scattered in some fifty locations all over northwest Iowa and parts of Minnesota. Each day during honey season he travels alone in his pick-up truck to check his hives, wearing only a straw hat with a net over his face for protection. "Gloves just seem to get in the way," he said with a shrug. "Oh, I get a few stings now and then, but you get pretty immune to it after awhile."

Bob Vande Hoef has his own system for choosing his locations. "If I see a nice spot for putting some hives, I'll just ask the farmer if he'll let me use some of the land in exchange for some honey," he said. "They're

usually glad to. A lot of them say the bees help pollinate their soybean fields, which improves their yields."

Besides soybeans, alfalfa and white clover are good sources of Iowa honey. "But big, yellow sweet clover seems to produce the best honey," he said. Unlike the dark Minnesota honey produced by bees that feed on pollen from sunflowers, Vande Hoef finds that Iowa honey is lighter and has a milder flavor.

After a long winter under a protective cover, the bees take their first flight outside the hives to collect pollen from apple blossoms, honeysuckle hedges, fruit trees, and wildflowers. Near the first of May they produce their first honey flow, strictly for their own use, which they will later build upon. The main honey flow, however, usually begins in June.

From August until mid-October, Vande Hoef extracts the honey by placing a fume pad which "smells like almond" on top of a tall stack of hives. The pungent aroma drives the bees down to the bottom of the

Bob Vande Hoef tending his hives

frames, leaving only the honey and wax. The wax is not disposed of when it is removed; instead, it is melted and sold for making candles, floor polish, and other products. "Every year, the fifth grade class at Floyd Valley Grade School here come to watch the honey being extracted," Shirley added. "They always send us lots of nice thank you letters."

Bob and Shirley both say they prefer honey to sugar in their coffee and on their cereal. And Shirley, an avid cook, is constantly seeking new ways to incorporate it into dishes. "I use it for freezing fruits, like rhubarb," she said. "As a rule, I eliminate the water and use about one-quarter less honey than I would sugar." She also frequently substitutes honey (about three-fourths cup to each cup of sugar) in cakes and cookies and uses it for homemade breads. She finds it makes tasty salad dressings and glazes for meat and poultry dishes. And since the Vande Hoefs raise a few sheep in addition to bees, she's also come up with some intriguing lamb recipes which call for honey.

Here are a few of the family favorites.

Honey Lemon Lamb Shoulder

1/4 cup chopped fresh parsley
Salt and pepper
1 shoulder of lamb (about 4 to 5
  pounds), precarved through the
  bones and tied firmly; or boned,
  rolled, and tied; or with a
  pocket cut

1 medium lemon, thinly sliced
1/3 cup honey
2 tablespoons orange juice
1/8 teaspoon ground allspice

Preheat oven to 325 degrees. Sprinkle parsley, salt, and pepper on all sides of lamb. Cut lemon slices in half and insert them in between lamb slices, if using precarved, or in between folds of meat, if using boned. Or, stuff them in the pocket and then tie it shut. In a small bowl, blend together honey, orange juice, and allspice. Place roast uncovered on a rack in a greased pan in oven. Roast about 30 to 35 minutes per pound, or until meat thermometer registers 170 degrees for medium doneness. During the last 10 minutes of cooking time, baste occasionally with the honey–orange juice mixture. Let stand 10 to 15 minutes before slicing. Makes about 8 servings.

Poppyseed Salad Dressing

1/3 cup honey
1/2 teaspoon salt
1/3 cup vinegar

3 tablespoons mild prepared
  mustard (such as Dijon)
1 1/4 cups salad oil
2 1/2 tablespoons poppyseeds

Place all ingredients in an electric blender; blend until oil disappears. Makes about 2 1/2 cups.

Busy Bee Peanut Bars

3 cups all-purpose flour
1 cup (2 sticks) margarine or
  butter, softened
1/2 cup packed brown sugar
1/4 teaspoon salt

1 12-ounce package butterscotch
  chips
3 tablespoons margarine or butter
3 tablespoons water
1/2 cup honey
3 cups salted peanuts

Preheat oven to 375 degrees. In a bowl, mix together flour, margarine or butter, brown sugar, and salt (the mixture will be crumbly). Press into an 11 × 14-inch pan. Bake about 20 minutes, or until lightly browned. Meanwhile, in a saucepan combine over medium-low heat butterscotch chips, margarine or butter, water, and honey; cook and stir until dissolved. Stir in peanuts. Pour over baked crust and bake 8 minutes longer. Cool and cut into squares. Makes 36 bars.

Special K Bars

½ cup granulated sugar
½ cup honey
¾ cup peanut butter
1 teaspoon vanilla

3 cups Special K cereal
½ cup chocolate chips
½ cup butterscotch chips
2 tablespoons butter

In a medium saucepan, bring sugar and honey to a boil; remove from heat. Add peanut butter, vanilla, and cereal; stir until well blended. Press into a greased 7 × 11-inch Pyrex pan. Let cool. In a double boiler over simmering water (or in a microwave) melt together chocolate chips, butterscotch chips, and butter. Spread over cooled bars. Makes about 24 bars.

Oven Barbecue Chicken

¼ cup (½ stick) butter, melted
1 tablespoon lemon juice
1 tablespoon paprika
*½ cup mayonnaise-type salad
    dressing*

¼ cup hot ketchup
2 tablespoons honey
1 3-pound frying chicken, cut up

Preheat oven to 350 degrees. In a baking pan, combine all ingredients except chicken. Arrange chicken in a single layer over mixture, turning once to coat. Bake in preheated oven 45 to 60 minutes or until done, basting every 15 minutes. Makes 5 to 6 servings.

FISH, FOWL, AND FRESH
MUSKMELON

Mark Twain didn't stick around Muscatine long enough to pen his first novel. But if he had, the young apprentice for the *Muscatine Journal,* who would later delight the world with his tales of high adventure on the Mississippi, wouldn't have had to look far for inspiration. For 150 years or better, the maple syrup–colored waters separating this classic old river town from its Illinois neighbor have provided a favorite playground for countless real-life Huck Finns and Tom Sawyers. In the summer they fish for bass in hopes of winning a tournament championship and for catfish in anticipation of a neighborhood fish fry. Come fall or spring the river becomes a hunter's paradise, when congregations of migrating ducks and geese en route to warmer climates stop there to feed.

The river's been a second home to Elmer Weggen for more than sixty years. Even now he takes as much delight in lugging home a stringer laden with "whoppers" as his young grandson Jeff, his most frequent fishing companion. "That kid's some fisherman, I tell ya," Weggen said this hot August afternoon, beaming with pride. His son Larry had just phoned to tell him his grandson had won the first-place trophy for catching the biggest bass in the Kids' Fishing Contest sponsored by the Muscatine Bass Club during the city's annual Great River Days celebration. "Never will forget the time I carried him with me down to Chicken Creek. It was a little late for the catfish to be biting. But wouldn't you know it, we caught us a seven-pounder, with just a little plastic worm. That kid's eyes like to have popped!"

Shoving a well-worn fishing cap over his crewcut, Elmer climbed behind the wheel of his pick-up, his little dog Barney tucked in the crook of his arm. Just a few blocks away from his house the riverfront was buzzing with throngs of folks who'd turned out for the four-day celebration. Besides fishing contests, there would be Venetian boat rides, parades, ski shows, hot air balloon rides, even a presentation by a local Mark Twain impersonator.

Weggen drove right past, heading for places that interested him more. Chomping his fat cigar, he pointed out the window to some weed-choked railroad tracks. That's where he used to hide his fishing pole—a willow branch with a string tied to the end—on his way home from a day's fishing.

"Gosh darn, I like it here," he said emphatically, as the truck bumped along the dusty back roads leading to other favorite fishing spots. It was here that he learned to catch catfish with "part of a weenie," carp with "big yellow grasshoppers," snapping turtles with his bare hands. Every year before duck season opened, he recalled, he and his buddies were busy making decoys by "rasping out parts of old-time telephone poles, then painting 'em all different colors."

"At night time, us boys used to go up and down the river, hunting for leopard frogs. Sometimes, when it was too dark for us to see and real, real quiet, we'd come right up to one without even knowing it. Then all of a sudden they'd make this big noise—BRUMPH!!" He howled with laughter. "Sounded just like a big ol' moose. You should have seen us all jump, it scared us so bad."

Weggen, who retired several years ago after forty-two years in the door department at the Roach and Musser Sash and Door Company, has watched his hometown grow and change from all directions. "Back when I was a boy, this place was nearly all wilderness; where I lived, timber wolves would come right up underneath my window and howl."

His uncle had a little truck farm where he sold watermelons, muskmelons, tomatoes, and other produce which still flourishes throughout the 30,000 acres of the extra-rich bottom land on Muscatine Island. It was there that Weggen earned his first pocket money by picking cucumbers, tomatoes, green beans, and baby onions for ten cents a basket for the Heinz canning factory. He later had a hand in building Wildcat Den Park, putting locks on the dam, and laying the baseball diamond at Kent-Stein State Park.

The highlight of the summer, he recalled, was when his Baptist church Sunday school class took its annual steamer excursion up the Mississippi to Davenport. "Looking out on that water from the steamboat was just like watching slow-motion photography," he mused. Most of those trips were all-day affairs which climaxed in Davenport, where the children were allowed to ride the steam calliope until it was time to head for

Kids' fishing tournament, Great River Days, Muscatine

home. "But one time, we took a moonlight excursion," he added. "They had all that southern dancin' in this one room where all the grown-ups went. And fancy food—real expensive, too."

Weggen never acquired much of a taste for haute cuisine, not when he could cook up a catfish feast his family claims can't be beat. His tasty but rather unorthodox coating includes crushed graham crackers, which add crunchiness and a slightly sweet flavor.

A younger generation of fishermen in the area also have theories on the best way to serve their catch. "At least three or four times a year, a bunch of us relatives get together for a fish fry," said Jim Larson, a construction worker by trade who said he's "pretty tied up with fishing through the whole summer." Larson usually fixes them one of two ways: "rolled in cornmeal or flour, or dipped in beer batter. Homemade potato salad and muskmelon are the standard accompaniments."

The river's influence on the diet here is evident in cooler weather as well, when duck appears as the main attraction at game dinners sponsored by hunting clubs such as the Izaak Walton League and in private homes. In the Larson home, the favored way to prepare duck is to stuff it first with onion, apple, and celery to absorb some of the gamy flavor and then oven-roast it with bacon strips laid across the top for extra moistness.

Here are just a few ways Muscatine residents savor the gifts of the river.

Jim Larson's
Beer Batter Catfish

3 cups flour
1 cup yellow cornmeal
2 eggs, beaten
1½ cups milk

½ of a 12-ounce can of beer
About a dozen medium-sized
catfish, cleaned
Fat for deep frying

In a large bowl, stir together flour and cornmeal. Add eggs, milk, and beer and mix thoroughly, adding more beer to thin, if necessary. Cover and refrigerate 2 hours or longer. Dip fish in batter and fry in hot (375-degree) oil until golden brown. Serve with bread, potato salad, and fresh muskmelon. Makes 8 to 10 servings.

Elmer Weggen's
Coating for Fish and Game

"For each skilletful, I mix up a tablespoon of flour with about 6 graham crackers, crushed up, but not too fine. I take my pieces of fish or game and roll them in the coating while they're still a little damp. Then I melt some shortening in my skillet and fry them up."

Muscatine-Style Duck

1 duck, wild or domestic, dressed
and cleaned
½ apple, chopped

2 or 3 stalks celery, chopped
½ onion, chopped
2 strips bacon

Preheat oven to 325 degrees. Prick duck lightly with fork to allow fat to escape. Stuff cavity with apple, celery, and onion. Criss-cross bacon strips on top. Place in roasting pan and roast in preheated oven about 20 minutes per pound. Makes 2 to 3 servings.

Note: For a delicious accompaniment, try roasting quartered new potatoes in the duck drippings alongside the duck about 45 minutes, turning to brown on all sides. On a platter, surround duck with potatoes, orange wedges, and parsley sprigs.

Del Jones, area chairman of the Great River Bend Chapter of Ducks Unlimited and an avid duck and goose hunter, frequently gives cooking demonstrations for duck. With goose, he admits, he rarely does more than roast it and serve it with cranberry sauce on the side. "Wild goose has such a sweet, delicate flavor, I wouldn't want to doctor it up." Duck, however, is a different story. Often, he'll soak it in wild grape wine and then smoke it. "It's great for snacking in the duck blinds," he said. He also likes to roast duck and serve it with an orange sauce, or fillet the breast and then bread and fry it "as for chicken-fried steak." Another specialty is Oriental stir-fried duck breast and vegetables, a recipe which varies according to whatever vegetables he happens to have on hand. Here is one rendition.

Duck Breast
and Vegetable Stir-Fry

2 whole duck breasts (¾ to 1 pound), skinned, boned, and cut into strips

2 tablespoons soy sauce

2 tablespoons dry sherry

1 clove garlic, crushed

1 tablespoon cornstarch

2 tablespoons vegetable oil

1 small onion, peeled and thinly sliced

2 medium carrots, peeled and cut crosswise on sharp diagonal into ¼-inch slices

1 sweet red pepper, cored, seeded, and cut into ¼-inch strips

2 cups fresh snow peas, trimmed

Salt to taste

¼ to ½ cup water or chicken or duck stock

Hot, cooked rice

In a nonaluminum container, combine duck breast strips, soy sauce, sherry, garlic, and cornstarch. Marinate, refrigerated, 3 to 4 hours. In a wok, heat 1 tablespoon of the oil over medium-high heat. When hot, add onion and stir-fry 2 minutes. Add carrots and stir-fry 2 minutes longer. Add red pepper and stir-fry 1 minute longer. Add snow peas and stir-fry 1 to 2 minutes longer, or until crisp-tender. Season to taste with salt and remove to a bowl.

Add remaining tablespoon of oil to wok. With a slotted spoon, add duck strips, reserving marinade, and stir-fry 2 minutes, or until browned on both sides but still slightly pink in middle. Add reserved marinade and just enough water or stock to make a sauce. Return vegetables to wok and stir-fry about 1 minute to heat through. Remove to platter and serve with hot rice. Makes 3 to 4 servings.

If you should have some leftover catfish or other white fish, try this recipe adapted from the December 1975 issue of the *Iowa Conservationist.*

Fish Chowder

¾ cup cubed salt pork
½ cup sliced onion
2 cups water
1 teaspoon salt
2 cups cubed potatoes
4 cups flaked cooked or canned
   fish, bones removed

6 cups hot milk
1 lemon, thinly sliced
⅛ teaspoon pepper
Paprika
Chives

In a skillet, fry salt pork to golden yellow, add onion, and cook, stirring occasionally until pork is crisp and onion is light yellow. Pour off grease. Add water and salt, bring to a boil, and transfer to a 2½-to-3-quart saucepan. Add potatoes; cover and cook 20 minutes. Add fish; simmer 5 minutes to heat thoroughly. Just before serving add hot milk, lemon slices, and pepper; sprinkle with paprika and chives. Makes 6 to 8 servings.

In the summertime, a standard accompaniment to fried catfish or just about any other dinner specialty is fresh melon, particularly muskmelon, which grows in profusion in Muscatine. Mrs. Kenneth Shoultz, who sells melons and other family-raised produce in one of many local roadside stands, offered this recipe for cantaloupe jam, popular among Muscatine farm women. It has a wonderful, honeylike flavor.

Muskmelon Jam

*3 medium, fully ripened
   cantaloupes or muskmelons
7 cups granulated sugar*

*½ cup Certo
1 teaspoon vanilla*

Remove seeds from melons; pare and cut into squares. Cook slowly without adding water until soft. Mash and continue cooking until very tender. To 3½ cups pulp, add sugar and bring to a boil for 3 minutes, stirring constantly to prevent scorching. Remove from fire and add Certo and vanilla. Remove foam, pour into sterilized jars, and seal with paraffin or in boiling water bath 5 minutes. Makes 7 half-pints.

Part Three

SPECIAL PLACES

LIVING HISTORY FARMS

There were a few things those newfangled home economics classes Karin Kliewer took in college didn't prepare her for when she began cooking regularly at Living History Farms near Des Moines. They didn't teach her how to light a wood-burning stove with corncobs, stuff freshly butchered pork into sausage casings made from hog intestines, or churn butter in a crock with cream straight from the cow.

When Karin came to work at the state's largest outdoor agricultural museum in 1978, she quickly learned the true meaning of living off the land with the same driving forces her ancestors used: perseverance, patience, and lots of elbow grease. She and the other interpreters at the farms tell the story of Iowa's agricultural development not by merely serving as tour guides; rather, they step back into the lives of the ordinary, hard-working pioneers responsible for transforming the huge prairie into a breadbasket plentiful enough to feed a big chunk of the world.

Carts pulled by tractors transport the 100,000 or so tourists who visit the farm each year to its major attractions. Each represents a different phase of Iowa history: a 1700 Ioway Indian site, a pioneer farm of the 1840s, a 1900 horse farm, a farm of the future, and the bustling little pioneer town of Walnut Grove. The town's general store, one-room schoolhouse, textile house, and carpentry, pottery, and blacksmith shops are all in full operation. The fully restored Flynn Mansion recreates the regal opulence of the Victorian era.

In 1980, the Interfaith Church of the Land was erected on the six hundred–acre site where Pope John Paul II preached the importance of good stewardship of the soil to more than 400,000 spectators in October of the previous year during one of Iowa's most fruitful corn harvests. That was the same message William Murray hoped to convey to fellow Iowans and visitors to his home state when he came up with the idea for Living History Farms back in the 1960s. On visits to other museums Murray had noticed, much to his dismay, that the static displays of farm and household goods used by his forefathers were all too often overlooked. With the support of others who shared his sentiments, he planted the seeds for a repository with another dimension: real people who would "interpret" those bygone days by reliving them themselves.

"I really feel like this is my house," said Karin as she decorated sugar cookies inside the quaint kitchen of the two-story 1900 farmhouse. Other women, attired as she was in ankle-length cotton print dresses with white aprons, poured cups of steaming cider from an antique tea-pot for the guests waiting outside the white picket fence. The men mean-while went about their regular chores outside, tending the horses and raising enough corn, wheat, oats, beef, and pork to feed the household—relying solely on turn-of-the-century farming methods.

Although the women also render lard for soap, wash clothes and linens by hand, and keep their household spotless, most of their daily routine revolves around food. Each day they must provide a hearty noonday meal for themselves and the other interpreters without the convenience of electricity, running water, refrigeration, or manufactured foods. Their menus are confined to products they raise themselves, with the exception of a few staples from the general store. "We do grind some of our wheat, but we occasionally buy white flour as well," Karin con-fessed. "Back then, you were considered higher on the social scale if you could afford storebought flour. The same was true for more highly re-fined sugar."

The women also help gather eggs from the henhouse, milk the cow, and pick fruits and vegetables from the orchards and gardens. The pro-duce is then canned in Mason jars and sealed with lard. During harvest season they prepare a threshers dinner with all the trimmings for the extra farmhands hired to help ease the workload. Donna Miles, who spins and weaves at the farms' textile house, was among the researchers who scoured old cookbooks and diaries so they could recreate authen-tic meals for such occasions. Threshing, she explained, was a commu-nity effort; one farmer owned the threshing machine and some fifteen to thirty neighbors would pitch in to help. "Other women in the community would help the wife of the farmer who owned the threshing machine plan a huge feast for the farmers when they returned from the fields," she said. "A big banquet table was spread with a white linen tablecloth and a mirror was hung on the dinner pole outside so the farmers could wash up and comb their hair before eating." The threshers dinners they prepare at the farms, she said, typically consist of "roast beef and fried chicken, green beans with side meat, boiled potatoes, scalloped corn, sliced tomatoes and onions, pickled beets and cucumbers, homemade breads, lemonade, and coffee. For desserts we usually have apple and cherry pies, rhubarb pudding, and chocolate and spice cakes."

Donna's husband, Dave, rarely experiences fare so elaborate at lunch-time. By day he is part of a more primitive era as site manager for the Pioneer Farm. Built in 1970, the forty-acre site was selected by its modern-day "pioneers" with the same foresight Iowa's first settlers would have used. It possessed all the features needed for supplying their fundamental necessities: fertile prairie, forest, and well-watered bottom land along a stream. They chopped trees to build a crude log-and-sod cabin, a smokehouse, and a corn crib. Dave also trained oxen to pull the heavy plows through the root-entangled prairie sod and split the rails for the fence that zigzags around the entire site to keep unwelcome varmints away from the crops.

The meals are all hearth-cooked; soups and stews are prepared in a black cast-iron pot, meats and eggs are fried over the fire in a heavy skillet, and breads and pies are placed in a Dutch oven underneath the coals, explained Mary Schmidt, who helps run the primitive household. A challenge greater than preparing the food, she added, is finding ways to store it. "We smoke a lot of our meats and dry things like beans, peas, corn, and apples," she said. "We store vegetables like potatoes, rutabagas, turnips, and winter squash in our root cellar." Typical noonday meals prepared at the farm include ham and beans with corn bread, fried pork chops with Dutch oven–baked biscuits, squash or pumpkin mush, freshly butchered chicken boiled with homemade noodles, and seasonal vegetables.

The staff at Living History Farms are dedicated not only to portraying the hard work behind early farm life but also the pleasures that went along with it. During the season, visitors are invited to take part in an Old-Fashioned Fourth of July, a Traditional Music Festival, a Homemade Pie Social, a Quilt Show and Raffle, a Husking Bee, a Grain Harvest Festival, and a traditional Christmas celebration.

The Victorian Weekend Celebration is just one of many opportunities visitors have not only to observe but to sample the old-fashioned delicacies of previous eras for themselves. The staff shared a few of those recipes along with some of the other old-time favorites they're just as likely to prepare in their own kitchens.

1900 Farm
Bread-and-Butter Pickles

1 gallon cucumbers
8 small onions, peeled
½ cup noniodized salt
1 quart cracked ice
5 cups granulated sugar

½ teaspoon ground cloves
2 tablespoons mustard seed
1 teaspoon celery seed
1½ teaspoons turmeric
5 cups vinegar (5 percent acidity)

Slice cucumbers and onions paper thin; you'll be happy that you did later. Mix together cucumbers, onions, and salt in a noncorrodible container. Bury ice in center of vegetables; cover and let stand for 4 to 6 hours. In a 6-quart kettle, combine sugar, cloves, mustard seed, celery seed, turmeric, and vinegar. Heat until sugar dissolves. Drain cucumbers and onions and add to kettle. Cook over medium-low heat until bubbling. Pour into sterilized canning jars, being careful not to pack the cucumbers too tightly. Wipe jar rims and put on lids according to manufacturer's instructions. Process in boiling water bath 5 minutes for pints, 10 minutes for quarts, making sure water comes an inch over tops of jars. Cool on rack or cloth away from drafts. Next day, check seals and store in a cool, dry place. If you prefer not to process you can store pickles in refrigerator. Makes about 6 pints.

Legend has it that a fisherman, tired of waiting for his lazy wife to bake bread, baked his own, grumbling, "Anna, damn her!" Hence the name of this sturdy corn and wheat bread.

1900 Farm Anadama Bread

7 to 8 cups unsifted all-purpose
  flour ("You can use 3 cups
  whole wheat flour as part of
  this. We prefer to do it this
  way.")
1¼ cups yellow cornmeal

2½ teaspoons salt
2 packages dry yeast
⅓ cup butter, melted
2¼ cups very warm water
⅔ cup molasses

In a large bowl, thoroughly mix 2½ cups flour, cornmeal, salt, and undissolved yeast. Add butter. Gradually add very warm water and molasses to dry mixture and beat. Add remaining flour ½ cup at a time,

beating after each addition. Knead, cover, and let rise until doubled in bulk. Punch down and shape into 3 loaves. Place on cookie sheets, cover, and let rise again. Preheat oven to 375 degrees. Bake bread in pre-heated oven 40 to 50 minutes. Makes 3 loaves.

The following desserts have all been served at the Victorian Weekend Celebration.

1850 Gingerbread

¼ cup dark brown sugar
1 large egg
½ cup sour milk or buttermilk
1 cup dark molasses
2 cups flour, sifted
1 tablespoon ground ginger
1 teaspoon baking soda

½ teaspoon salt
5½ tablespoons butter
¼ to ½ cup candied ginger root,
  thinly sliced
⅓ cup seedless raisins
Whipped cream (optional)

Preheat oven to 325 degrees. In a large bowl, beat together brown sugar and egg. Add milk and molasses (to substitute sweet milk, add 1½ tablespoons white vinegar to 1 cup lukewarm sweet milk and let stand 10 minutes). Sift together flour, ginger, baking soda, and salt and add them to the wet mixture. Melt butter and add to batter. Do not overbeat. Fold in ginger root and raisins. Pour into greased and floured 8-inch square pan. Bake in preheated oven for 55 to 65 minutes, or until cake tester inserted in middle comes out clean. Do not overcook! Serve warm with whipped cream, if desired. Makes 6 to 8 servings.

A good, old-fashioned pound cake with a thick, sugary crust and a slight lemony flavor . . .

1876 Pico Lo Mino Cake

1 cup (2 sticks) butter
3 cups granulated sugar
5 eggs, well beaten
4 cups all-purpose flour

½ teaspoon baking soda
1 teaspoon cream of tartar
1 cup milk
1 teaspoon lemon juice

Preheat oven to 350 degrees. In a mixing bowl, cream together butter and sugar until fluffy. Add beaten eggs to creamed mixture. Sift together flour, baking soda, and cream of tartar. Alternately add dry ingredients and milk to creamed mixture; stir in lemon juice. Bake in greased and floured angel food cake pan for 1 hour to 1 hour and 15 minutes, or until cake tester inserted in middle comes out clean. Makes 10 to 12 servings.

Nineteenth-Century Seedcake

2 cups sifted all-purpose flour
¼ teaspoon salt
¼ teaspoon nutmeg
1 cup (2 sticks) butter
1 cup granulated sugar
2 teaspoons caraway seeds

6 egg yolks
2 tablespoons brandy
6 egg whites, stiffly beaten
Caraway Comfits (sugared
    caraway seeds) or crushed
    lump sugar

Preheat oven to 350 degrees. Sift together flour, salt, and nutmeg and set aside. Work butter until creamy, then gradually work in sugar until mixture looks and feels fluffy. Stir in caraway seeds and beat in egg yolks one at a time, beating hard after each addition. Add flour mixture and brandy, alternately, and then fold in the stiffly beaten egg whites, gently but thoroughly. Spoon batter into a greased and lightly floured 9-inch tube pan. Sprinkle Caraway Comfits or crushed lump sugar on top. Bake in preheated oven for 1 hour, or until cake pulls away from sides of pan. Cool in pan about 10 minutes, then turn out onto cake rack to cool completely. A day or so of mellowing, tightly wrapped, develops the flavor. Makes 10 to 12 servings.

THE AMANA COLONIES

Neither the Old World surroundings nor the hearty German-style cuisine at the Ronneburg Restaurant in the Amana Colonies has changed much since the days when Elsie Oehler's grandmother was in charge of the kitchen more than half a century ago. Inside the large, ivy-colored brick building the antique tables are still heavily laden with fare substantial enough to stuff the hungriest of field hands: cold pickled ham, locally butchered meats with separate bowls of gravy, hearth-baked bread, crusty dumplings and hash browns, sauerkraut, tangy cottage cheese with green onions, an array of vegetables, old-fashioned pies and cakes.

Relics from the past, from the ornate, handmade iron molds feather cakes were baked in to the big straw baskets used for gathering onions and potatoes, are displayed on walls and shelves. Enlarged old photographs depicting dusty roads filled with horse-drawn wagons, sturdy buildings of brick, stone, and plank, abundant front-yard gardens and orchards surrounded by wooden fences also serve as reminders of the way things were.

Yet other features of the restaurant today would have been unheard of in its early years: the jovial hosts in lederhosen, the joking and laughter in the upstairs beer garden, the music provided by the zither player. That was back when the followers of a religious movement known as the Community of True Inspiration staunchly abided by a cardinal rule of precommunal living. All property was held in common and both church and secular affairs were governed by the same leadership.

A group of Lutherans who in the 1700s broke away from the church in Germany emigrated in 1842 to Ebenezer, New York, just outside of Buffalo, to escape religious persecution. As the area became more urbanized, its members decided to seek a new home base more conducive to their self-sufficient, God-fearing life-style apart from the outside world. That new site was eastern Iowa, where in 1859 they began establishing a cluster of seven villages with two main hubs of activity: the church and the communal kitchen.

"None of the families had kitchens of their own; they found it much more efficient to do everything as a community," Mrs. Oehler said. The home she grew up in served as one of sixteen communal kitchens. Her grandmother held the esteemed position of kitchen boss, in charge of making up menus and dividing the available food among the forty or so diners. Her staff consisted of nine or ten young girls who did all the cooking and a handful of older women who picked the vegetables from the garden.

Though the communal kitchens were abandoned before Mrs. Oehler was born, Henry Schiff, the sprightly director of the Amana museum, now in his eighties, recalls them vividly. "We used to eat all of our meals in our 'home kitchen': breakfast, lunch, dinner, and two elaborate coffee breaks," said Schiff. "The meals were huge—I stress to you, HUGE!" He said he particularly looked forward to the days when pork was served. "It was a chop that was cut just a wee bit differently than it is to-day, dipped in batter and fried in a cast-iron skillet. There were always lots of fresh vegetables from the fields, and potatoes, lots of potatoes. For dessert we had fruit pies made with apples, wild plums, or wild gooseberries."

The children were expected to attend school year-round with breaks at harvest and planting time so they could help in the fields, harvesting apples, plowing vegetable patches, picking potato bugs off the vines. "Each day a school lunch was brought to us; it could be beef or mutton, and always sweets," Schiff added.

Both children and adults were expected to attend prayer meetings every evening, as well as Wednesday and Saturday mornings. "During harvest time that always meant sacrificing an extra hour or two of sun-light for working in the fields. To compensate, we would sometimes have 'fast days.'"

After graduation, Schiff remembers meeting with a group of young men for a drawing to select their occupations. "We used to have shops for every trade imaginable," Schiff said. "We even had an umbrella maker and a lampshade maker." Schiff was assigned to work in the woolen mill. "My father was a farm manager and my brothers worked in the fields. I guess three guys coming home every night smelling like horses was enough!" Despite their lack of choice in the matter, Schiff added that "they would never try to put a square peg in a round hole."

The system sustained its people for nearly a century. But with the onset of the Great Depression in the 1930s it soon became apparent that the Amanas would not be able to survive in isolation forever, particu-larly after a fire destroyed the colonies' two greatest sources of live-

Three Arts Inc.

Hearty Ox Yoke Inn fare

lihood: the woolen factory and the flour mill. In 1932, a plan was drawn up by the community's leaders to separate church and state. But according to Schiff, "it wasn't a decision based on the sentiments of our people. There were 1,997 of us—just three shy of 2,000—that had to be fed and clothed somehow. That was just the cruel, harsh truth. We had only two choices: to abandon everything we'd ever strived for, or to tighten up our belts a couple of notches and do our best to retain our togetherness."

Today, the Amanas are still noted for their fine craftsmanship, particularly in their Amana refrigeration products and hand-crafted furniture.

And they've tried to preserve as much of their heritage as possible. Each year thousands of tourists come to visit their museum and gift shops filled with reminders of those traditions. There's a bakery where breads and coffee cakes are baked in a brick oven, meat markets where the local butchers stuff their sausages by hand, several wineries that produce wines ranging from elderberry to dandelion with the juices from their own orchards and vineyards. And every colony has at least a restaurant or two with menus based on the German-American cooking typical of the communal kitchens.

After "the change" from communal cooking, Mrs. Oehler's family purchased the house they'd been assigned to live in. Like the other Amana families, she said, they had to add a sink and stove to their home "in any room where there was a chimney." In 1950, she and her mother, Helen Zimmerman Graichen, decided to put the kitchen back into use by converting it into a restaurant. They named it the Ronneburg after a medieval fortress in Hesse, Germany, which sheltered their ancestors from persecution more than two hundred years ago. While their repertoire of entrées has expanded over the years, Mrs. Oehler still abides by many of the culinary principles set forth by her grandmother. She bakes virtually everything from scratch—from the sauerbraten to the rhubarb pie. And she's constantly looking for appetizing ways to stretch a limited ingredient or take advantage of exceptionally abundant produce. "Our ancestors wasted nothing, especially when it came to food," she said. "Back then, even pine trees in the yard were considered frivolous; only fruit-bearing trees were permitted." The kitchen bosses were exceptionally thrifty in the communal kitchens. "Bread crumbs were used to extend stewed tomatoes and spinach, and onions and apples were mixed in with the pickled herring. My mother used to say that after they sat in the icebox for a while the apples began to taste just like the herring."

Several years ago, Mrs. Oehler compiled the restaurant's house specialties, along with some other area favorites devised by herself and her ancestors, into a little cookbook entitled the *Ronneburg Recipe Album* (RR 255, Amana, Iowa 52203). Along with a sampling from her book, I've included several other area specialties.

I never got excited over a bowl of cottage cheese until I visited the Ronneburg. Not only is it refreshing and delicious, it's probably the only low-cal item on the menu!

Ronneburg Cottage Cheese

1 16-ounce carton cottage cheese
1 green onion, including some of
   the top, chopped

2 tablespoons buttermilk
1/4 teaspoon salt
Dash pepper

Combine all ingredients. Makes 4 servings.

This popular luncheon item at the Ronneburg was an overwhelming hit in my kitchen—a fabulous way to take advantage of excess garden produce.

Harvest Casserole

2 medium eggplants, peeled and
   diced
4 medium zucchini, sliced
4 teaspoons salt
2 pounds hamburger
3 tomatoes, chopped
2 green peppers, chopped
2 medium onions, chopped

4 ears raw sweet corn, cut off the
   cob
1 1/2 cups cooked rice
3 tablespoons chopped parsley
1/4 teaspoon pepper
1/2 cup (1 stick) melted butter
2 cups grated Parmesan cheese

Place eggplant and zucchini in colander. Sprinkle with 2 teaspoons salt. Let stand for 30 minutes so juices can drain. Preheat oven to 375 degrees. Cook hamburger until redness is gone; drain. In a large bowl, combine eggplant, zucchini, hamburger, remaining vegetables, rice, and parsley. Sprinkle with remaining 2 teaspoons salt and pepper. Place into buttered baking dish and pour butter over all. Cover tightly and bake 45 minutes in preheated oven; uncover, sprinkle cheese on top, and bake until vegetables are tender and cheese is melted, about 10 minutes more. Makes 10 to 12 servings.

A tangy, refreshing accompaniment to a hearty meat dish such as rouladen.

Pickled Red Cabbage

1 pound red cabbage, shredded	*1 cup vinegar*
1 teaspoon salt	*1 cup water*
1 cup granulated sugar	

Put cabbage in bowl and sprinkle with salt. Let stand 30 minutes. In saucepan, combine sugar, vinegar, and water and bring to a boil. Pour over cabbage and stir well. When cool, refrigerate at least 12 hours before serving. Will keep up to a week if refrigerated. Makes 4 servings.

These delicious braised, stuffed beef rolls are reserved at the restaurant for special occasions. They do take a little time to make, but they're well worth it, especially when served with the bread dumplings which follow.

Rouladen

2½ pounds round steak, ¼ inch   2 tablespoons lard
  thick, cut into 4 × 8-inch pieces   1½ tablespoons shredded carrots
3 tablespoons German-style   1½ tablespoons chopped celery
  mustard   1½ tablespoons chopped onion
⅔ cup finely chopped onion   1½ tablespoons chopped parsley
6 slices bacon, cut in half   2 to 3 cups water
3 whole dill pickles, each cut into   4 tablespoons all-purpose flour
  4 pieces lengthwise   ¼ to ½ cup cold water

Preheat oven to 350 degrees. Lay pieces of steak flat. Cover each with the mustard and the onion. Across the narrow end of each piece place 1 piece of bacon, then 2 pieces of dill pickle. Top with another piece of bacon. Roll up like a jelly roll, starting at the narrow end. Tie the rolls at least twice with kitchen cord. In a skillet over high heat, melt lard and brown the rolls on all sides. Transfer browned rolls to a baking dish large enough to hold them in one layer. Sprinkle with carrots, celery, onion, parsley, and water. Cover tightly and place in preheated oven for 1½ hours. Transfer rolls to a heated platter and keep warm. Combine flour and cold water, making a smooth paste, and slowly stir it into the hot liquid in the pan. On top of the stove, over medium heat, cook for several minutes, stirring constantly. Pour over rolls and serve. May be covered and kept warm at this stage up to 1 hour. Makes 6 servings.

Bread Dumplings

¾ pound white bread (very dry is   2 eggs, beaten
  best)   1½ cups milk
9 tablespoons butter   2½ cups all-purpose flour
½ teaspoon salt   ¾ cup bread crumbs

Cut crust from bread into very small pieces. Sauté in 4 tablespoons butter until lightly browned. Set aside. In a large bowl, break up the bread into small pieces. Sprinkle with ½ teaspoon salt. Combine beaten eggs and milk and pour evenly over the bread. Toss until milk mixture has soaked into bread. (Mixing is best done with your hands.) Drizzle with 2 tablespoons melted butter. Gradually add flour and mix well. Add crusts and blend them into the dough. Dipping hands into flour, gently form 12 round dumplings and place on a floured surface. Cook in enough lightly salted water to cover dumplings for 20 to 25 minutes.

While dumplings are cooking, in a small skillet melt remaining butter. Add bread crumbs and cook until golden brown, stirring constantly. Remove dumplings with a slotted spoon; sprinkle with bread crumbs. Makes 6 servings.

Sauerbraten and rhubarb custard pie are standbys in most of the Amana Colonies restaurants. These two outstanding versions are from the Ox Yoke Inn, which has been dishing out hearty Old World fare since the doors of its more than 125-year-old facility opened for business in 1940.

The Ox Yoke Inn's Sauerbraten

1 4-to-5-pound top round roast
1 cup cider vinegar
2¼ cups water
1 lemon, cut up
1 medium onion, cut up
2 bay leaves
1½ teaspoons salt
½ teaspoon whole black peppercorns
½ teaspoon whole cloves
2 cups water
⅓ to ½ cup all-purpose flour
⅓ cup granulated sugar
2 gingersnap cookies, crushed
Kitchen Bouquet (about 2 teaspoons)

Place roast in an earthenware crock or stainless steel stock pot. (Container should be approximately the same size as roast to obtain maximum coverage when marinade is added.) In another stainless steel pot, combine vinegar, water, lemon, onion, and spices; bring to a boil. Pour hot marinade over roast, then cool to room temperature. Place container in refrigerator and let roast marinate for 3 days. Baste roast frequently and turn twice a day to assure proper penetration of marinade.

After 3 days, remove roast from marinade and place in an uncovered roaster pan. Set marinade aside. Preheat oven to 275 degrees. Place roast in preheated oven and cook until tender, about 1½ to 2 hours. Remove meat from roaster and let stand.

Add meat juices from roaster to the reserved marinade; strain, then add 1 cup water and bring to a boil. To remaining cup water, add flour and mix well. Stir into marinade mixture to thicken gravy; bring to a boil again. Remove gravy from heat and add sugar, crushed gingersnaps, and Kitchen Bouquet to make gravy a rich, brown color. Slice meat and add gravy before serving. Makes 8 servings.

At the Ox Yoke Inn, this wonderfully tart/sweet pie is topped with a meringue, which to me seems a bit superfluous. If you prefer, however, you can separate the eggs and use only the yolks for the filling and the whites for a meringue to be added during the last 15 minutes of baking.

Rhubarb Custard Pie

3 eggs, lightly beaten
¼ cup half-and-half
1½ cups granulated sugar
1 tablespoon flour

⅛ teaspoon salt
4 cups chopped rhubarb
1 9-inch unbaked pie shell

Preheat oven to 375 degrees. In a large bowl, mix eggs and half-and-half. Add sugar, flour, salt, and rhubarb and mix thoroughly. Pour mixture into unbaked pie shell. Place pie in oven and bake 15 minutes; lower heat to 350 degrees and bake 30 to 45 minutes longer, or until set. Makes 6 to 8 servings.

A "most requested" at the Ronneburg, this makes a refreshing and delicious side dish any time. But Mrs. Oehler particularly recommends it in the summer with sliced tomatoes and corn on the cob.

Cucumbers in Cream Sauce

*4 medium cucumbers, peeled and
  thinly sliced*
1 medium onion, sliced
2 teaspoons salt

CREAM SAUCE:
*½ cup whipping cream (not
  whipped)*
2 tablespoons vinegar
¼ teaspoon salt
⅛ teaspoon pepper

In a large bowl, combine cucumbers, onion, and salt. Let stand at room temperature about 1 hour. Drain well. Combine ingredients for cream sauce, add to cucumber/onion mixture, and stir. Chill several hours before serving. Makes 4 to 6 servings.

THE WILTON CANDY KITCHEN

If you thought soda fountains went out with sock hops and hula hoops, you've obviously never stopped in for a Green River, a Brown Jersey, or any of the other soda fountain specialties at the Wilton Candy Kitchen. Since 1910, the turn-of-the-century general store across from the Wooden Nickel Saloon along Wilton's main street has been attracting customers from near and far to its soda fountain. Until recently, it was still possible to order sodas made with home-churned ice cream, sundaes dripping with secret syrups, and bubbly phosphates in a rainbow of colors—all advertised in large, handwritten letters on the mirrored walls.

Until his death at the age of ninety-two, Gus Nopoulos, the Candy Kitchen's founder, showed up to work faithfully every day, often spruced up in his gray suit complete with bow tie and red carnation to reminisce with the regulars, shake hands with the newcomers, and perhaps serve up a multifruit-flavored phosphate called a Dipsy Doodle to a young video game champ. The work was left to his son George and daughter-in-law Thelma and any of their four children when they happened to be in town. They also offered soup and sandwiches at lunchtime. For seventy-seven years the store stayed open from 7:00 A.M. to 1:00 A.M. seven days a week, including holidays. In 1987, when George and Thelma announced their plans to retire and close the store, the news hit the front pages of Iowa papers, and Iowans and their neighbors are still hoping that the Candy Kitchen will open its doors again.

Gus Nopoulos left his Greek homeland at the age of sixteen to work as an apprentice candymaker under his uncle, who ran a confectionary in Davenport. Two years later, the ambitious teenager decided to start his own business in a little whistlestop called Wilton Junction, hoping to attract business both from the townspeople and those waiting to catch the Rock Island train. He set up a little candy case and a soda fountain in the two-story building he rented for seven dollars a month. In a back room was an ice house where he made his ice cream in wooden tubs and even crushed up the ice to freeze it. He also roasted his own peanuts for peanut clusters that were dipped by hand in chocolate and sold for thirty cents a pound.

Nopoulos quit making his own candy a number of years ago because, he said, "it just got to be too much work." But all of the ice cream dishes and their embellishments were authentic, from maple-flavored ice cream to the crushed blackberry and strawberry toppings George claims were "made with genuine fresh fruit." A favorite standby was a phosphate called the Hadacol, a root beer and cherry syrup concoction named after the cough syrup. George's explanation: "We hadda call it something." Not all the items withstood the test of time so well. One that was removed from the menu due to low ratings was the Egg Malted Milk: one raw egg blended in a malt for those who "didn't have time for breakfast in the morning," Gus used to say. "It used to take three eggs in a chocolate malt to get me going in the mornings."

The Candy Kitchen's popularity reached its zenith during World War II, when gas was rationed and citizens were limited to finding entertainment closer to home. "Wednesday nights were always packed," recalled Thelma, who started washing dishes at the store more than forty years ago when she was ten years old and never left. "That was the night everyone would come downtown to see if their names would be drawn out of a barrel to win cash prizes offered by the local merchants." Added George: "Things were always real hectic on Saturday nights, too; all the bands would get together and play on the street corners 'til real late."

But business didn't fall off once transportation became easier. If anything, it increased. A guest register the Nopouloses used to keep shows that within one three-month period they received guests from forty-three different states and twenty countries.

In recent years, the Candy Kitchen has received nationwide recognition—from CBS news, which filmed the soda fountain for a feature segment; from the *Chicago Tribune,* which named Gus "Father of the Year" in 1979; and from the Coca-Cola bottlers, who presented father and son with a plaque of appreciation for seventy years of dedicated service. It wasn't surprising, then, that it was standing room only for the three days in June 1980 set aside to commemorate the kitchen's seventieth anniversary. Prior to the event, Thelma hand-painted 1,500 Coke glasses with the year of the anniversary. A local florist provided arrangements of carnations set in ice cream cones. And throughout the festivities the Nopouloses snapped pictures of their guests which now fill a bulging scrapbook. Among them are shots of five generations of Candy Kitchen regulars as well as one of a couple who'd celebrated both their engagement and their fiftieth anniversary in one of the booths.

In the summer of 1982, the thousands of cyclists who pedaled across Iowa in the state's annual Ragbrai bike ride rerouted the trip just so the Candy Kitchen could be included in their itinerary. Here were a few of the treats that were in store for them.

Green River

LEMON SYRUP:
1 gallon boiling water
15 pounds granulated sugar
1½ ounces lemon extract
½ ounce citric fruit acid

LIME SYRUP:
1 gallon boiling water
15 pounds granulated sugar
1½ ounces lime extract
½ ounce citric fruit acid

Crushed ice
Carbonated water

To make lemon syrup, pour boiling water over sugar. Cool and strain. Add extract and citric fruit acid. Pour into gallon jug and store. Follow same method for preparing lime syrup. When ready to serve, pour 1½ ounces of each syrup into 8-ounce glasses. Fill with crushed ice and carbonated water. Stir and serve. Makes 88 servings.

High School Special

2 scoops chocolate ice cream,
    preferably homemade
1 to 2 ounces chocolate syrup

1 to 2 ounces marshmallow syrup
    (marshmallow creme diluted to
    running consistency with simple
    syrup; see p. 252)
Handful of Spanish peanuts

Place ice cream in a large dish. Top with syrups and peanuts and serve. Makes 1 serving.

Brown Jersey

2 scoops vanilla ice cream,
    preferably homemade

1 to 2 ounces chocolate syrup
1 tablespoon malt powder

*Three generations of the Nopoulos family.
From left: Nic, George, and Gus.*

Place ice cream in a large dish. Top with syrup and sprinkle with malt powder. Makes 1 serving.

Candy Kitchen
Ham Salad Spread

2 pounds spiced luncheon ham
5 hard-boiled eggs
1 medium onion
5 tablespoons pickle relish

5 tablespoons mayonnaise-type
  salad dressing (or enough for
  spreading consistency)

Grind together ham, eggs, and onion. Stir in relish and salad dressing. Refrigerate. Makes enough for about 12 to 15 sandwiches.

Chocolate Malted Milk

1½ ounces chocolate syrup,
  preferably homemade
Generous amount of homemade
  chocolate or vanilla ice cream

Milk
1 or 2 tablespoons malt powder

Place all ingredients in a malt mixer and blend. Makes 1 serving.

THE WHITE WAY

I 'm far from being an exotic cook," confesses Carroll Marshall without a note of apology in his voice. "I cook the things that *I* like." Marshall may not be a connoisseur of haute cuisine, but when it comes to the subject of unpretentious, down-home Iowa cooking, there's probably no better authority around. Since opening the White Way Restaurant in Durant in 1967, Marshall has built a reputation for dishing out the kind of fare that represents the best the Cornbelt has to offer. "We're big on top-grade pork and top-grade beef; that's what we're most famous for," noted Marshall, a former army cook who picked up his first culinary lessons on the farm he grew up on in West Liberty. "And there's always plenty of it."

Located on the main drag of this quaint little farming community, the White Way—which is actually rustic brown, not white—was named after the Great White Way (now Highway 6 across Iowa). In 1985, the Iowa Pork Producers Association presented the White Way its Iowa restaurant award, and no wonder. Every day the menu features seven pork items: barbecued ribs, braised ribs with sauerkraut, hefty smoked chops, grilled chops, fork-tender Iowa chops smothered in mushroom sauce, grilled ham, country sausage. There's also roast beef and gravy, batter-dipped fried catfish, fried chicken, and—as Marshall puts it—"good ol' common Swiss steak" to choose from. All come with bread and a choice of baked, French-fried, or crusty, freshly made hash brown potatoes.

But the real show-stopper at the White Way is the salad bar, which is as steeped in Midwestern Americana as the entrées. And it could easily be just as filling, should you get carried away and try to sample all twenty-five items. There's nothing nouvelle here, either—just plenty of cool, homespun concoctions that would be right at home at a church potluck or family reunion in the Heartland. The items aren't labeled, but Marshall's wife, Bonnie, is on hand to offer any explanations. Along with the sparkling, traditional pea salad with sweet pickles and hard-boiled eggs found in Mom and Pop restaurants all over the state, Marshall makes a crunchy variation with raw cauliflower, celery, and shredded carrot, bound together with the peas in seasoned mayonnaise dressing. Other options include a mustardy potato salad, taco-flavored kidney bean salad with crushed tortilla chips, tangy sauerkraut salad flecked with pimiento, marinated pickled beets, an old-fashioned macaroni salad, a more contemporary version made with spiral pasta, a marshmallow-studded pineapple salad mixed with whipped topping called, appropriately enough, White Fluff, and a creamy, pink-tinted rice salad so rich and sweet it could easily pass for dessert.

A typical soup of the day would be chicken noodle, but one that bears no kinship to the stuff that comes out of a can. In its fragrant, steamy broth are tender chunks of chicken and vegetables along with plump, made-from-scratch noodles. Not only are there crackers to go with it, but Marshall's ultrarich liver pâté for spreading as well.

There isn't likely to be much room left for dessert, but a wedge of Marshall's deep-dish pies—most notably, the coconut cream and raisin cream—are well worth the price of a little extra discomfort. For years all the pies served at the White Way were made at home by Marshall's mother; after she died, Marshall tinkered around with her recipes until he could duplicate them himself. "I'm a damn good pie maker," Marshall said with conviction. "I'm a firm believer every pie needs a quarter teaspoon of salt; it can make the difference between a good pie and a bad pie. To bring out the best flavor, you've got to have the perfect balance between sugar, salt, and vanilla."

Besides his mother's files, Marshall said he gets much of his inspiration from local church cookbooks, particularly the Catholic ones, because they tend to have more large-quantity recipes designed for bigger families.

Here are some of his specialties which seem to disappear the fastest.

White Way Coconut Cream Pie

¾ cup granulated sugar
4 tablespoons cornstarch
¼ teaspoon salt
2 cups milk
¾ cup heavy cream
4 egg yolks
1 teaspoon vanilla

A good handful (¾ to 1 cup) grated coconut
1 baked 10-inch deep-dish pie shell
Meringue (recipe follows) or whipped cream
Additional coconut for garnish (optional)

In a heavy saucepan, combine sugar, cornstarch, and salt. Gradually stir in milk and cream. Cook and stir over medium heat until mixture is thick and bubbly. Reduce heat; cook and stir 2 minutes more. Remove from heat.

In a medium bowl, lightly beat the egg yolks. Gradually stir about half the hot mixture into the yolks; immediately return to mixture in pan and bring to a gentle boil, stirring constantly. Cook and stir 2 minutes more. Remove from heat and add vanilla and coconut. Let cool slightly. Pour into baked crust. Preheat oven to 350 degrees. Make meringue, if using (see following recipe), and spread over warm filling, sealing to edge of pastry. Sprinkle with additional coconut, if desired. Bake in preheated oven 12 to 15 minutes, or until meringue is golden. Let cool to room temperature 4 to 6 hours; cover and refrigerate. Dip knife in water before cutting pie to prevent sticking. Makes 8 servings.

Meringue

4 egg whites
½ teaspoon cream of tartar

Pinch of salt
½ cup granulated sugar

In a large bowl with electric mixer, beat egg whites with cream of tartar and salt until frothy. Gradually add sugar; beat until stiff but not dry peaks form. Spread over pie as directed. Makes a meringue for 1 10-inch pie.

Raisin Cream Pie

1 cup raisins
1 cup granulated sugar
½ cup all-purpose flour
¼ teaspoon salt
1 cup heavy cream
½ cup milk

4 egg yolks
1 tablespoon butter, melted
1 teaspoon vanilla
Baked pastry shell for 1 10-inch
  deep-dish pie
Meringue for 1 10-inch pie

Place raisins in a saucepan; cover barely with water. Cook over medium heat just until tender. Drain raisins, reserving liquid. In a measuring cup, pour in 1 cup of the raisin liquid.

In a heavy saucepan, combine sugar, flour, and salt. Gradually stir in cream, reserved raisin liquid, and milk. Cook and stir until thickened and bubbly. Reduce heat; cook and stir 2 minutes more. In a medium bowl, lightly beat egg yolks. Gradually stir about 1 cup of the hot mixture into egg yolks; immediately return to mixture in saucepan and bring to a gentle boil. Cook and stir 2 minutes more. Remove from heat; add butter and vanilla. Fold in raisins. Let cool slightly. Preheat oven to 350 degrees. Pour filling into pie shell, spread with meringue, and bake for 12 to 15 minutes. Cool to room temperature (takes 4 to 6 hours), then cover and refrigerate. Makes 8 servings.

Iowa Pea Salad

2 10-ounce packages frozen peas,
  thawed
3 hard-boiled eggs, chopped
½ cup chopped celery
3 to 5 tablespoons chopped sweet
  pickles

½ cup mayonnaise-type salad
  dressing (or to taste)
3 to 4 ounces cheddar cheese,
  shredded or diced

In a large bowl, stir together all ingredients. Makes 6 to 8 servings.

Cauliflower-Pea Salad

1 large head cauliflower, trimmed   *½ cup chopped celery*
  and broken in flowerets   *1 cup shredded carrot*
1 10-ounce package frozen peas,   *2 cups mayonnaise*
  thawed   *Seasoned salt to taste*

In a large bowl, combine cauliflower, peas, celery, and carrot. In a smaller bowl, stir together mayonnaise and seasoned salt. Add mayonnaise mixture to vegetables and combine well. Makes 6 to 8 servings.

Midwest meets Southwest in this spicy White Way salad bar specialty which could easily be a meal in itself.

Carroll Marshall's Taco Salad

½ pound ground beef   *1 16-ounce can chili beans in*
½ package (2 tablespoons) taco   *gravy*
  seasoning mix   *½ cup mayonnaise-type salad*
1 teaspoon (or less) salt   *dressing*
1 head iceberg lettuce, chopped   *¼ cup chili sauce*
1 medium onion, chopped   *A little chili powder to taste, if*
1 large tomato, diced   *desired*
4 ounces cheddar cheese, grated   *2 or 3 cups broken taco-flavored*
                                               chips

In a skillet over medium-high heat, brown ground beef with taco seasoning mix and salt. In a large bowl, toss together lettuce, onion, tomato, and cheese. Add meat (drained) and beans and toss. In a small bowl, mix together salad dressing, chili sauce, and chili powder. Stir into salad. Just before serving, mix in chips. Makes 4 to 6 main-course salads.

TERRACE HILL

O n the third floor of the stately, rose-colored Victorian mansion, the lady of the house and her cook checked over last-minute details of the evening's menu. Standing rib roast was in the oven, assorted vegetables were marinating, potatoes were stuffed and ready to bake, ice cream dessert was freezing. Early that morning formal place settings, candles, and fresh flowers had been arranged on the antique lace tablecloth covering the formal dining room table.

This lady of the house was a stickler for perfection, to maintain her reputation not only as a hostess but also as first lady of the state. During her husband, Robert's, unprecedented sixteen-year stint as Iowa's governor, Billie Ray became accustomed to entertaining such high-powered dinner guests as Prince Faisal of Saudi Arabia, Ambassador Shirley Temple Black, Governor John Connally, and Vice-President George Bush, to name but a few. On other occasions, not-so-famous Iowa citizens were extended invitations to dine at the governor's residence. Each Thanksgiving, she remembered, the Rays had a tradition of sharing their feast with "people who may have had no one to eat with that day. One year we had some nursing home residents for dinner; another time we invited some handicapped citizens."

Until her husband stepped aside for a new administration in 1983, Billie Ray played a leading role in restoring the governor's residence, Terrace Hill, to its original timeless elegance that once inspired writers to describe it as "the finest home west of the Hudson River." "Some people had their doubts, but I always thought it would be just lovely," mused Mrs. Ray.

It took noted Chicago architect William W. Boyington more than four years to complete the mansion for millionaire banker Benjamin Franklin Allen and his wife, Arathusa, in 1869. That year, on the couple's fifteenth wedding anniversary, the couple sent out one-thousand invitations to a housewarming gala to show off their dream house. A chef from a famous Chicago restaurant was brought in to prepare the delicacies: turkeys in colored aspic, oysters, a variety of meats, a twenty-five-pound lady cake, two gargantuan fruit cakes, and an ice cream sculpture of George Washington.

Only fifteen years after they'd moved in, however, financial difficulties forced the Allens to sell their home. It was purchased for a meager $60,000 by Frederick Marion Hubbell, a shrewd businessman who, at his death, was proclaimed the richest man in Iowa history. The Hubbell family continued to occupy the mansion until Frederick's youngest son, Grover, died in 1956. It remained inhabited only by caretakers until 1976, when Governor Ray and his family moved into the private quarters—five years after Frederick Hubbell's heirs presented the house as a gift to the state of Iowa.

Now a showplace for visitors to tour, the mansion has twenty rooms on the first two floors which have been refurbished during the past two decades with chandeliers, tapestries, and exquisite nineteenth-century antiques.

To help raise money for the renovation, the Terrace Hill Society in 1979 sponsored a dinner dance patterned after the Allens' grandiose housewarming 110 years earlier. More than six hundred guests purchased tickets to stroll through the mansion's freshly decorated interior, dance to the six-piece band, and sample the sumptuous fare on the buffet table: cold lobster mousse in pastry shells, whole breast of turkey en gelée, sliced tenderloin of beef, roast crowns of lamb, potato nests filled with peas, decorated Victorian lady cakes, strawberry tarts, and whole wheels of Stilton cheese. That menu was later recaptured in *A Taste of Terrace Hill* (Terrace Hill Society, Des Moines, Iowa 50265), a cookbook put together by Mrs. Ray and a group of friends as another effort to raise money for Terrace Hill's restoration. Along with recipes popular with Terrace Hill guests, the hardback book also features photographs of the mansion's renovations.

"It seemed that as soon as my husband was elected into office, requests began pouring in for our favorite recipes," she said. "We must have sent out hundreds of them to churches, schools, everybody. That made us think that there might be interest in a cookbook." She added that, with the help of several friends who test recipes for *Better Homes and Gardens* magazine, located in downtown Des Moines, "we tried to select a nice variety of tried-and-true favorites that were somewhat unique; not twenty-five meatloafs and ten brownie recipes." She admitted, however, that more than a few of the recipes are for ice cream desserts. "My husband is an ice creamaholic," she laughed. "Probably 90 percent of the desserts we serve here lean toward ice cream."

The high-brow social functions, however, aren't the only memories

Billie Ray looks back on when she thinks of her years spent at Terrace Hill. "Whether we were on our way to the main dining room for a formal reception or to the cookie jar in our kitchen for a snack, Terrace Hill always felt like home to us," she reflected. "The governor's residence we lived in before was much more public than this; we had very little privacy, even in our living quarters. But here we found that we could keep our public and private lives separate. That's what made it a home."

Here are some of the recipes the Rays have enjoyed together as a family and with guests at Terrace Hill.

Tuna Mountain

1 cup (2 sticks) butter or
*   margarine*
1 8-ounce package cream cheese
2 6½-ounce cans tuna, drained
2 tablespoons chopped green
*   onions*
1 tablespoon lemon juice
1 tablespoon capers

¼ teaspoon salt
¼ teaspoon dried tarragon,
*   crushed*
Dash pepper
¼ cup finely snipped parsley
1 hard-cooked egg yolk, sieved
Radishes

In a mixing bowl with electric mixer, food processor fitted with steel blade, or blender, cream together butter and cream cheese. Beat in tuna, onions, lemon juice, capers, salt, tarragon, and pepper until smooth. Shape into a mountain on a serving plate. Sprinkle parsley around base. Chill. Sprinkle top with sieved egg and garnish mountain with whole radishes. Serve with crackers or rye bread. Makes 3½ cups spread.

Cheesey Chowder

1 cup peeled, chopped potatoes
½ cup chopped carrots
½ cup chopped celery
½ cup chopped onion
½ cup chopped green pepper
4 tablespoons butter or margarine
3 cups chicken broth

Dash of white pepper
2 cups milk
½ cup all-purpose flour
12 ounces shredded sharp
*   processed American cheese*
1 tablespoon snipped parsley

In a Dutch oven over medium heat, cook potatoes, carrots, celery, onion, and green pepper in butter or margarine until tender but not brown. Add chicken broth and pepper. Cover and simmer 30 minutes. Blend milk into flour and add to chowder with cheese and parsley. Cook and stir until thickened and bubbly. Makes 7 to 8 servings.

Grand Avenue Party Chicken

6 slices bacon
3 whole chicken breasts, split, boned, and skinned
¼ cup water
1 3-ounce package sliced smoked beef

1 10¾-ounce can condensed cream of onion soup
½ cup dairy sour cream
1 tablespoon flour
Paprika

In a skillet, cook bacon until crisp. Remove, crumble, and reserve. Drain bacon drippings. Place chicken breasts and water in same skillet. Cover and simmer 10 minutes. Pour off water. Fold 6 slices of beef in half and wrap 2 around each breast. Return chicken to skillet. Combine soup, sour cream, and flour. Cut up remaining smoked beef and add to sour cream mixture. Spoon over chicken in skillet. Sprinkle with paprika. Simmer, covered, 8 minutes, or until hot. Serve garnished with bacon. Makes 6 servings.

Iowa Ham Balls

1 pound ground ham
1½ pounds ground pork
2 cups soft bread crumbs
2 well-beaten eggs
1 cup milk
1 cup brown sugar, packed

1 teaspoon dry mustard
½ cup vinegar
½ cup water
½ cup horseradish sauce
½ cup heavy cream, whipped

Preheat oven to 325 degrees. Combine ham, pork, bread crumbs, eggs, and milk and form into balls larger than golf balls. Place in an 11 × 16-inch pan. Combine brown sugar, mustard, vinegar, and water in saucepan and heat until sugar is dissolved. Pour over ham balls. Bake in preheated oven 1 hour, covered, and 1 hour, uncovered. Serve with horseradish sauce mixed with whipped cream. Makes 10 servings.

L'Abricot et Amande Dessert

1½ cups crushed vanilla wafers
⅓ cup melted butter
⅔ cup toasted almonds
1 teaspoon almond flavoring
½ gallon vanilla ice cream

1 20-ounce jar apricot jam
3 tablespoons orange-flavored
   liqueur
12 maraschino cherries (optional)

Mix first 4 ingredients together, reserving ⅓ cup for topping. Using a 9 × 13-inch pan, press half the mixture firmly in bottom. Add 1 quart ice cream. Put in freezer to refreeze ice cream. When firm, coat with about 10 ounces apricot jam mixed with liqueur. Repeat layers and top with remaining crumb mixture. Put into freezer until just before serving. Cut into squares or serve in sherbet glasses and top with a cherry, if desired. Makes 12 servings.

Try this with fresh Iowa muskmelon in late summer!

Cantaloupe Buffet Salad with Black Pepper Dressing

*3 cups thin, sliced fresh
   cantaloupe or muskmelon
1 cucumber, peeled and thinly
   sliced*

*Black pepper dressing (recipe
   follows)
Crisp lettuce
Finely snipped parsley*

Gently toss melon and cucumbers with black pepper dressing. Cover and chill 2 hours or longer. To serve, arrange on lettuce-lined chilled serving platter or individual plates. Spoon dressing over and sprinkle with chopped parsley. Makes 4 servings.

Black Pepper Dressing

*½ cup salad oil
3 tablespoons fresh lemon juice
¾ teaspoon Dijon-style mustard*

*½ teaspoon salt
½ teaspoon freshly ground black
   pepper*

In a jar, shake together all ingredients. Makes a scant ¾ cup dressing.

RAILROAD TOWN

U nlike most Creston citizens, neither Bob Berning nor any of his family has ever worked on the railroad. But when his customers tell him they're coming down the track for a Rail-Splitter, he has no trouble interpreting the lingo.

In layman's terms, the "track" refers to the bars customers slide their trays along during lunchtime at Berning's Cafe and Motor Inn, trying to choose between the potpourri of filling entrées, some forty different salads, vegetable casseroles, and homemade cream pies piled high with meringue. The Rail-Splitter is what they usually order: a locally butchered steak accompanied by their favorite salad, a baked potato, and homemade Vienna bread.

For more than forty years, Berning's family has been accommodating the heavy lunchtime traffic from the railroaders who work at Creston's historical passenger depot across the street from the hotel restaurant. That's why their menu has always included plenty of meaty, substantial entrées sure to satiate the appetite of many a hard-working brakeman or engineer.

"Since the railroad's the major industry in this town, the bulk of our business has always been railroaders and passengers," Berning said. Besides feeding the noontime regulars, he also serves a group of retired railroaders who meet there for coffee once a month. In the evenings, he frequently entertains visiting railroad officials with a more lavish menu that includes such classic selections as beef Wellington wrapped in puff pastry carved at the table and flaming cherries jubilee for dessert.

Berning's Cafe is only one place where the railroad's impact on this bustling southern Iowa city of about 10,000 is evident. It has molded the history and character of Creston for more than a century. Now served by Amtrak and Burlington Northern Rail System, Creston's railroad dates back to the 1870s, when the Burlington and Missouri River Road Company obtained a special grant of public lands from the federal government in hopes of connecting up with the old rail lines spreading westward from Chicago. By the 1890s, more than one thousand men were employed there as machinists, boilermakers, switchmen, firemen, and engineers. Unlike other rural towns on the Midwestern frontier, Creston was set in urbanized, industrial surroundings that earned for it the nickname Little Chicago.

Rail construction gangs and labor union dissension spawned crime and corruption. Lifetime Creston resident Opal Leach recalled that "as a child, I wasn't allowed to go down Pine Street because of all the taverns and 'loose women' there." But the town's rowdy side was tempered by an air of opulence and sophistication. With the influx of prosperity brought in by the railroad, the humble structures of the frontier construction camp were replaced by elegant homes of distinctive architecture: Italianate, with projecting eaves supported by brackets and corner porches; Queen Anne, with multiple steep roofs; functional bungalows, with gently pitched gables and large front porches; Gothic, with arched windows and high-pitched roofs. Railroad organizations frequently gave fashionable parties and formal balls. One of the top social privileges was to receive an invitation to attend the annual dance sponsored by the Order of Railway Conductors.

Creston hotels were familiar stopover places noted for their luxurious accommodations and fine cuisine. And the Renaissance Revival–type depot built in 1910 by two renowned Chicago architects drew visitors from miles around, especially when such notables as Franklin Roosevelt and Harry Truman delivered speeches from the back of the trains on whistle-stop tours.

Railroaders have always been treated with utmost respect in Creston. "It's a mortal sin to say anything against the railroad men in this town," said Mrs. Rudolf Weisshaar, the daughter of a railroader. "In my neighborhood, many of the men like my father would leave early in the morning for work and wouldn't come home until late that evening. It was hard, heavy work, but they were very, very dedicated. They lived their jobs." Opal Leach agrees. Not only was her stepfather an engineer; her brother was a brakeman and her husband a conductor. The "way car," or caboose, was their second home, she said. "When the men would have to travel somewhere overnight, they'd take their bedrolls back there to sleep on. They had a little monkey stove and skillet to cook their meals with. And they could cook! They'd make pancakes, biscuits, eggs, or cornmeal mush with applesauce for breakfast, and for supper they'd usually fry steaks. T-bone was their favorite."

They frequently talked about "Bright Eyes," the toothless waitress at

Pacific Junction, "a little hole in the road" where they'd often stop en route to their destinations. "The railroaders used to have the dizziest names for things," Opal Leach said, laughing. "Whenever they wanted coffee, they'd ask Bright Eyes to bring them a cup of 'iodine.' Or if they wanted two poached eggs on toast for breakfast, they'd order 'Adam and Eve on a Raft.'"

Creston reached its heyday during the age of the steam engine, when the powerful Pufferbellies with their diamond-shaped smokestacks roared and hissed their way toward Creston's depot twenty-four times a day. "This depot used to be a beehive of activity, especially when we had our roundhouse," Mrs. Leach recalled. At one time, she noted, it was re-puted to be one of the largest of its kind in the country, with sixty stalls for maintaining the massive locomotives. "It was a real beauty," she re-flected. "It was so big that they had to have 'call boys' to relay messages on bicycles between the different workmen."

Some of Mrs. Leach's most memorable dining experiences were on board the train. "They had such wonderful food in the diners!" she mused. "Things like big bowls of chicken pot pies, strawberry shortcake, turkey with corn bread dressing, hot mince pie with brandy sauce." The service, she said, was equally impressive. "Each table was covered by a pink tablecloth, with a vase holding a pink carnation on top. The dining car waiters were dressed up in tuxedos, and they'd take orders until five in the morning. It was all very expensive, and of course you never forgot to tip!"

With the advent of the diesel, the roundhouse was no longer needed. The frenetic activity once associated with the depot diminished. But the charm and romance of those days haven't disappeared from this town completely. Thanks to a group of dedicated Crestonians, the depot still stands as an enduring legacy to its colorful past. In addition to serving as a waiting room its interior, with its polished marble floors and ornate molded ceilings, also contains public offices, meeting rooms, and space for senior citizens' congregate meals. And every year it's the center at-traction during the town's annual Railroad Heritage Days celebration, honoring the railroad system and the Crestonians who played a role in its development. Historical films are shown, free train rides are offered, and many of the stately homes are open for tours. Sandwiches, home-made pastries, and ice cream are sold at a sidewalk cafe. And right across the street Bob Berning is putting his culinary skills to work, cre-ating a meal fit for a railroader.

One of the long-standing favorites which he often makes for special groups is baron of beef, a seventy-five or eighty-pound side of beef that's seasoned and slow-roasted until it's extra tender and then carved table-

side. Here's his method, adapted for home use by substituting a smaller cut of beef. His homemade Vienna bread, characterized by a crusty exterior and soft interior, would be ideal for sopping up the savory juices.

Baron of Beef

*1 top round beef roast (5 to
   7 pounds)
1 small, fresh tomato, peeled and
   chopped
1 stalk celery, chopped*

*1 medium carrot, cut up
1 small onion, chopped
1 clove garlic, cut in half, or garlic
   powder
Salt and pepper to taste*

Preheat oven to 275 degrees. In a large roasting pan, combine roast with tomato, celery, carrot, and onion. Rub roast with cut garlic clove or sprinkle all over with garlic powder. Sprinkle all over with salt and pepper. Roast for 3 to 4 hours, depending on desired doneness (140 degrees on meat thermometer for rare, 160 degrees for medium, 170 degrees for well done). Makes 12 to 15 servings.

Vienna Bread

2 cups hot water
2 tablespoons shortening
3 tablespoons granulated sugar
1 package (1 tablespoon) dry
  yeast

7 cups all-purpose flour (more if
  necessary)
1 tablespoon salt

In a large bowl, combine water, shortening, and sugar, stirring until dissolved. When lukewarm (105 to 110 degrees), add yeast. Let stand until bubbly. Combine flour and salt. Stir half the flour/salt mixture into other ingredients until smooth. Add rest of flour, cup by cup, and stir until stiff. Add extra flour if necessary. Knead on a floured counter until smooth and elastic. Cover, set in a warm place, and let rise until doubled in bulk, 2 to 2½ hours. (Rub with softened butter to prevent drying.) Punch down, let rise again for 2 to 2½ hours. Punch down; divide dough into 3 sections.

With floured rolling pin, roll each section into a 6 × 12-inch rectangle. Fold each side toward the center, then fold again at center. Pinch edges together so that seam is invisible. Make diagonal slashes across each loaf about 2 inches apart. Place on greased cookie sheets; cover and let rise again for about 45 minutes. Preheat oven to 400 degrees. Bake about 30 minutes. Makes 3 loaves.

One of the pleasant, unexpected touches which come with Berning's dinners is a bountiful relish tray, which includes a creamy lobster and rice salad. That recipe and the next one were both featured in the November 1986 issue of *Ford Times* magazine.

Lobster or Crab Salad

1 cup cooked lobster or crabmeat
  chunks
2 cups cooked white rice
¼ cup diced celery

¼ cup diced onion
¼ cup diced green pepper
1 cup mayonnaise
Salt and pepper to taste

Gently mix the salad ingredients and chill for at least 1 hour before serving. Makes 4 servings.

Rhubarb Crisp

4 cups diced rhubarb   *½ cup brown sugar*
⅔ cup granulated sugar   *½ cup rolled oats*
1 tablespoon grated orange peel   *½ cup flour*
Pinch of salt   *⅓ cup butter or margarine*

Preheat oven to 350 degrees. In a large bowl, mix rhubarb, granulated sugar, orange peel, and salt together and place in a buttered 9-inch square baking dish. Combine brown sugar, oats, and flour and sprinkle on top of rhubarb. Top with dots of butter or margarine. Bake in preheated oven for 30 to 45 minutes, or until bubbly. Makes 6 to 8 servings.

THE MASON HOUSE

Buretta Redhead has always had a deep-rooted interest in the arts: watercolor painting, china painting, doll making, sewing. But she never cared a lick about cooking until 1980, when she began serving meals at the Mason House, the historic inn she and her husband, Herb, purchased some twenty-five years earlier in the near ghost town of Bentonsport along the lower Des Moines River in Van Buren County. "Food is an art, too. You can make it fun," she said. "I don't believe in getting all unstrung and nervous in the kitchen; I don't sweat it. I do whatever I feel comfortable doing."

Although simple, home-style Iowa cooking is the inn's specialty, all of the dishes are served with flair. On this particular morning, for example, the highlight of the hearty breakfast is baked French toast, a cross, you might say, between French toast and bread pudding, glazed with local maple syrup and topped with fresh sliced strawberries and bananas. To go with it there are scrambled eggs and bacon brought to the guests at the eight-leaf walnut thresher's table on blue calico plates garnished with nasturtiums. "Herb is used to my decorating the plates; he thinks that's the secret to my cooking," the ebullient innkeeper, attired in circa 1900 garb, said with a twinkle in her eyes. "I like to use fresh flowers, different kinds of fruit."

In the kitchen, she said, the philosophy is "nothing fast and nothing fried. We stick mostly to meat and potatoes. We do lots of casseroles. Fresh butter, fresh cream, fresh milk, fresh herbs—that's our emphasis." For years Mrs. Redhead was assisted in the kitchen by local Amish women who passed along many of the recipes used at the inn today: breads and sweet rolls baked from scratch, casseroles made with seasonal local produce, home-canned preserves and relishes, old-time desserts from molasses cookies to apple dumplings. The breakfast cooks begin mixing the dough for fresh cinnamon rolls or Danishes sometimes as early as 3:00 A.M. To wake the guests, "we just fling open the door to the upstairs and let them smell the rolls."

It isn't just the home cooking that draws visitors to the Mason House

Jo Futrell

The Mason House as seen from across the Des Moines River

but the charm of the inn itself. Built in 1846, the twenty-one room brick Federal-style structure was once a stopping place for riverboat captains and other travelers back in the days when Bentonsport was a prosperous river town. An avid Iowa history buff, Mrs. Redhead first laid eyes on the landmark in 1954 while traveling through southeast Iowa as secretary of the state centennial celebration. At that time it was being used as a summer home by the Mason family. "I told Herb, 'Gimme a dollar bill, and I'm making an offer,'" she remembered. Soon after, the couple and their two young daughters gave up everything, including their large antique shop in Des Moines, to preserve this piece of Iowa history in one of the poorest areas of the state. "If you see a purpose, you fufill it," she said with a shrug. "Either you're dedicated or you're not dedicated."

Renovating the structure was a full-time, labor-intensive job for both of them. Before the heat was working properly the winters were miserable, "especially when we'd have to bathe in that old copper tub in the bitter cold." The Redheads furnished the house with the early trappings which were still intact when they arrived as well as many of their own family antiques of the pre–Civil War era. Today it functions as both an inn and a gift shop which sells antiques and works by local craftsmen, including the hand-sewn Amish dolls made by local Amish women from patterns designed by Mrs. Redhead.

Other sites in Bentonsport, which in 1972 was designated a National Historic District, have since been renovated: the Greef General Store, which now contains antique and crafts shops; the Odd Fellows Hall, a former furniture factory which houses a museum featuring Indian artifacts and other curios; the Bank of Bentonsport, now occupied by a potter; and an old-fashioned English garden along the riverfront. Behind the Mason House is a cottage also restored by the Redheads which serves as a bridal suite. A special breakfast and dinner are prepared for the couple and delivered to their doorstep.

The inn is open for guests from April to November. For more information, write the Mason House Inn, Rural Route 2, Keosauqua, Iowa 52565.

Here are some of the specialties preserved in the Mason House recipe files.

Amish Meat Loaf

1½ pounds ground beef
1 cup quick-cooking oats
1 cup grated carrot
⅓ cup finely chopped onion
2 eggs, slightly beaten
1½ teaspoons salt

1½ teaspoons Worcestershire
  sauce
¼ teaspoon pepper
3 hard-cooked eggs, peeled
Gravy (optional)

Preheat oven to 350 degrees. In a large bowl, combine beef, oats, carrot, onion, eggs, salt, Worcestershire sauce and pepper. Form half the mixture into a rectangle and place in an 8 × 4-inch baking pan. Arrange hard-cooked eggs lengthwise down the center of the meat. Form remaining meat into a rectangle slightly larger than the first. Place over eggs. Press the 2 layers of meat together to form a compact loaf. Bake 50 to 60 minutes. Serve with gravy, if desired. Makes 6 to 8 servings.

Sweet Potato and Cashew Bake

½ cup packed brown sugar
⅓ cup broken cashews
½ teaspoon salt
¼ teaspoon ground ginger

2 pounds sweet potatoes, cooked,
  peeled, and cut crosswise into
  thick pieces
1 8-ounce can peach slices, well
  drained
3 tablespoons butter or margarine

Preheat oven to 350 degrees. Combine brown sugar, cashews, salt, and ginger. In a 10 × 6 × 2-inch baking dish, layer half the sweet potatoes, half the peaches, and half the brown sugar mixture. Repeat layers. Dot with butter or margarine. Bake, covered, in preheated oven 30 minutes. Uncover and bake mixture about 10 minutes longer. Spoon brown sugar mixture over potatoes before serving. Makes 6 to 8 servings.

Sauerkraut Casserole

½ pound sliced bacon
2 cups chopped onion
2 32-ounce jars sauerkraut,
  drained and rinsed
2 cups chopped apples

2 cups chicken broth
⅓ cup packed brown sugar
½ teaspoon pepper
½ teaspoon thyme
1½ cups dry vermouth
Apple wedges

Preheat oven to 325 degrees. In a large skillet over medium-high heat, fry bacon until crisp. Drain on paper towels. Sauté onion in bacon drippings until limp. Stir in remaining ingredients. Spoon mixture into a 3-quart baking dish. Cover and bake until liquid is absorbed, about 2 to 2½ hours. Top with reserved bacon and apple wedges. Makes 10 to 12 servings.

Mason House Molasses Cookies

1 cup (2 sticks) butter or
  margarine
1½ cups granulated sugar
1⅓ cups sorghum molasses
2 eggs, lightly beaten
5 cups all-purpose flour

1 teaspoon baking powder
1 teaspoon baking soda
3 teaspoons cinnamon
1 teaspoon cloves
1 teaspoon ginger
1 cup chopped nuts (optional)

Preheat oven to 350 degrees. In a large bowl, cream butter or margarine with sugar until fluffy. Blend in molasses and eggs. Sift together flour, baking powder, baking soda, cinnamon, cloves, and ginger. Add to creamed mixture, mixing well. Fold in nuts, if using. Drop tablespoons of batter on foil-lined cookie sheets, leaving 3 inches between each cookie. Bake 10 to 12 minutes for soft cookies, a few minutes longer for crisp cookies. Makes about 4 dozen 3-inch cookies.

Baked French Toast

¾ stick butter
½ cup maple syrup, honey, or
  brown sugar
7 or 8 slices white or wheat bread
  (or combination), cut in half
  horizontally

6 eggs
3 tablespoons milk
Sliced bananas and strawberries

Preheat oven to 375 degrees. Combine butter and sweetener in a 9 × 13-inch baking dish. Set in preheated oven until butter is melted. Remove from oven and layer half-slices of bread in two rows, overlapping edges of bread. Beat eggs with milk in mixing bowl. Pour mixture over bread. Bake at 375 degrees for 15 minutes, until bread is firm. Remove from oven. With a spatula, remove rows of toast, one at a time, and flip over onto a platter so that the glazed side is up. Cover with bananas and strawberries and serve. Makes 4 to 6 servings.

THE LITTLE BROWN CHURCH
IN THE VALE

Protestants all over the world know "The Church in the Wildwood" as
one of their best-loved hymns. But to Paul and Ardith Goings, "the
little brown church in the vale" is more than the subject of a song. It's
the church they grew up in, the church they were married in, and the
church where they've continued to pursue a spiritual life together for
more than forty years.

The Little Brown Church in the Vale still stands in Nashua, Iowa,
among "the trees where the wildflowers bloom"—the exact spot where
composer William Pitts envisioned such a church one summer day in
1857. Though the congregation's membership today barely exceeds 130,
some 50,000 visitors enter its humble doors each year and between 700
and 800 couples choose it as the perfect spot to exchange their wedding
vows. "We have a very different kind of ministry here," said John Christy,
the church's twenty-ninth pastor, who considers the fact that the imagi-
nary church in Pitts's song became in reality a "miracle of God's divine
providence."

Legend has it that the young music teacher discovered the church's
picturesque site after the stagecoach he was riding to visit his bride-to-
be in Fredericksburg stopped for a rest in Bradford, a once-thriving Iowa
farm community a few miles from Nashua. As he strolled through a
nearby wooded glen he became enchanted by its pastoral beauty: the
gentle breeze rustling the leaves of the ancient trees, the birds chirping
in melodious harmony. Shortly after returning to his home in southern
Wisconsin he set those impressions to music with a hymn he titled "The
Little Brown Church in the Vale." His composition remained stashed in
his desk drawer until he came back to Bradford several years later to
teach music at Bradford Academy. Upon his arrival in town he hopped
on his horse to ride to his favorite spot, where, to his amazement, he saw
the foundation for a small church being laid, just as he had imagined.

The day the church was dedicated, Pitts's vocal class performed "The
Little Brown Church in the Vale" for the first time in public. Soon after he
sold the song to a Chicago publisher for twenty-five dollars to help pay

his medical school tuition. The hymn was sung regularly by the congregation until the 1900s, when the railroad bypassed Bradford and went to the neighboring community of Nashua instead.

As the community dwindled, the weeds around the church grew waist-high. Its fresh coat of brown paint faded. The song might have been forgotten altogether had it not been for the Weatherwax Quartet of Charles City, some twelve miles from Nashua. One of the country's most popular gospel groups at one time, they recalled the song from a visit to the Little Brown Church years earlier and decided to introduce it on their radio program. The response was so favorable that "The Little Brown Church in the Vale," or "The Church in the Wildwood," eventually became their theme song, performed not only on the air but at chautauquas and revivals all over the country.

A revival eventually pulled the church back on its feet. And the extra effort put forth by its stout-hearted congregation kept it thriving. Paul Goings, who now teaches Sunday school there, remembers when his father used to go door to door taking up a collection to hire a pastor. The advent of the automobile introduced another means of support when couples from all over began seeking what Mrs. Goings calls its "quiet simplicity" for exchanging marriage vows. "I always thought I would get married here, or I wouldn't get married at all," she said, smiling. Mrs. Goings, who got acquainted with her husband at a "young people's Bible reading" at church, recollects her own ceremony well. "Two sisters and two brothers were our attendants, and we had a flower girl. A soloist sang 'Because' and 'I Love You Truly.' Then the church bell was rung and the organist played 'The Church in the Wildwood.'" After the ceremony, miniature angel food cakes, punch, and coffee were served in the fellowship hall along with slices of the tiered wedding cake baked by Mrs. Goings's sister-in-law.

The ceremonies Christy performed during his years at Nashua (Pastor Robert Middleton assumed those duties in 1987) were much like the Goingses', though each was unique in its own special way. He's conducted them as early as sunrise and as late as quarter 'til midnight. He once married a couple from Germany enchanted by the church on a visit to Iowa with the assistance of an interpreter. One bride, he recalled, had as her bridesmaids her daughter and granddaughter, while her mother served as matron of honor.

Some brides choose to furnish their own refreshments. But upon request, the ladies of the church will prepare the tiered cake and the homemade mints, punch, coffee, and nuts. The first Sunday of every August, Mrs. Goings said, the ladies rise "very, very early in the morning" to

John Christy at the Little Brown Church

begin making preparations for the annual reunion of the couples married at the Little Brown Church. "We've had two thousand or more show up for it," she noted, adding that one year there were fifty-six couples in attendance who'd been married more than fifty years. Along with a huge picnic on the grounds, one of the event's highlights is a fashion show entitled "Love Never Goes out of Style," put on by the brides who can still squeeze into their wedding gowns. Whether or not the special ceremony has any long-term effects one can only speculate. But Christy estimated that "of the marriages that have started here, only about 10 percent have ended up in divorce."

But the life of the church isn't entirely centered around weddings. Each fall the members dress up in old-fashioned clothes for a chili supper commemorating Founder's Day. And they can always expect a heavy turn-out Easter Sunday for the sunrise service, followed by a special breakfast prepared by the women of the church. "We used to have all different kinds of eggs: fried eggs, scrambled eggs, colored Easter eggs," said Mrs. Goings. "Then we discovered an egg dish we could make up the night before that everyone seems to like." Here is the recipe, along with the punch and mints that receive compliments at nearly every wedding.

Little Brown Church
Easter Breakfast Dish

5 tablespoons margarine
2 tablespoons all-purpose flour
½ teaspoon salt
⅛ teaspoon pepper
2 cups milk
1 cup processed American cheese,
   shredded

1 cup diced meat (ham, bacon, or
   sausage)
¼ cup minced onion
12 eggs, lightly beaten
1 3-ounce can mushrooms,
   drained
2½ cups soft bread crumbs

Make a cheese sauce by melting 2 tablespoons margarine over medium heat. Stir in flour, salt, and pepper; cook and stir 2 minutes. Slowly stir in milk; cook and stir until bubbly. Stir in cheese until melted; set aside.

In a skillet over medium heat, fry together meat and onion until thoroughly cooked. Transfer to a large bowl. In the same skillet over low heat, cook eggs in 3 tablespoons margarine until barely set. In a large bowl, combine eggs, meat mixture, mushrooms, cheese sauce, and bread crumbs. Place mixture in a 9 × 13-inch pan. Cover and refrigerate overnight. Remove from refrigerator and let stand at room temperature for 30 minutes. Meanwhile, preheat oven to 325 degrees. Bake, covered, until heated through, 40 to 50 minutes. Makes 10 servings.

Nashua Wedding Punch

3 6-ounce cans frozen lemonade
9 6-ounce cans water
1 cup granulated sugar
Ice ring

2 46-ounce cans pineapple-
  grapefruit juice
2 1-liter bottles 7-Up
Few drops food coloring

In a 3-quart container, combine lemonade, water, and sugar. Stir until sugar is dissolved. Pour about 4½ cups of this mixture into the punch bowl with the ice ring. Add 1 can pineapple-grapefruit juice and pour 1 bottle of 7-Up down the side of the bowl; add food coloring; stir gently, just enough to mix. When needed, refill with remaining lemonade mixture, pineapple-grapefruit juice, and 7-Up. Makes about 4½ quarts, or about 26 cups.

Bridal Mints

2 ounces cream cheese, softened
1⅔ cups powdered sugar
¼ teaspoon vanilla

Mint flavoring to taste
Few drops food coloring
Granulated sugar

Cream together cream cheese and powdered sugar until fluffy. Add flavorings and food coloring. Roll into marble-size balls. Roll in granulated sugar; press with a fork. These mints freeze well. Makes about 2½ dozen. Keep chilled until ready to serve.

THE OLD CREAMERY THEATRE

The sleepy little farm town of Garrison, which consists of little more than two taverns, a post office, and a farmer's mercantile, may seem a peculiar site for a theater company. But Tom Johnson, artistic director of the Old Creamery Theatre in the hub of this hamlet, doesn't think so. "I find the audiences no more provincial than those who attend the plays I directed in Los Angeles and Hollywood," he said with a shrug. "Just because people haven't been exposed to the theater doesn't mean they can't appreciate it."

A former drama professor at Iowa State University, Johnson and his wife quit their jobs to escape campus unrest during the Vietnam War for "a little burg in the middle of nowhere." Already a group of potters and sculptors had settled there to establish an arts community. "I envisioned Garrison as a place where the theater and the arts could exist hand-in-hand," he said.

The nonprofit company has come a long way since the original cast, consisting of Johnson and nine other Iowa State students and faculty members, performed its first production, an outdoor mime, at the Garrison Brick and Tile Works during the summer of 1971. Now located in a refurbished brick building which was once a canned corn factory, the theater attracts more than 30,000 theatergoers a year.

During theater season, performances are held on both the main stage and a smaller thrust stage by members of the regular cast, who also double as ushers when they aren't performing, and an occasional guest performer from New York or Hollywood. The theater also has an educational touring company which travels throughout the country putting on benefit performances for groups of people who would otherwise have no opportunity to see a stage production, such as those confined to county care facilities and nursing homes. It has received extensive funding from the Iowa Arts Council and the National Endowment for the Arts and, in 1980, Governor Robert Ray presented the company the Distinguished Service Award for its contributions to cultural life in Iowa.

"You can pay a big price to see theater in Chicago and New York, but some of the plays I've seen here are just as good to me—especially *Jesus Christ, Superstar,*" commented Alberta Owen, a former dietitian in Rochester, New York, who has since retired to her hometown of Peli. "The atmosphere here is much warmer and friendlier than in the city, and it's great when you get to know the cast and see them in different roles."

Before the performances, ticket-holders can dine on basic, home-style entrées ranging from fried chicken to carved roast beef in the Old Creamery Theatre Restaurant. But the showstoppers of the menu are the special desserts created by Todd Kemmerer, a young actor in the company who manages the restaurant in between performances during the theater's season from May to October. "The dessert changes for each show," said the Colo, Iowa, native who has been with the company since 1981. Though his home base is now Minneapolis, he calls Garrison his "second home."

One of his specialties which went over particularly well was the decadent Edgar's Revenge, a liqueur-soaked, layered pound cake and ricotta cheese dessert based upon an Italian classic. It was named in honor of a character in a recent performance of "The Murder Room."

Edgar's Revenge

½ pound (2 sticks) butter
1⅔ cups granulated sugar
5 eggs
2 cups all-purpose flour
½ teaspoon salt
½ teaspoon vanilla
½ teaspoon almond flavoring
¼ cup Grand Marnier mixed with
  ¼ cup Triple Sec (or other
  desired liqueurs)

6 ounces ricotta cheese
3 grated Hershey's chocolate bars
  (1.65 ounces each)
Chocolate buttercream (recipe
  follows)
Fresh sliced strawberries for
  garnish

Preheat oven to 325 degrees. Butter and lightly flour a 9 × 5-inch loaf pan. In a mixing bowl, cream butter. Slowly add sugar, beating until light. Add eggs one at a time, incorporating each well. Stir in flour, salt, vanilla, and almond flavoring. Bake in preheated oven for 1¼ to 1½ hours or until cake passes the clean toothpick test. Do not overbake! Cool slightly and turn onto rack to cool completely.

Slice cake lengthwise into 4 or 5½-inch layers with serrated knife.

Place layers on rack. Brush bottom layer with liqueur mixture. Spread thin layer of ricotta cheese on top and sprinkle well with some of the grated chocolate. Alternate this with each layer, except top, until assembled. (I find it best to slice off uneven and crusty edges at this time.) Brush top layer with liqueur and let stand 15 minutes until absorbed. Frost with chocolate buttercream and garnish top with sliced strawberries. Looks very elegant served on a silver tray and finished with decorations piped with excess buttercream. Makes 10 to 12 servings. Edgar, eat your heart out . . .

Chocolate Buttercream

½ pound (2 sticks) butter
2 cups powdered sugar
2½ ounces real semisweet
  chocolate, melted and cooled

Few drops half-and-half (or more)
½ teaspoon vanilla
½ teaspoon almond extract

In a mixing bowl, cream butter. Add powdered sugar ¼ cup at a time until very stiff. Incorporate chocolate until creamy. Add more sugar or half-and-half until desired consistency is reached. Add vanilla and almond extract and beat until creamy.

Phil Laughlin, a former chef at Lawrence Welk's restaurant in Escondido, California, who manned the theater's kitchen when it was called the Stagedoor Restaurant, was in charge not only of the restaurant offerings but also of the more lavish spreads served for patrons' parties held in the sunken brick courtyard adjoining the theater after the performances. For those events a fire would be lit in the courtyard and patrons and cast members would mingle with one another over champagne and hors d'oeuvres prepared by Laughlin.

Hot Bacon and Chicken Livers

Wrap chicken livers in thinly sliced bacon. Skewer with toothpicks and place on rack in oven. Broil until bacon is crisp and brown. Insert fresh skewers and serve.

Cream Cheese Balls

Season cream cheese to taste with A-1 Steak Sauce. Shape into bite-size balls. Roll in chopped, salted almonds. Skewer on toothpicks.

Spiced Cheese Spread

2 tablespoons butter
½ pound sharp cheddar cheese,
 run through a meat grinder or
 finely grated by hand

2 tablespoons cream
¼ cup dry sherry
1 teaspoon dry mustard
Salt and pepper to taste

In a mixing bowl, cream butter. Beat in cheese; moisten to a smooth paste with cream and sherry. Stir in mustard, salt, and pepper. Use as a cracker spread. Makes about 1¼ cups.

Pickled Shrimp

1½ pounds large shrimp, cooked,
 peeled, and cleaned
¾ cup Sauterne
3 tablespoons lemon juice
3 tablespoons sugar
1 minced garlic clove
2 tablespoons dry onion soup mix
1 teaspoon Worcestershire sauce

2 tablespoons minced parsley
½ teaspoon celery salt
¼ teaspoon dried sweet basil
½ teaspoon seasoned salt
2 drops Tabasco
Dash of paprika
Lemon wedges and parsley sprigs
 for garnish

Place shrimp in a crock. Blend together remaining ingredients in a bowl and pour over shrimp. Cover and refrigerate, turning shrimp occasionally. Leave in pickling liquid 3 hours or longer. Serve on a relish tray, garnished with lemon and parsley. Serves 12 to 15 as an appetizer.

ELK HORN'S DANISH WINDMILL

The days when windmills were used for grinding grains into flour ended in Denmark long before 1976. In Elk Horn, Iowa, however, they were just beginning. That was the year practically the whole town pitched in to turn local farmer Harvey Sornson's dream into a reality: erecting an authentic Danish windmill just a few miles from his home. The windmill project, which took first place in the Iowa Community Betterment Contest during the Bicentennial, now stands as an impressive monument to the Danish ancestry of the Elk Horn–Kimballton area.

Visitors from all over climb the wooden steps of the six-story, eight-sided structure to observe the inner operations of the mill. On windy days its graceful wings, or "swoops," turn in the breeze like a giant pinwheel, while Sornson, the community's official miller, grinds corn, wheat, and rye into flour. The flours are then packaged by hand and sold in the mill's gift shop, which was modeled after the old mill house used for storing grains brought in by the farmers to its original location in Norre Snede, Denmark, more than one hundred years ago.

While vacationing in Denmark, Sornson was saddened to see that the windmills which once dotted the countryside were no longer in operation; most, in fact, had been torn down. Before they became completely obsolete, he thought, why not try to revive this piece of his heritage back home? The community sought contributions to test the project's feasibility, and within three days $30,000 worth of pledges had been made. Following a series of many overseas phone calls, a mill was finally located. It was shipped to America from Norre Snede and then delivered to Elk Horn on a double-wide flatbed truck—in a shambles.

"A lot of the wood was rotten; it was in terrible shape," recalled Lisa Riggs, who runs the windmill gift shop. "Everybody was a little depressed at first." But that didn't stop some three hundred determined citizens—nearly half the town's population—from contributing their time, labor, and hard-earned dollars into carrying out their plans.

When the main timbers were raised, the structure was crowned with a "rejsekrans," a good luck symbol of three evergreen wreaths encircling a flag of Denmark. Several months later, a crowd of spectators cheered and clapped as a crane hoisted the two crossbars into an X position on the face of the mill. That spring the wings revolved, turning the stones inside which ground the first batch of corn into meal. Every year since the mill has been the center attraction during Danish Days on Memorial weekend, a celebration featuring folk dancing, Danish movies, a parade, and lots of Danish treats from picturesque open-faced sandwiches to aebleskiver, a puffed doughnut baked in a "monk pan," a special skillet with rounded depressions into which batter is poured.

At Christmastime, the mill sponsors an open house, during which rosettes, Danish cookies and pastries, and various imported cheeses are served. "Christmas is my favorite time of year here," mused Lisa Riggs. "There's always goose or duck, potatoes cooked in brown sugar, rice pudding, Danish beer, and, of course, lots of pastries. After we eat we sing and dance around the Christmas tree."

Another celebration the community commemorates in true Danish spirit is Sankt Hans Dag, a Lenten celebration which is similar to Halloween. "We have a big bonfire in the park, where we burn a witch made out of black construction paper, to get rid of evil spirits," Lisa explained. Citizens then take turns hitting, with a bat, a papier-mâché black cat filled with candy. Afterward, fastelavnsboller, a sweet yeast roll similar to hot cross buns, is served.

Danish traditions are also observed at local weddings. In the shop's showcase window Lisa pointed out the Danish wedding cake—a tower of oblong, almond-filled pastries built in concentric circles around a wine bottle. "My mother made a wedding cake for me just like this when I was married; I didn't even have a regular cake," she said. With all such dishes, these Iowa cooks of Danish descent take the same kind of artistic care in perfecting the fine details that the hundreds of volunteers took in rebuilding the windmill. At no place could the point be better illustrated than at the Danish Inn, run by Jan and Don Larsen, right across the street from the windmill. The couple is carrying out the traditions started twenty-five years ago by Jan's retired parents, Henry and Dorothy Mortensen, who began serving coffee, Danish pastries, and open-faced sandwiches to farmers who wandered in from the fields at any hour of the day. Since the opening of the mill they've expanded the menu to include more substantial Scandinavian specialties such as rodspaetter, a flounder from the North Sea, and morbrad, stuffed loin of pork.

Mrs. Mortensen, who learned many of her culinary tricks on numerous trips to her family's native country, taught her daughter to make sure every dish sent to the table was as pretty as it was appetizing. She was always particularly fussy about the presentation of her smorsbrod (open-faced sandwiches).

Danish Inn Smorsbrod

Bread: white
Filling: pickled herring or cooked shrimp
Garnish: dollop of horseradish sauce

Bread: wheat or rye
Filling: cooked pork slices
Garnish: prune, twist of orange, parsley sprigs

Bread: rye
Filling: sliced beef or rullepolse (recipe follows)
Garnish: narrow slices of beef aspic, criss-crossed on top

Bread: white
Filling: Danish cheese slices (Tybo, Tilsit, Blue, Havarti)
Garnish: radish slice

Bread: rye or wheat
Filling: cold leverpostej slices (recipe follows)
Garnish: teaspoon of cooked red cabbage or cucumber slices

"There are definite rules to follow when making a Danish open-faced sandwich. The bread should be very thin and spread with lots of butter. It should be completely covered with fresh greens; no bread should be visible to the eye. There should be an odd number of garnishes, which must match the appropriate filling and bread. The combination possibilities are endless."

DOROTHY MORTENSEN

This liver loaf is delicious served warm, like any other meat loaf, but even better cold, as a pâté with coarse-grained mustard or for open-faced sandwiches.

Leverpostej

1½ pounds beef or pork liver   *3 eggs, beaten*
1½ pounds pork shoulder   *2 tablespoons flour*
1 small onion   *1 tablespoon salt*
2 slices bread   *½ teaspoon pepper*
1 cup milk   *½ teaspoon allspice*

Preheat oven to 350 degrees. Grind together liver, pork, and onion. (You can use a food processor for this.) Soak bread in milk. Mix together with remaining ingredients and pour into 2 9 × 5-inch loaf pans lined with aluminum foil. Place loaf pans in a pan of water and bake in preheated oven 2½ hours. Let stand at least 10 minutes before cutting. Makes 2 loaves, enough for about 2 dozen open-faced sandwiches.

Several meat lockers in the Elk Horn–Kimballton area make rullepolse, a spiced meat roll similar to corned beef and used mainly for open-faced sandwiches. A few ambitious cooks in the area produce it at home to sell to restaurants and individuals. I had fun trying this home version provided by Lisa Riggs in my own kitchen, and it was actually far less laborious than I'd imagined.

Rullepolse

BRINE: *2 tablespoons salt*
2½ quarts boiling water   *½ teaspoon saltpeter*
2 cups salt   *1 teaspoon pepper*
½ teaspoon saltpeter   *1 onion, chopped*
                                      ½ teaspoon allspice
MEAT: *3 or 4 thin slices pork, about ½*
1 flank beef or lamb, about 2 to   *pound total*
   2½ pounds

Combine all ingredients for brine; let cool. Remove sinew from meat and cut meat so it forms a rectangle. Flatten out (if necessary, by pounding slightly with a meat pounder) and sprinkle with salt, saltpeter, pepper, onion, and allspice. Lay pork slices on flank. Roll meat tightly so when it is cut it will slice across the grain. Sew ends and sides; put in cold brine and refrigerate for 10 days.

After 10 days, remove meat from brine, tie securely with cord, and put into boiling water. Reduce heat and simmer, covered, for 2 hours, or until tender. Remove from water and press between 2 flat surfaces until cold. Serve thin slices on bread. Makes enough meat for about 2 dozen open-faced sandwiches.

Another contribution from Lisa Riggs, these delicious citron-studded sweet rolls—similar to hot-cross buns—are traditionally served on the evening of Sankt Hans Dag.

Fastelavnsboller

1½ cups milk, scalded
½ cup butter or margarine
⅓ cup granulated sugar
1 teaspoon salt
2 eggs, beaten
1 package yeast, dissolved in ¼ cup lukewarm water
4½ to 5½ cups all-purpose flour, divided

1 cup raisins
⅓ cup chopped citron
½ teaspoon ground cardamom
Melted butter
Powdered sugar glaze (½ cup powdered sugar mixed with 2 tablespoons butter and 1 tablespoon hot water)

In a large bowl, combine milk, butter or margarine, sugar, salt, eggs, dissolved yeast, and 2 cups flour; beat until bubbly. Add raisins, citron, cardamom, and 2½ cups flour. Knead well, adding more flour if necessary, until dough is smooth and elastic. Place in a greased bowl and let rise until double. Form into small balls (about the size of golfballs) and let rise on a lightly greased cookie sheet until light. Preheat oven to 375 degrees. Brush buns with melted butter. Bake 15 to 20 minutes. When baked, spread with powdered sugar glaze. Makes about 1½ dozen buns.

The next two recipes were given to me by Lauri Nisson of Atlantic, who grew up in the Elk Horn area. These tiny, peppery nuggets are served in candy dishes around the holidays.

Pepper Nuts

1½ cups shortening
1½ cups granulated sugar
2 eggs
1 cup milk
1 teaspoon salt

1 teaspoon cardamom
4 teaspoons baking powder
Flour to make a stiff batter (6 to
    7 cups)

In a large mixing bowl, cream together the shortening and sugar. Blend in eggs and milk until creamy. Mix in seasonings and baking powder. Stir in enough flour to make a stiff dough.

Preheat oven to 300 degrees. Roll dough in narrow strips like pencils, cut into small (½-inch) cubes, place on ungreased baking sheets, and bake like cookies in preheated oven for about 30 minutes. Makes about 3½ quarts.

Aebleskiver means "apple pancake balls," because originally the pancakes had a slice of apple or dab of applesauce in the middle. But because the filling has a tendency to leak into the pan, most Danish cooks these days make them plain, with applesauce served on the side.

Aebleskiver

2 cups all-purpose flour
½ teaspoon salt
1 teaspoon granulated sugar
2 cups buttermilk

2 egg yolks
1 teaspoon baking powder
2 egg whites, stiffly beaten
Butter
Monk pan

In a large bowl, mix flour, salt, and sugar. In another bowl, beat together buttermilk and egg yolks. Add to flour mixture. Stir in baking powder. Fold in egg whites. Put a little butter in each hole of the monk pan and heat until melted. Pour batter into each hole but do not quite fill them. Cook over low heat and turn quickly when half-done to brown other side. Serve very hot with jelly, sugar, butter, and applesauce. Makes 28 pancakes.

BONAPARTE

I t's been ages since the long wooden paddles of a mighty water wheel churned the waters of the Lower Des Moines River, powering the more than 150-year-old grist mill gracing the riverbank in Bonaparte. Yet the mill still draws visitors from miles around. These days, however, they come not for freshly ground flour and meal but for the home-cooked Iowa dishes served in an atmosphere reminiscent of the steamboat era.

Lifetime area residents Ben and Rose Hendricks were determined to revive the dying monument to that colorful phase of Iowa history. So in 1976 they transformed the dilapidated three-story brick structure into the Bonaparte Retreat, one of the state's most highly acclaimed restaurants. The couple did almost all the refurbishing themselves, including rebuilding the foundation, remodeling the interior with hardwood floors and soft bricks left over from an old brick factory, and collecting riverboat relics and artifacts to enhance its nostalgic decor.

The simple, hearty dishes which have become their trademark are all prepared by Rose, who relies on the culinary techniques passed down from her mother along with her own ingenuity. "We don't use fancy sauces or anything like that," she said. "We just try to make sure that what we serve is plain and good and that there's plenty of it."

Main courses vary from extra-thick Windsor (smoked) chops and center-cut ham slices to seafood and Iowa prime steaks. The most unique item on the menu, a real throwback to bygone days, is home-canned beef: cubes of rib-eye or New York strip served in the Mason jar in which they're pressure-cooked. Appetizers include French-fried vegetables, shrimp cocktail, and Rose's homemade soup of the day, which varies from beef barley to clam chowder to cheddar cheese. All orders are accompanied by a helping of savory wild-rice dressing and crunchy pan-fried bread, sometimes referred to as "railroad biscuits."

The Hendrickses are part of a renaissance that's been developing for the past decade or so in Bonaparte as well as the other river towns that make up Van Buren County, the only county left in the state without a single stoplight.

"Know what that is?" asked Ben, pointing out the window to a large concrete slab jutting out of the water. "That's one of the last remaining lock walls left on the Des Moines River." The locks once allowed the passage of steamboats and paddlewheelers transporting new goods and merchandise to supply the businesses and industries dotting the riverbanks, back when Bonaparte was one of the Midwest's major commercial centers.

Bonaparte's roots can be traced back to the arrival in 1836 of William Meek, a prominent Michigan businessman in search of a spot to build a grist mill. There in the wilderness he met up with N. N. Cresap, M.D., another ambitious pioneer looking for investment opportunities. Together they built the foundation for a new community called Meek's Mills. Later, Meek changed the name to Bonaparte in honor of his favorite war hero.

The river provided power not only for a grist mill but for a saw mill, woolen mill, and dam as well. Other businesses and industries sprang up as a result: a brick yard, a glove factory, a pants factory, three millinery establishments, a pottery house, a jewelry store, two furniture stores, a photography studio. Hordes of visitors came to Bonaparte in horse-drawn wagons to check out the latest goods and fashions and to have their grains ground at the grist mill. Before the bridges were built they often had to wait their turn for days to cross the river on the ferry at a fare of a nickel per passenger and a quarter per oxen, horse, or mule team. The ferries were connected by ropes attached to grooved wheels which traveled along sturdy cable stretched between two huge maples on either riverbank.

"Going to the mill was like a holiday to those people," Ben Hendricks explained. "They'd camp out across the river and fish and play cards to pass the time." An old ice house, where the fish were stored until the visitors were ready to leave, can still be seen through the trees.

"They used to call it 'poker hill' up there," said Mary Warner, who runs the Aunty Green Museum around the corner. "That's where the steamboat captains would set up their poker tables on their stops through town." Back then the museum was one of several hotels which catered to river travelers. Its rooms have since been refurbished with many of the original furnishings from its heyday.

Though steamboat traffic disappeared with the advent of the railroad before anyone living there now can remember, the grist mill was still in full operation during Ruth Meek's childhood. Mrs. Meek, whose husband was a descendant of the town's founder, attributed its steady stream of

business to the quality of the flour and the fishing. "We used to buy fifty-pound sacks of flour for sixty-five cents," she recalled. "Mama always said she could make better bread out of that flour than any other. Sometimes the neighbor ladies would trade bread to see who made the best."

A trip to the mill nearly always meant fresh fish for supper: catfish, carp, bass, spoonbills. "One year," she said, "there were so many fish that they clogged up the water wheel and shut off the power. You should have seen the wagonloads of fish they pulled out of there."

While most of the men spent their leisure fishing, the women would gather at the community center to spin wool or meet in each other's homes for a light lunch of chicken salad and finger sandwiches, with cake and ice cream for dessert. "Caramel ice cream was our favorite," Mrs. Meek said. "In the winter, we'd set it out on the porch to freeze. Then we'd cut it in slices just like bread."

The early prosperity of Van Buren County, however, was destined to fall. The river was no longer a feasible method of transporting merchandise. The mills shut down when they could no longer compete with the larger markets. And many of the remaining industries and homes were destroyed in fires and cataclysmic floods. The population, which was once close to 1,500, dwindled to less than 500. But the folks in this area aren't about to let their heritage die. The Bonaparte Retreat and the Aunty Green Museum are just a few of the well-preserved links to the past this town has to show. In the summertime Bonaparte is a haven for fishermen and water sports enthusiasts, particularly since the establishment of Bonaparte's Navy, a canoe club with members from all fifty states. On the Fourth of July thousands of spectators come to view a canoe race between Bonaparte and the small town of Bentonsport. The women of the Historical Society serve hot chicken sandwiches and in the evening the crowds head for the shore for pit-roasted hog and beer.

But any time of the year you can get a taste of an old Iowa river town by concocting one of these Bonaparte dishes at home.

The Retreat's Wild Rice Dressing

1 6-ounce package wild rice mix   *1 cup chopped onion*
1 pound bulk sausage   *8 slices toast, cubed*
1 cup chopped celery   *2 10¾-ounce cans chicken-rice*
    soup

Cook wild rice according to package directions. In a skillet, cook together sausage, celery, and onion until meat is browned and onion and celery are soft. Stir in cubed toast and soup; cook until hot and most of liquid has evaporated. Dressing may be placed in a casserole dish and refrigerated overnight. Before serving, bake at 350 degrees until heated through. Makes 8 to 10 side-dish servings.

Sometimes called "railroad biscuits," these crispy loaves which accompany every meal at the Bonaparte Retreat are always a hit with customers. Generally, Rose serves them unadorned, but "for ourselves, I sometimes shake them in a sack with cinnamon and sugar."

Pan-Fried Bread

Make any favorite yeast bread recipe or thaw a loaf of frozen bread dough. Pinch off pieces of dough the size of an egg and flatten out with a rolling pin to a ¼-inch thickness. Prick each piece in several places with a fork. In a skillet, heat at least 2 inches of lard or vegetable oil to about 350 degrees. When hot, add bread to skillet and fry until lightly browned. Serve immediately.

Meek's Mills Caramel Ice Cream

1 pint milk
2 cups granulated sugar
2 eggs

1 tablespoon all-purpose flour
3 pints cream

In a saucepan, scald milk. Whisk together 1 cup of the sugar and the eggs until light yellow, then whisk in the flour. Gradually add the milk, whisking until smooth. Stir the mixture in a double boiler over boiling water until it is thick enough to coat the back of a metal spoon. Do not boil. Melt remaining cup of sugar in a skillet. Cook until a deep golden brown. Carefully whisk it into the hot custard. Chill mixture, then add cream. Beat it up and let freeze.

Ruth Meek says her mother used to freeze this in a loaf pan and then slice it like bread. However, she said it may be removed from the freezer when partially set and whipped with a mixer. We tried freezing it both in a loaf pan and an electric ice cream maker and found we actually liked it best in the loaf pan; it was denser and thus had a much more intense caramel flavor. If making it in an ice cream maker, we would suggest reducing the amount of cream by 1 or 2 cups for a more intense flavor. Makes about 2 quarts.

Part Four

CELEBRATIONS

PELLA TULIP TIME

During Pella Tulip Time, you won't find Ralph and Howard Jaarsma anywhere among the Dutch-costumed citizens dancing to the accompaniment of an accordion player on a neatly manicured lawn ablaze with tulips. Nor will you spot them in any of the festival's six parades around the town's picturesque square. But you don't have to see these two lifetime Pella residents to recognize the contribution they make each year to one of the Midwest's most popular ethnic events. Bite into one of their Dutch letters instead.

The Jaarsmas spend virtually the entire celebration, day and night, in the huge kitchen adjoining their family's long-standing bakery making sure no one has to miss sampling at least one of the flaky, melt-in-your-mouth pastries. "Our ovens will be full of letters from the beginning 'til the end of Tulip Time," Howard said, as he and a couple of assistants rapidly filled sweet dough with almond paste. Each year they bake some 12,000 Dutch letters to sell in the bakery and in roadside stands around town. "We sell them just as fast as we bake them," he added. Along with the Dutch letters, the Jaarsmas also bake hundreds of other Dutch delicacies based on many of the techniques passed down to them from their Netherlands-born grandfather: Saint Nick cookies, hearty rye bread, meat-filled saucijzebroodjes (pigs in a blanket), crunchy Holland rusks, and deep-fried currant fritters called olie bolen.

Local cake decorator Julia Hagens carves and frosts cake replicas of wooden shoes and windmills for the storefront window, adorned like most of the downtown shops in delicate lace curtains. But both Ralph and Howard contend that no bakery creation can match the popularity of the Dutch letters. Originally molded in the shape of each family's initials, the letters are now more uniformly baked into S-shapes or straight strips. During the summer of 1981 the Jaarsmas set a Guinness world record by baking a Dutch letter three blocks long as a fund-raising project for the Pella Historical Society.

The original Jaarsma bakery, opened by their grandfather more than eighty-five years ago, still stands in the province of Friesland in the Netherlands, Ralph said. He and his wife have visited the building frequently on trips to their ancestors' homeland to purchase many of the items for his wife's gift shop around the corner from the bakery: antiques, fine lace, and authentic blue and white Delft pottery.

Like their grandfather, the Jaarsmas make everything from scratch, even the jams and jellies for their coffee cake and doughnuts. But production has increased tremendously since they first began greasing pans as children for their father's bakery, adjoining the home they grew up in in Pella. "In Holland it's traditional for the baker to live in the same building as his business," Ralph explained while keeping a watchful eye on the buns baking on revolving racks in the huge oven. "We used to have to throw wood in our brick ovens to keep it hot enough. We always baked the things that required hot temperatures, like yeast breads, first. Then when it cooled a bit we'd put in our cookies."

Now a city with a population of about 8,500, Pella was founded in 1847 by Hendrik Scholte and 800 Dutch immigrants. They fled from their homeland to avoid persecution for rebelling against the Dutch state church, which they regarded as despotic, and established a new settlement of grass-roofed sod dugouts in the middle of an Iowa prairie. They named their new home Pella, City of Refuge, after the Asia Minor city of Pella, which had been a refuge for Christians in A.D. 68. The immigrants were invited to return to their original homeland twenty years later by the new Dutch king, who believed they had been mistreated. The Pella citizens declined the offer. Despite that decision, the city still derives much of its strength from the Dutch customs and traditions retained from the settlers' ancestors.

As a means of preserving that heritage, the community in 1935 decided to have a Tulip Day, a community-wide picnic followed by an operetta at the Pella High School entitled *Tulip Time*. Since the event was organized in less than a month, there was no time to plant tulips, so a local cabinetmaker built fourteen four-foot-tall wooden ones instead. The celebration was such a success that the following year fresh blooms were imported from Holland and spectators from all over were encouraged to attend. "We really don't get to see too much of the festivities, but it's a good business thing for us and the other merchants," Howard said. "It has really put Pella on the map."

The Pella tulip queen and her court ride in both the afternoon and evening parades, which are preceded by a band of street scrubbers who spruce up the brick roads with long-handled brushes and buckets of

Street scrubbers in parade

water hanging from wooden shoulder yokes. Each night the Tulip Turen, a sixty-eight foot white-columned tower in the park, becomes a stage for a variety show.

Millers, spinners, weavers, potters, and wooden shoemakers practice their trades of yesteryear in the Pella Historical Society Village. And the Pella Garden Club, awarded a plaque for "artistic presentation of flowers and plants for public enjoyment" from the Society of Florists, presents a three-day flower show.

After the parades, hungry spectators flock to the meat market for a ring of Pella bologna, to the churches for homemade split-pea soup, to the nationally acclaimed Strawtown Inn Restaurant, which specializes in more refined Dutch delicacies, and, of course, to the bakeries for a Dutch letter and perhaps some other ethnic pastries to take home. Authentic recipes for many of those items can be found in the eighth edition of the *Pella Collector's Cookbook,* compiled and published by the Central College Auxiliary (Central College Auxiliary, Central College, Pella, Iowa 50219). The split pea soup, fish fillets, and Dutch lettuce recipes are adapted from that book. The recipe for Jaarsma's Dutch letters first appeared in the June 1987 edition of *Midwest Living* magazine (published by the Meredith Corporation, Des Moines, Iowa 50309).

Jaarsma's Dutch Letters

4½ cups all-purpose flour
1 teaspoon salt
1 pound (4 sticks) butter
1 egg
1 cup water

1 8-ounce can almond paste
½ cup granulated sugar
½ cup brown sugar
2 egg whites
Milk
Granulated sugar

In a large mixing bowl, combine flour and salt. Cut butter into ½-inch slices. Stir into flour mixture, coating each butter piece to separate it. In a small bowl, combine egg and water. Add all at once to flour mixture. Mix quickly. (Butter will still be in ½-inch pieces and flour will not be completely moistened.) Turn the dough onto a lightly floured surface and knead it 10 times, pressing and pushing dough pieces together to form a rough-looking ball. Shape dough into a rectangle. (Dough still will have some dry-looking areas.) Flatten dough slightly. Working on a well-floured surface, roll out dough to a 15 × 10-inch rectangle. Fold the 2 short sides to meet the center, then fold in half to form 4 layers (this should give you a 5 × 7½-inch rectangle). If dough is very sticky, chill it 20 minutes. Repeat rolling and folding process once. Cover the dough with plastic wrap; chill it for 20 minutes. Repeat rolling and folding 2 more times and chill 20 minutes more.

Meanwhile, in a small mixing bowl combine almond paste, ½ cup granulated sugar, brown sugar, and egg whites; beat until mixture is smooth and set aside. Cut dough crosswise into 4 equal parts. Keep unused dough chilled. Roll each part into a 12½ × 10-inch rectangle. Cut into 5 10 × 2½-inch strips. Preheat oven to 375 degrees. Spread 1 slightly rounded tablespoon of the almond mixture down center third of each strip. Roll up each strip lengthwise. Brush edge and ends with milk or water. Pinch to seal. Place seam side down on an ungreased baking sheet, preferably lined with parchment, shaping each into the letter S. Brush with milk and sprinkle with sugar. Repeat with remaining dough and filling. Bake in preheated oven 25 to 30 minutes, or until golden. Cool on wire racks. Makes 20 letters.

Erwtensoep (Split Pea Soup)

2 cups green split peas
4¼ quarts water
1½ teaspoons salt
2 pigs feet
4 leeks, trimmed of root end and
*   all but 2 inches of green tops,*
*   chopped*

1½ cups chopped celery
½ pound smoked sausage, cubed
*   or sliced*

Soak peas in 3 cups water for 12 hours. Drain; add remaining water to peas. Add salt and bring to a boil. Skim; add the pigs feet, leeks, and celery. Simmer for 3 to 5 hours, or until pigs feet are quite tender and the meat loosens from the bone. Lift out the pigs feet and discard skin and bones. Add meat bits to soup. During the last half hour of cooking, add sausage. Makes 8 servings.

This recipe comes from *Dutch Treats,* compiled by Carol Van Klompenburg (Penfield Press, 215 Brown St., Iowa City, Iowa 52240). Its contributor, Mina Baker Roelofs, says that pigs-in-a-blanket are a traditional pastry for Dutch coffee time, mid-morning or mid-afternoon. I made them for an hors d'oeuvre to take to a party and they disappeared in a matter of minutes.

Pigs-in-a-Blanket

DOUGH:
2 cups all-purpose flour
½ teaspoon salt
2 teaspoons baking powder
½ cup shortening
1 egg, beaten
½ cup milk

FILLING:
1 pound lean pork sausage
½ pound hamburger
2 Dutch rusks, crushed, or ¼ cup
*   dry bread crumbs*
2 tablespoons cream
Salt and pepper

Sift together flour, salt, and baking powder. With pastry blender or two knives, cut shortening into flour mixture. Mix beaten egg with milk (mixture should total ¾ cup liquid). Add to first mixture. Blend and knead 8 to 10 times on floured board. Divide dough into 2 parts. Roll each half of dough to a thickness of ¼ inch. Make 15 rounds of dough from each half using a medium-size cookie cutter.

Preheat oven to 350 degrees. Blend all filling ingredients. Form 30 small rolls shaped like link sausages. Place on pastry round, roll up, and seal edges. Place filled pastries on a baking sheet with raised edges and bake in preheated oven for 40 minutes. Serve hot. May be refrigerated or frozen after baking and reheated for serving. Makes 30 appetizers.

The Strawtown Inn's Schol
Uit de Oven (Fish Fillets)

6 thin sole fillets (5 to 6 ounces
  each)
1 tablespoon fresh lemon juice
1 teaspoon salt
3 tablespoons softened butter
6 bacon slices
1 cup all-purpose flour
¼ teaspoon dill weed

¼ teaspoon nutmeg
Freshly ground pepper
¼ cup grated Gouda cheese
⅓ cup soft, fresh bread crumbs
¼ cup slivered blanched almonds
3 tablespoons chilled butter,
  cut in bits

Pat fillets dry. Sprinkle both sides with lemon juice and salt. Set aside (at room temperature) for about 30 minutes. Preheat oven to 500 degrees. Spread 2 tablespoons of the softened butter over bottom and sides of a shallow enameled baking dish large enough to hold fish in one layer. Cut a piece of waxed paper to fit snugly inside baking dish; place inside baking dish and spread remaining tablespoon of butter on top. Set aside. In a skillet, fry bacon over medium heat until it begins to crisp. Remove and drain on paper towels. Pat fillets dry and fold lengthwise in half. Press edges together to hold them in shape. Dip fish in flour and shake gently to remove excess. Sprinkle both sides with dill weed and nutmeg. Arrange side by side on buttered waxed paper and lay a strip of bacon on each one. Grind a little pepper over top. Combine cheese, bread crumbs, and almonds. Scatter mixture evenly over the fish. Dot with chilled butter. Bake in upper third of oven for 7 to 10 minutes, or until topping is brown and fish is opaque. Serve at once. Makes 6 servings.

There are many varieties of this hot salad served both in Pella homes and local restaurants. This one, which features layers of hot mashed potatoes, lettuce, and hard-cooked eggs doused with a tangy hot bacon dressing, is hearty enough for a meal in itself.

Dutch Lettuce

1 tablespoon butter
1 tablespoon all-purpose flour
½ cup water
2 egg yolks, or 1 whole egg
½ cup granulated sugar
½ cup vinegar
6 servings hot boiled potatoes,
    riced or mashed

4 hard-boiled eggs, sliced
6 servings coarsely cut lettuce,
    with a little chopped onion
    added
6 strips bacon
⅓ cup vinegar
⅓ cup water

In a small saucepan over medium heat, melt butter, then add flour. When well blended, add water and bring to a boil while stirring. Beat egg yolks, add sugar and ½ cup vinegar, and blend and stir into the hot sauce. Let come to a boil. Remove from heat and set aside. (May be made several weeks ahead and refrigerated.)

Have ready potatoes, hard-boiled eggs, and lettuce. Cut bacon into small pieces, fry in skillet until nicely browned, and add 3 or 4 tablespoons above sauce, vinegar, and water. Bring to a boil in skillet and keep hot. Place a layer of hot riced or mashed potatoes in bowl; then a layer of lettuce, 2 sliced hard-boiled eggs, and several tablespoons hot bacon dressing. Add remainder of potatoes, lettuce, and sliced eggs. Pour rest of dressing over this and serve immediately. Makes 6 servings.

THE IOWA STATE FAIR

The Iowa State Fair is more than just another mammoth-size carnival. Perhaps no one has come up with a better description than Iowa native Phil Stong, whose 1932 novel *State Fair* was made into a movie starring Will Rogers. In a 1948 essay he called the inspiration for his best-seller "the greatest food festival in the world." Though the crowds get bigger, the rides get scarier, and the grandstand entertainment gets more spectacular every year, the underlying theme hasn't changed since the first fairgoers unhitched their covered wagons and pitched tents on the Fairfield fairgrounds in 1854. It's still a celebration of Iowa's bounty.

The expansive Agricultural Building features displays ranging from life-size dairy cows sculpted out of butter to dolls made from corn husks. Inside the huge barns, 4-H'ers lovingly groom the coats of prized livestock for the show ring. Meanwhile, pork and beef producers entice hungry passersby with thick grilled chops, barbecued ribs, beef burgers, and ham sandwiches—served with corn on the cob and cinnamon-laced applesauce underneath big canvas tents.

Inside the auditorium of the Family Life Center, not only are the best foods of Iowa recognized but the top cooks as well. Contenders in the foods categories and their families watch intently as home economists sample food entries lining the long tables in front of the red velvet curtain. Taking sips of water from Styrofoam cups between each bite, the judges ponder each decision before marking their scorecards, on which they record points for flavor, color, texture, aroma, and appearance. After announcing the winners at the 1982 fair, judge Ellen Thomas offered the audience a few pointers: "On the orange cookies, a pink frosting kind of throws me. A yellow frosting makes me think it's a lemon cookie. I would advise using white next time."

Down the hall in a well-lit display room, spectators strolled past the tall glass showcases with shelves lined with cookies, cakes, breads, pies, pastries, biscuits, jams, jellies, and every confection imaginable. Some paused to examine them more scrupulously. "Just look at those beautiful kolaches," sighed one woman. "And that bread! My loaves never rise that high and pretty."

For years, the culinary artworks that nearly always captured a second admiring glance were those made by Mrs. Keith Phillips of Centerville. If her name was attached to them, a good guess was that a blue ribbon was, too. Of the 128 entries she brought to the 1981 fair, 99 received ribbons. She was a three-time winner of the Archway Cookie Award of a hundred-dollar bond, not to mention scores of cookbooks offered as grand prizes in other categories. "But I slowed down a little this year," she admitted. "I only entered 79." Generally she said she starts baking about three weeks before the fair and works "all day, as long as I don't wear out."

Mrs. Phillips's entries could be found in every category, from home-canned pickles and relishes to fancy cakes and cookies. "Breads are my favorite, but I only bake them for the fair," she confessed. "Heavens, if I made them all the time, I wouldn't be able to waddle!"

Mrs. Phillips, who tests all her recipes on her husband of more than fifty years ("he somehow manages to stay skinny"), has no untold secrets to her success. "Oh, whenever I can my cherries I use my little nut pick to take out the seeds to keep them pretty. As for my peas, I sort them out real carefully and use only the prettiest ones. And I always make sure my cucumber cubes are all the same size. Just silly little things like that."

Tough to beat as her entries were, she'd been getting some pretty stiff competition in more recent years from another ubiquitous name at the fair, Robin Tarbell, also of Centerville. At twenty-one, she'd only been entering her baked goods for about five years, yet had already lost count of her blue ribbons. Mrs. Phillips, however, never minded losing out to this newcomer. Robin is her granddaughter, and Robin credits most of her culinary skills to her grandma.

Though Mrs. Phillips is no longer baking for competitions, Robin's collection of blue ribbons from the fair continues to flourish. Following are recipes for Robin's delectable jam thumbprints and her grandmother's cucumber cubes, also a fair winner, although Mrs. Phillips can't pinpoint the date.

Jam Thumbprints

²⁄₃ cup butter	*1½ cups all-purpose flour*
⅓ cup granulated sugar	*2 egg whites, slightly beaten*
2 egg yolks	*¾ cup finely chopped nuts*
1 teaspoon vanilla	*Strawberry preserves*
½ teaspoon salt	

Preheat oven to 350 degrees. In a mixing bowl, cream butter and sugar until fluffy. Add egg yolks, vanilla, and salt. Beat well. Gradually add flour, mixing well. Shape into ¾-inch balls. Dip in egg whites, then roll in nuts. Place 1 inch apart on greased cookie sheet. Press down center of each cookie with thumb. Bake in preheated oven for 10 to 12 minutes. Cool slightly, then remove from pan to rack to cool completely. Just before serving, fill centers with preserves. Makes about 3 dozen cookies.

These cucumbers completely lose their identity and take on the color of an evergreen and a taste reminiscent of candied crabapples. They make a tasty and decidedly different accompaniment to roast meats and are a colorful addition to a holiday table.

Cucumber Cubes

1 gallon cold water
1 cup pickling lime
7 pounds cucumbers (peeled and seeds removed, then cut like French fries)
1 quart cider vinegar (5 percent acidity)
6¾ cups (3 pounds) granulated sugar

1 tablespoon green food coloring
1 tablespoon celery seed and ½ tablespoon whole pickling spice, tied in a cheesecloth bag
1 tablespoon ground cinnamon
¾ tablespoon noniodized salt

In a 4-quart noncorrodible container, combine water, lime, and cucumbers. Let stand for 3 hours. Stir occasionally and let stand for 24 hours. Rinse 4 times to completely remove lime; drain thoroughly. Wash container and return drained cucumbers to it.

In a 4-quart saucepan, heat vinegar and sugar. Add green coloring, celery seed and pickling spice, cinnamon, and salt. Bring to a boil, then pour slowly over cucumbers. Let stand overnight or up to 24 hours.

Stir several times, then boil all ingredients together 25 minutes. Ladle into hot, clean canning jars, being careful not to pack the cucumbers too tightly. Wipe jar rims and apply lids according to manufacturer's instructions. Process in a boiling water bath 5 minutes for pints, 10 minutes for quarts, making sure water comes an inch over the tops of the jars. Cool on rack or cloth away from drafts. (If you do not want to process, you can store the pickles in the refrigerator). Next day, check the seals and store in a cool, dry place. Makes 5 half-pints.

Here are more blue-ribbon winners featured in *Winners Every One!*, the fourth edition of the *Iowa State Fair Cookbook* (Statehouse, Des Moines, Iowa 50319). It features both prize-winning recipes from the 1985 competition as well as a special section of winners from previous years as a special tribute in honor of the one hundredth anniversary of the purchase of the present fairgrounds site in Des Moines.

Carlisle resident Maryel Waddill stumbled upon this recipe while looking through some old cookbooks of her grandmother's. "It was a winner from a Pillsbury Bake-Off Contest back in '54 or '55. I was looking for something unusual to enter at the fair, but I had no idea what the outcome would be." Apparently this irresistible layered cream pie has withstood the test of time, as evidenced by her blue ribbon.

Hawaiian Chocolate Pie

1 8-ounce can crushed pineapple
1⅓ cups granulated sugar
½ cup all-purpose flour
½ teaspoon salt (or less)
3 cups milk
3 egg yolks, slightly beaten
2 tablespoons butter
2 teaspoons vanilla
1½ to 2 ounces unsweetened chocolate, melted
¾ cup pecans, finely chopped
1 9-inch pastry shell, baked

Drain pineapple; set aside. Combine sugar, flour, and salt in a heavy saucepan. Gradually add milk; blend well. Bring to a boil, stirring constantly; cook over medium heat until thick. Blend small amount of hot mixture into egg yolks; add to hot mixture in saucepan. Cook 1 minute, stirring constantly. Blend in butter and vanilla. Divide filling in half. Stir drained pineapple into one portion and blend chocolate into second. Cover; cool to lukewarm. Spoon half of chocolate mixture into crust. Cover with pineapple mixture; top with remaining chocolate mixture. Sprinkle nuts over top. Cool completely. Makes 1 9-inch pie.

Cynthia L. Weed of Indianola took a first place in the Hy-Vee Supermarkets Meat-of-Iowa Casserole Contest with this gussied-up version of chicken pot pie.

Chicken and Corn Pot Pie

1/4 pound bacon
2 tablespoons butter
3 pounds chicken breasts
1/4 to 1/3 cup all-purpose flour
2 large carrots, diced
1 pound small boiling onions
8 ounces fresh or frozen corn
1 1/4 cups chicken stock

3 whole cloves
1/8 teaspoon cardamom
Salt and pepper to taste
1 tablespoon parsley flakes
Cornmeal-chive pastry (recipe
    follows)
1 egg, beaten

Chop bacon and fry in butter in skillet until browned. Remove bacon with slotted spoon. Dredge chicken in flour; brown. Remove chicken; drain off all but 3 tablespoons of fat. Add carrots, onions, and corn to skillet; sauté 3 minutes. Add stock, seasonings, chicken, and bacon. Bring to a gentle simmer. Cover; cook 30 minutes. Remove chicken; set aside to cool. Heat remaining sauce over high heat until rich in flavor and reduced to half its volume. Skin and bone chicken. Cut into bite-size pieces. Add to sauce; refrigerate overnight.

Preheat oven to 400 degrees. Roll cornmeal-chive pastry to fit a greased 6-cup casserole. Fill casserole with chicken mixture; top with pastry and seal edges. Brush with beaten egg. Bake in preheated oven 50 to 60 minutes, or until sauce is bubbly and crust is brown. (If crust browns too quickly, cover lightly with foil.) Makes 4 to 6 servings.

Cornmeal-Chive Pastry

1 1/2 cups all-purpose flour
2/3 cup yellow cornmeal
1/4 cup cake flour
1/2 teaspoon salt

3 tablespoons chives or green
    onion tops, minced
1/2 cup (1 stick) plus 2 tablespoons
    cold, unsalted butter
1/2 cup cold water

Combine dry ingredients and chives (cake flour adds extra tenderness to pastry). Using pastry blender, cut in butter until mixture resembles coarse cornmeal. Add water. Mix with fork only until dough is moistened and can be gathered into a loose ball. Do not overwork pastry. Let dough rest. Wrap and chill at least 30 minutes. (After initial rest, dough can be wrapped in an airtight container and frozen up to 3 months.)

Another winner from Cynthia Weed, this one in the cake doughnut category. These doughnuts are delicious plain, but they're even better—in the estimation of our tasters—coated with cinnamon-sugar. To coat them, place them in a bag, while they're still hot with a mixture of granulated sugar and cinnamon and shake until they're well coated.

Spicy Spud Doughnuts

4 cups all-purpose flour
2 tablespoons baking powder
1 teaspoon salt
½ teaspoon ground cloves
½ teaspoon cinnamon
3 eggs, beaten

1 cup brown sugar, packed
1½ cups mashed potatoes, cooled
2 tablespoons shortening, melted
1 5⅓-ounce can evaporated milk
Oil for deep-fat frying

In a large bowl, stir together flour, baking powder, salt, cloves, and cinnamon. In another bowl, beat eggs and sugar until thick. Stir in potatoes, shortening, and milk. Gradually add dry ingredients to potato mixture, stirring until combined. Chill at least 3 hours. Roll dough on lightly floured surface, half at a time, to a ½-inch thickness. Cut with floured doughnut cutter; chill cut doughnuts 15 minutes before frying in deep, hot fat (375 degrees). Fry 1 to 1½ minutes per side, turning only once. Makes 3 dozen doughnuts.

An avid baker for the last decade, Chuck Baumhover, a salesman for the Principal Financial Group in Des Moines, did lots of experimenting before he decided to enter the fair. "I fed all the failures to my hunting dog," he chuckled. "I think he was glad when I finally learned to bake; his stomach was getting kind of heavy."

Before entering his cinnamon rolls, he tested the recipe out on the kids in the neighborhood. "They said there wasn't enough cinnamon, so I really laid it on. After I baked them, though, they looked so terrible that I decided not to enter them." Later he reconsidered and resolved to give it a shot anyway. Despite their less-than-perfect appearance, the rolls earned him first place in the cinnamon roll division as well as a hundred-dollar U.S. savings bond from Tone's for the best cinnamon rolls in the Iowa Boy's Great Cinnamon Roll Search. ("Iowa Boy" is the column in the *Des Moines Register* written by Chuck Offenburger, who judged the cinnamon roll contest for several years.)

Blue-Ribbon Cinnamon Rolls

1 package active dry yeast
¼ cup warm water
¼ cup shortening
½ cup honey
2 teaspoons salt
1 cup milk, scalded

4 cups all-purpose flour, sifted
1 egg, beaten
2 tablespoons butter or
  margarine, melted
½ cup granulated sugar
2 tablespoons cinnamon

Dissolve yeast in warm (110-degree) water. Combine shortening, honey, salt, and milk in mixing bowl. Add 1 cup flour. Beat in egg and yeast. Add remaining flour until a soft and pliable dough is formed. Knead on a lightly floured surface until dough is smooth and elastic. Cover in a greased bowl; let rise until doubled. Punch down; let rise again until doubled. Roll into an 8 × 16-inch rectangle. Mix melted butter, sugar, and cinnamon. Spread on surface of rectangle. Beginning at long side, roll tightly, seal edge, and cut in 1¼-inch sections. Place rolls in greased 9 × 9 × 2-inch pan. Cover; let rise until doubled. Preheat oven to 375 degrees. Bake in preheated oven 25 minutes. Makes 9 rolls.

Unlike other culinary competitions, those vying for a ribbon in the Scripture Cake Contest must follow one specific recipe as if it were the Gospel. That's because it *is* the Gospel. Ruth Ellen Church, a graduate of Iowa State and former food editor of the *Chicago Tribune,* devised this formula with ingredients culled from these passages: 1 Kings 4:22, Judges 5:25, Jeremiah 6:20, 1 Samuel 30:12, Nahum 3:12, Judges 4:19, Numbers 17:8, 1 Samuel 14:25, Amos 4:5, 2 Chronicles 9:9, Leviticus 2:13, and Jeremiah 17:11.

Scripture Cake

½ cup (1 stick) butter
2 cups granulated sugar
2 tablespoons honey
6 beaten egg yolks
1½ cups sifted flour
2 teaspoons baking powder
2 teaspoons ground cinnamon
½ teaspoon ground ginger

1 teaspoon ground nutmeg
½ teaspoon ground cloves
Pinch of salt
½ cup milk
2 cups chopped figs
2 cups raisins
2 cups chopped almonds
6 egg whites, stiffly beaten

Preheat oven to 300 degrees. In a large mixing bowl, cream together butter, sugar, and honey. Add egg yolks. In a second bowl, sift together flour, baking powder, cinnamon, ginger, nutmeg, cloves, and salt. Add alternately to creamed mixture with milk. Stir in figs, raisins, and almonds. Fold in egg whites. Turn batter into a well-greased 10-inch tube pan and bake in preheated oven for about 1½ hours, or until cake tester inserted in middle comes out clean. Makes 12 to 15 servings.

A MESQUAKIE INDIAN POWWOW

Like drops of rain, a shower of drumsticks fell upon the taut rawhide, softly at first, gradually building up to a thunderous downpour of rhythmic rolls. The drummers chanted a fervent "yi-yi, yi-yi," while dancers in full regalia cantered around them in a snakelike procession, whirling, stamping, and gyrating to the drumbeats. Outside the danceground, curls of pungent gray smoke rose from black, pot-bellied kettles hanging over smoldering logs, where copper-skinned women, white to the elbows in flour, were preparing a feast of Indian corn soup and fry bread.

For more than seventy-five years, native American Indians from all over the country have been converging annually at this clearing on the outskirts of the Mesquakie settlement for an authentic Indian powwow. During the four-day celebration they set up tents and wigwams, don their finest buckskins and headdresses, and share with each other their centuries-old ancestral tribal dances, crafts, and foods. Unlike earlier powwows, however, non-Indians, too, may observe and even participate.

Each year, the colorful dance performances attract thousands of spectators, yet the Mesquakies contend that there are no special rehearsals or elaborate preparations prior to the event. "We were brought up observing the ceremonies," explained Louis Mitchell, a wiry, soft-spoken Mesquakie in his seventies, as he spread out the wares he hoped to sell during the powwow: bracelets and necklaces of silver and turquoise, feathered earrings, miniature tomahawks, hand-carved pipe stems. "My grandmother taught me how to do these things," he said, holding out a tiny beaded ring in his callused palm. "She taught us the language; we always spoke it in our home."

Mitchell was chairman of the tribal council, which has governed the affairs of the Mesquakies since the last Mesquakie chief died in 1918. Besides helping the tribe survive in the modern world, the council also struggles to preserve the customs, values, and beliefs of its people.

Also known as the Fox and Red Earth people, the Mesquakies, along with the Sacs, or Yellow Earth people, occupied the area long before the white settlers arrived. In 1845 both tribes were ordered off the land and sent to a reservation in Kansas. With the government payments they'd frugally saved, however, they gradually began buying back their homeland until they'd accumulated 3,200 acres along the Iowa River near the town now known as Tama.

Through the years, the Mesquakies have faced unending pressure from the U.S. government to adapt to white customs. Nevertheless, even in the modern world they've managed to retain a number of the tribal customs practiced by their ancestors centuries ago. They still hold traditional worship services with dancing and tribal feasting, sometimes in the elaborate costumes worn at the powwow. The costumes, some valued at as much as seven hundred dollars, are handmade by the women with the skins, feathers, and other ornaments provided by their husbands.

Behind many of the frame homes are bark houses covered with brushes woven together called wickiyaps. "In the summer, we stayed in the wickiyap, and in the winter, we lived in the frame house," Mitchell explained. "Our grandma refused to live in the frame house, even in winter," said Shirley Eagle, who came back from South Dakota to take part in the powwow with relatives. "Sometimes we'd spend the night with her when she'd have a fire going to keep us warm. The next day we'd have to go to school smelling like bark," she laughed.

The household Mrs. Eagle grew up in was "very strict. We were never allowed to sit. We had to wash every piece of clothing and every blanket by hand. We never had to be told more than once to do our chores. We knew by our grandmother's voice and eyes we'd better obey." Some of their duties were more tolerable than others. In addition to household chores, their grandmother also taught them how to make dolls and jewelry, which they sold at craft shows and powwows.

The meals were never fancy. "We usually could get by on one or two pots a day," said Marge Mauskemo, Mrs. Eagle's sister. "Indian soup" was the staple of the diet. Generally, it was a hodgepodge of Indian corn, beans, and whatever meat was on hand: diced pork, chicken, beef, game. They particularly looked forward to dinnertime, when the men came in from a productive hunt. "We might roast a raccoon, have pheasant and dumplings, or boil deer meat and then serve it with flour gravy," Mrs. Mauskemo remembered. Possum and muskrat were also frequently served, Mrs. Eagle added. "Whenever we'd have muskrat, the kids would always fight over the tail!"

Dessert was rarely much more than dried squash, which was boiled and sweetened with sugar. "But we did have one special treat," Mrs.

Eagle said. "We used to go out in the woods and collect sap from the maple trees. Then we'd take it to a shed where we'd boil it down to syrup. When it turned to liquid, we'd mix in some walnuts and then put it in little bowls to harden. That was always our favorite. We had to work so hard for it!"

Mitchell recalls other dishes his grandmother used to make which were only found in nature: wild potatoes, which are "a lot stronger tasting than regular potatoes," and milkweed, which was breaded and fried.

"And of course we always dry plenty of Indian corn in the summertime," said Beverly Roberts, who still does most of her cooking in a "cook shack" behind her house because "food just always seems to look better and taste better when it's cooked outside." For breakfast she often fixes "Indian oatmeal," which is actually Indian corn that's first toasted in a skillet and then ground. "We cook it in water until it's soft, then we serve it in a bowl with a little lard and sugar." Her specialty, however, is fry bread, a Mesquakie staple served for most meals. In fact, one year she took first place in the National Fry Bread Contest in Arkansas with the delectable golden circles she serves hot from the kettle they're fried in each year at the powwow. Traditionally, they're eaten plain or sprinkled with sugar, but during the powwow a more contemporary Tex-

Making fry bread

Mex version is also offered: fry bread wrapped around a filling of seasoned taco meat, grated cheese, lettuce, and tomatoes.

The following recipe for fry bread is based upon the technique Mrs.
Roberts demonstrated at the powwow.

Indian Fry Bread

4 cups all-purpose flour　　　　　*1 cup warm water (about 115*
1 tablespoon baking powder　　　　　*degrees)*
1 teaspoon salt　　　　　　　　　*Oil for deep-fat frying*

In a large container, mix together flour, baking powder, and salt. Make a
well in the center of the flour mixture. Slowly stir in water until mixture
is the consistency of biscuit dough. (Add more water if necessary.)
Knead lightly, folding over about 10 times or so, until dough is easy to
handle but not stiff. Pull off a fistful and flatten it with floured hands to

about ¼-inch thickness by slapping dough lightly from one hand to another. Cut a 2-to-3-inch slash completely through the dough about an inch away from the edge. Stick a long-handled fork through the slash and transfer to a pot of oil hot enough for deep frying, about 375 degrees. Remove when surface is golden brown and bubbly. Drain on paper towels. Serve hot, either plain or with butter and sugar, or make an Indian taco by topping with beans, seasoned meat, lettuce, tomato, and grated cheese. Makes about 12 to 16 5-inch circles.

THE GRANT WOOD ART FESTIVAL

During the Grant Wood Art Festival each June, fans of Iowa's best-known and probably best-loved painter can immerse themselves in the legends and lore of the village that inspired many a Grant Wood painting. They can observe artists and artisans at work in the great stone barn of the Green estate, one of the last remaining original structures built near the turn of the century with the vast resources of nearby stone quarries. Also on the agenda are art exhibits, seminars, jam sessions, and folk dancing.

Born on a farm near Anamosa in 1891, Wood attended the Handicraft Guild in Minneapolis after graduating from high school and later taught at the University of Iowa. On a trip to Europe during this period, he became intrigued by Flemish and German primitive art forms and, as a result, decided to return to his home state to paint the scenes with which he was most familiar in the style that made him famous. He died in 1941 and is buried in Riverside Cemetery on the southeast edge of Anamosa.

Wood's painting *American Gothic,* depicting a solemn farm couple in front of their whitewashed homestead, achieved worldwide recognition and earned notoriety as the subject of universal parody. Many of these caricatures are on display at the old blacksmith shop, a scheduled stop on the guided bus tours through Grant Wood country during the festival.

When Wood and his followers left Stone City in 1933, so did the town's life and vitality. It remained virtually dormant until William Weber purchased the quarries in the 1950s and started the Weber Stone Company, which is now run by his son-in-law, Frank Deutmeyer. Weber staunchly supported efforts to preserve the community's graphic heritage, and several decades later a group of citizens banded together to form the Stone City Community Club for the sole purpose of preserving the history, beauty, and lore surrounding this picturesque landscape.

The old general store, built in 1897, is now a music hall with an underground pub. It's the scene for most nighttime entertainment, from fireside square dances complete with a fiddler to performances by top-name jazz musicians. Worshippers can still attend mass at St. Joseph's

Catholic Church, characterized by kaleidoscopic stained glass imported from Munich, Germany, an Italian white Carrara marble altar, and a ten-foot native stone fireplace in the basement. A blacksmith shop once used for the care of the quarry horses is now a gift shop, and the former Stone City school, which was in use until 1947, has been converted into a community building. Only a small portion of the foundation of Columbia Hall, the fifty-six room hotel and opera house where Jenny Lind and Major Tom Thumb once performed, remains. Both Columbia Hall and the Green mansion, the center of the Stone City Colony and Art School, were destroyed in fires.

During the festival, any of the new generation of artisans who have begun filtering back into the community—a gunsmith, a puppetmaker, a precision tool maker, an old-time book printer—can tell you the legends of Stone City. But if you look hard enough, you can find some of the old-timers who can relate those accounts first-hand, like Jay Joslin. "My father and I, we used to work in the quarries back when the rocks had to be blasted out by hand," recalled Joslin, now in his early seventies. A retired grain hauler and co-op manager from Amber, he still spends most of his weekends at his cabin on the riverbank of his birthplace. He can well remember when Stone City was a bustling community with a population of more than one thousand, when the advent of the Portland Cement Company caused it to diminish to a ghost town, and when Grant Wood and his followers moved in.

The artists, Joslin noted, didn't exactly blend in with the rest of the townfolk, comprised mostly of the families of quarry workers. "People around here always thought they were oddballs. I used to think it was kinda like a half-way nudist colony. I was the general chore boy around there and lots of time I'd pass by and see some of the lady artists out sunbathing with half their clothes off." He remembers most distinctly the time watercolor instructor Adrian Dornbush called upon him to fetch a can of fly spray. "I walked in on his paintin' class, and found out what he needed the spray for. A fly was biting his nude model, and I was afraid for a minute he was going to ask me to spray her," he said, laughing. "Luckily, he didn't. Whew, I would've been mighty embarrassed!"

What Joslin remembers most about Grant Wood was his Studebaker car with the built-in sun roof, but not all the artists lived so lavishly. Times were hard and those who couldn't afford a dormitory room for $1.50 a week camped out in ice wagons. For $8.50 a week, however, an artist could receive board with "excellent cuisine" often prepared by Grant Wood himself. Several of those dishes are featured in the *American Gothic Cookbook* compiled by Joan Liffring-Zug (Penfield Press, 215

Brown St., Iowa City, Iowa 52240). Edwin B. Green of Iowa City submitted the recipe for Wood's famed strawberry shortcake, which previously appeared in a 1953 cookbook by the ladies of St. Edward's Parish, Waterloo. In the introduction, Grant Wood's sister, Nan Wood Graham, says of her brother: "On occasion, he would go into the kitchen and show his prowess at cooking. In no time, he could turn out the best potato salad I ever tasted. He was also noted for his Strawberry Shortcake. Once when mother and I were away and unexpected company arrived, Grant rose to the occasion and whipped up a Strawberry Shortcake that the guests later described as 'out of this world.' In telling my mother about it, Grant said in a surprised tone of voice, 'We could actually eat it.' After hearing it described as 'out of this world,' Grant never dared try making the shortcake again for fear of ruining his reputation as a cook."

Grant Wood's
Strawberry Shortcake

1 quart fresh ripe strawberries,
washed and hulled
½ to 1 cup granulated sugar
2 cups sifted all-purpose flour
3 teaspoons baking powder

½ teaspoon salt
6 tablespoons lard
¾ cup milk
Butter (fresh homemade is best)
Rich country cream

Place strawberries in a bowl and bruise and chop with a silver spoon. Cover with sugar to suit and let stand at room temperature to bring out the juice. Make a biscuit dough as follows. Preheat oven to 425 degrees. Sift together flour, baking powder, and salt. Cut in lard. Add milk and mix lightly, the less the better. Spread out in a greased pie tin with a spoon. Bake in hot oven until done (12 to 20 minutes).

Carefully break biscuit dough into 2 layers, using a fork to separate them. Lay top layer to one side (remove with a pancake turner if necessary). Butter the bottom layer and cover with crushed strawberries. Butter the top layer and put back on the strawberries. Top the cake with more strawberries. Cut in huge slices and serve with country cream. (This and coffee make a complete meal.) Makes 6 to 8 servings.

Mrs. Robert C. Armstrong of Cedar Rapids reports: "Grant Wood made this for Sunday supper at the Artist's Colony in Stone City. (We had it there.) He said it was his version of French potato salad which he liked in France."

Grant Wood's Potato Salad

6 potatoes cooked in skins,
peeled hot
1 clove garlic, cut in half
⅓ cup salad oil
3 tablespoons vinegar
¾ teaspoon salt
½ teaspoon pepper
½ onion, grated

2 or 3 tablespoons minced parsley
½ cup chopped celery
2 tablespoons chopped pickle
Cooked salad dressing to taste
(see page 83)
Hard-cooked eggs for garnish

Cook and peel potatoes. Rub a bowl well with garlic. Put in the oil, vinegar, salt, pepper, onion, and parsley. Blend this dressing well. Add diced warm potatoes and toss well. Add celery and chopped pickle. Cool in refrigerator for several hours. Add a little cooked dressing and mix well. Garnish with slices of hard-cooked eggs. Makes 6 to 8 servings.

This recipe comes from *Recipes from Our Annual Fourth of July Potluck Picnic for Friends and Relations,* also compiled by Joan Liffring-Zug (Penfield Press). It was submitted by Nan Wood Graham, of Riverside, California, model for *American Gothic* and sister of Grant Wood. She writes, "This is one of our favorite dishes and it never failed to please Grant."

Mrs. Wood's Stuffed Cabbage

1 head cabbage	*⅓ cup chili sauce*
1 pound ground beef ("Mother	*2 teaspoons Worcestershire sauce*
used half a pound of sausage	*½ teaspoon salt*
and half a pound of beef	*½ teaspoon marjoram*
instead of all beef")	*Few grains of pepper*
2 green peppers, finely chopped	*1 8-ounce can tomato sauce*
2 medium onions, finely chopped	*2 tablespoons butter or margarine*
2 tablespoons vegetable oil	*½ cup sour cream*
1 cup soft bread crumbs	

Core cabbage and cook 7 minutes in boiling water, covered. Drain; cool. Remove 12 large outer leaves. Cook ground beef, green peppers, and onions in oil until meat is browned. Add bread crumbs, chili sauce, Worcestershire sauce, and seasonings; mix well. Place equal amounts of meat mixture on each cabbage leaf. Roll and secure with wooden picks. Place in a large skillet. Pour in tomato sauce. Dot with butter or margarine. Cover and simmer about 1 hour. Remove cabbage rolls to platter. Stir sour cream into tomato sauce in skillet (this burns easily so watch carefully) and then pour some of this mixture over cabbage rolls. Serve remainder separately. Makes 6 servings.

HOUBY DAYS

In Czechoslovakia, the word *houby* means mushroom, or "gift of the forest." In Cedar Rapids, perhaps "gift of the meadow" would be a more accurate definition. Yet even without abundant timberland where mushrooms are most likely to flourish, Cedar Rapids's residents of Czechoslovakian descent take mushroom hunting as seriously as their ancestors did. In fact, they even have a festival to celebrate the annual spring ritual.

Houby Days takes place in the heart of Cedar Rapids's "Czech Town" every year in mid-May, the first weekend after Mother's Day when mushroom-hunting season is at its peak. Several weeks prior to the festival, avid mushroom hunters throw on their grubbies and head for the secret spots where they can expect to find goatsbeards, grass mushrooms, and perhaps the most highly valued fungus of all: the morel.

The festival is one of two celebrations put on by the Czech Village Association to help nurture the rich Czech heritage which has always characterized this quaint little neighborhood around Cedar Rapids's 16th Avenue. The weekend after Labor Day, the merchants of the businesses housed in European-style storefronts along the sidewalks also sponsor the Czech Village Festival, which features a kolache breakfast, a bake-off, a Sunday polka fest, and an antique show.

During both events, Czech villagers, garbed in puffy-sleeved blouses with colorful embroidered skirts or in wool pants and vests with brass buttons, demonstrate native crafts: egg decorating, rugmaking, cornhusk dollmaking, woodworking. Folk dancers polka and waltz to a band of accordion players providing lively accompaniment under a white gazebo. Spectators are invited to tour the town's Czech museum and library filled with authentic Czechoslovakian literature which dates back more than two hundred years. And citizens in local restaurants, bakeries, meat markets, churches, and outdoor tents offer favorite native dishes, from goulash and sauerkraut to kolaches (sweet buns filled with fruit, cheese, or ground poppyseeds) and, during Houby Days, mushroom fritters.

But the highlight of the Houby Days celebration is the judging of the mushrooms. After houby "experts" carefully examine each entry displayed on long tables in front of the bandstand, trophies are awarded for the largest, smallest, most oddly shaped, best display, and best houby in show.

Jana Fast, who can recall houby hunting with her father as a small child in Czechoslovakia, said that in her native country it is much more than just a sport. "Mushrooms are often called 'Poor Man's Bread,' for they are a staple of the Czech diet," she said. "Czechs have always lived off the land in every way they could. They pick the mushrooms when they are at their best, and those that aren't eaten right away are dried and used later in various dishes."

One way Czechs in Cedar Rapids as well as Europe like to eat mushrooms, especially the spongelike, aromatic morels, is sautéed in scrambled eggs. Some years, when the hunters have come back with a particularly abundant supply, scrambled eggs and mushrooms are served as the featured attraction at the merchants' breakfast on Sunday morning during the festival.

Throughout the celebration, local restaurants offer mushroom delicacies, and many townfolk have houby feasts in their homes, along with other dishes reminiscent of their heritage. Many of those dishes are featured in the *Czech Book* (Penfield Press, 215 Brown St., Iowa City, Iowa 52240), a collection of recipes, facts, and anecdotes about Czech traditions compiled by former Czech Village Association coordinator Pat Martin. Here is a sampling.

Morel Mushrooms
with Beef Sauce

1 pint morel mushrooms, washed and carefully dried (if morels are unavailable, goatsbeard or any fall or spring mushrooms can be substituted)
5 tablespoons butter
1½ teaspoons minced onion

½ teaspoon minced parsley
¼ teaspoon salt
⅛ teaspoon nutmeg
2 tablespoons flour
¾ cup beef broth or beef bouillon
1 teaspoon lemon juice (optional)

Slice mushrooms. In a skillet over medium heat, melt 3 tablespoons of the butter, add mushrooms, and sauté with onion, parsley, salt, and nutmeg for about 5 minutes. In a bowl, blend remaining butter and flour;

Mushroom judging

when smooth, add broth or bouillon. Add this to the mushroom mixture and simmer for another 5 minutes. Add lemon juice if desired. Serves 2 to 3 as a light lunch, or 4 to 6 as a side dish with dinner.

SHERYL BELLON

Sidonia Klimesh of Spillville says her pickled mushrooms are popular at potluck suppers and also make "a very nice gourmet gift."

Pickled Mushrooms

1½ cups vinegar
1 cup granulated sugar
½ cup sliced onion

Mushrooms, "as many buttons as
you have" (about 12 ounces)

In a saucepan, cook vinegar, sugar, and onion until the onion is nearly transparent. Add the mushrooms, stirring carefully. Let mixture come to a boil and simmer for 5 minutes. Pack mushrooms carefully into small sterilized jars, pour on liquid, and seal. (Mushrooms will keep for several weeks in the refrigerator.) Makes about 2 cups.

Vera Krasova Miller, who hunted mushrooms with her father in Czechoslovakia, said that when she moved to Cedar Rapids in 1962 she "had to learn from scratch as mushrooms of Iowa were mostly different varieties." Here's a delectable use for the fruits of her labor.

Hot Mushroom Sandwiches

2 cups chopped fresh mushrooms
2 tablespoons butter, softened
½ cup mayonnaise

¼ cup finely diced ham
Salt and pepper to taste
4 to 6 thick slices French bread
Grated cheddar cheese

Preheat oven to 400 degrees. Combine mushrooms, butter, mayonnaise, ham, salt, and pepper. Spread evenly on the bread slices. Sprinkle each with cheddar cheese. Bake in preheated oven until cheese is bubbly, about 7 to 8 minutes. Makes 4 to 6 generous servings.

Note: For the bread slices, trim the ends of a 14-ounce loaf of French bread with a serrated knife, cut the loaf in half lengthwise, then cut crosswise into 2 or 3 equal portions. For an irresistible hot hors d'oeuvre, spoon the filling atop rounds cut from a baguette, top with cheese, and bake as before.

Wenceslaus Square Goulash

½ cup lard or shortening
1 cup chopped celery
2 large onions, chopped
2 pounds lean pork, cut into cubes
2 bay leaves

2 cups tomato juice
1 tablespoon caraway seeds
1 cup red wine
1 teaspoon salt
1 tablespoon paprika
2 cups water

In a large skillet over medium heat, melt lard or shortening. Add celery and onions and sauté until soft. Add meat and fry over medium-high heat until lightly browned on all sides. Add bay leaves, tomato juice, caraway seeds, wine, salt, and paprika, stirring to coat meat evenly. Add water, cover, and simmer without stirring for ½ hour. Serve over dumplings. Makes 6 servings.

Note: The Wenceslaus Square Czech Restaurant was a restaurant in Cedar Rapids's Czech Village for several years.

ANNA KENJAR

These rich, positively irresistible buns come from Helen Horak Nemec, who grew up near Cedar Rapids's Czech village and worked in Sykora's Bakery. They are involved, but well worth the effort!

Kolaches

2 packages dry yeast
¼ cup lukewarm water
1 tablespoon granulated sugar
1 cup (2 sticks) butter or
   margarine
2 cups milk
2 whole eggs and 4 egg yolks
½ cup granulated sugar

½ teaspoon mace
1½ teaspoons salt
½ teaspoon grated lemon rind
6 to 7 cups all-purpose flour
Melted butter
Cherry or poppyseed filling
   (recipes follow)
Crumb topping (recipe follows)

Dissolve yeast in lukewarm water, add 1 tablespoon sugar, and let set until bubbly. Melt butter and add milk; heat until warm. Beat eggs and egg yolks and add sugar, beating until mixture becomes thick. Add warm milk with melted butter. Add yeast, mace, salt, and lemon rind. Next beat in flour, 1 cup at a time.

When dough becomes too thick to beat with a wooden spoon, turn out onto a floured board and knead until smooth and silky. Put in greased bowl and let rise in warm place until double in bulk. Turn dough out on floured board and divide into 6 large pieces. Cut each of these large pieces into 12 small pieces. Form into walnut-sized balls. (Roll dough under your hand and form with your palm.) Place on greased baking sheet 2 inches apart and brush each ball with melted butter. Let rise until almost double in size. Press center and fill with desired filling. Sprinkle with crumb topping, if desired. Let rise until light. Preheat oven to 400 degrees. Bake in upper third of preheated oven 7 to 10 minutes, until barely golden. Remove from oven and brush with melted butter. Makes 6 dozen.

Cherry Filling

1 cup granulated sugar	*1 teaspoon red food coloring*
6 tablespoons cornstarch	*1 teaspoon vanilla*
¼ teaspoon salt	*½ teaspoon almond flavoring*
2 1-pound cans sour red cherries	

In a saucepan, mix sugar, cornstarch, and salt. Add juice from cherries. Cook and stir over medium heat until thick. Add remaining ingredients. Makes enough filling for 3 dozen (at least) kolaches.

Poppyseed Filling

1 cup water	*½ teaspoon cinnamon*
½ pound ground poppyseeds	*1 cup granulated sugar*
1 cup milk	*½ cup crushed graham crackers*
1 tablespoon butter	*½ cup raisins, plumped in hot*
1 teaspoon vanilla	*water and drained*

In a saucepan, add water to ground poppyseeds and cook until thickened. Add milk and cook slowly for about 10 minutes, being careful that it doesn't scorch. Add butter, vanilla, and cinnamon, then sugar, and continue cooking for about 5 minutes; remove from burner. Add graham cracker crumbs and raisins. Makes enough filling for 3 dozen (at least) kolaches.

Crumb Topping for Kolaches

1 cup all-purpose flour
½ cup granulated sugar
¼ cup (½ stick) butter or
margarine

¼ teaspoon salt (omit if using
margarine)
¼ teaspoon cinnamon

In a large bowl with pastry blender, mix all ingredients together until crumbly. Makes enough for about 6 dozen kolaches. Also a good topping for coffee cakes.

NORDIC FEST

On most days, the meals that appear on the table of H. P. Field and his wife, Iduna, of Decorah would give no clue to their ethnic roots. But during certain times of the year such as Christmas and their hometown's annual Nordic Fest, it's a different story. That's when Mrs. Field and the other Decorah residents of Scandinavian ancestry pull out their handcrafted rosette irons, lefse grills, intricately patterned butter molds, and other special utensils passed down to them by their mothers and grandmothers to pay homage to their culinary heritage.

Throughout the two-day festival, which is held the last weekend of July, some 75,000 spectators have an opportunity to sample all kinds of Nordic delicacies prepared in sidewalk food stands, church kitchens, and public halls. In storefront windows along Water Street, citizens garbed in native dress demonstrate the fine art of making the waferlike flatbrod and the thin potato pancake called lefse, which is rolled out with a grooved rolling pin and baked on a special grill the size of a dinner plate. Handcrafted irons of various patterns are used for deep-frying rosettes, which are rolled in sugar and cinnamon; the rich Christmas pastry, sandbakkals, are baked in special tin forms. In one window, an expert Norwegian baker deftly twists pencil-thin strands of sweet dough into figure-eight shapes for kringle, while another rolls out thin, patterned cookies called goro.

On the Luther College campus, demonstrations are conducted for stuffing Scandinavian sausages and constructing a Norwegian wedding cake: a tower of almond-filled cookies. There's also a contest for eating lutefisk, or lye fish, so called because it's first preserved in lye and rinsed before baking, a native dish that perhaps only a true Scandinavian can appreciate. "When made properly, it's flaky, tender, and delicious," said H. P. Field, a lanky, white-haired dentist of Nordic descent. "But if some novice makes it who doesn't know what she's doing, it'll be as rubbery as an eraser." Lefse, he noted, also requires a certain finesse. "Otherwise, it can taste like an old dishrag."

The Fields also keep varieties of Norwegian cheeses around the house, but not gammelost. "That's the word for old cheese," Field said, grimacing. "My mother used to take the unprepared curds and put them under the bed to age. Some Norwegians around here think it's delicious. But I'd just as soon eat some cottage cheese mixed with snuff."

The Fields' cozy tomato-red house trimmed in white is fashioned similarly to the cottages in his father's native village in the craggy, unfertile mountains of Norway. There, he said, his father's family subsisted mainly on the products reaped from their small patches of barley, rye, and "bland corn," referred to as "mixed grains." They fished for trout, herring, and cod, kept a flock of goats for milk and cheese, and raised their own chickens for fresh eggs.

Soon after the Civil War, his father left his homeland with a band of fellow countrymen in hopes of finding greater prosperity abroad. "Things were booming in America then. They foresaw unlimited opportunities. Fertile soil. They would get rich," Field explained. "One of the old pioneers used to say, 'Back in Norway, you people never work. You putter! But when you Norwegians come to America, you work like crazy people!'"

The Norwegian pioneers originally settled in Wisconsin, then moved to Forest City, Iowa, before coming to Decorah. At first, they wondered if they'd made a terrible mistake. "They were afraid of the prairies. They thought if the trees wouldn't grow, the grain wouldn't grow." Nevertheless, Field's father was determined to give farming a try and immediately purchased the best team of oxen he could find. Much to his chagrin, however, the oxen refused to obey his commands. One day, as he was struggling with the ornery beasts to guide them down a dirt road, a local citizen spotted him and doubled over with laughter. "You know what the problem is, don't you?" the citizen called out to him. "Your oxen don't understand Norwegian." He taught the bewildered farmer a few English commands, and he never had a bit of trouble with them again.

As their language became more Americanized, so did their daily routine. At Christmastime, however, many of the Norwegian citizens still have a customary Norwegian "White Christmas," which refers not to the snow on the ground but to the spread on the dining room table. "Everything is white, even the tablecloth and candles," Field explained. "White fish, or lutefisk. White rice with sugar and cinnamon. A sweet, white porridge called rommegrot. Lefse, rolled up with butter and sugar. White cheeses." The children were particularly fond of white mice, a crescent-shaped cookie rolled in powdered sugar.

For many years, the town commemorated Norway's constitution on May 17 with a celebration called Sytende Mai, for which there would be plenty of "singing, dancing, feasting, and picnicking," Field remembered. Eventually that event was replaced with the Nordic Fest. Besides its food customs, other aspects of Norwegian history and culture are revived as well. Inside the Norwegian-American museum, one of the oldest immigrant museums in the country, artisans demonstrate birch root basket weaving, candle dipping, Hardanger violin making, wheel rug making, and the old Scandinavian art of burning designs on wood known as rose-maling. The Good Shepherd Church Puppeteers re-enact Scandinavian folk tales, including the children's classic "The Three Billy Goats Gruff." And the Decorah Kilties Drum and Bugle Corps, which performs throughout the Midwest, entertains thousands of spectators with a marching routine in front of the courthouse square.

The best places for a visitor to get a taste of Norwegian home-style cooking are at the smorgasbords put on by several local churches. At the Glenwood Lutheran Church the year I visited, the spread consisted of Norwegian meatballs in a mildly seasoned gravy, mashed potatoes, fruit soup, lefse, and a variety of Swedish cookies. Here are recipes for some of those dishes adapted from the *Glenwood Lutheran Church Cookbook* and the *Sons of Norway Cookbook*.

Fruit Soup or Sweet Soup

½ cup quick-cooking tapioca
2 quarts water
1 pound pitted prunes
1 pound raisins

½ cup lemon juice
1 to 2 cups granulated sugar
2 whole cinnamon sticks
1 quart grape juice

In a double boiler, cook tapioca in 1 quart of the water until clear. In a large kettle, cook prunes and raisins in remaining quart of water until tender. Add cooked tapioca to fruit, along with lemon juice, sugar to taste, and cinnamon sticks. Add grape juice last and cook only until heated through. Makes about 5 quarts.

White Mice

1 cup Crisco
1 cup (2 sticks) butter
*8 heaping tablespoons granulated
    sugar*
4 cups all-purpose flour

2 teaspoons vanilla
1¼ cups crushed pecans
Pecan halves (optional)
Powdered sugar

Preheat oven to 300 degrees. In a mixing bowl, beat together Crisco, butter, and sugar until fluffy. Add flour, vanilla, and crushed pecans. Stir in a few drops of water if mixture seems too dry. Shape in mounds or crescents by tablespoonfuls and place on ungreased cookie sheets. Option: a pecan half may be rolled in the center of each cookie. Bake in preheated oven 20 minutes. Roll in powdered sugar. Makes about 4 dozen.

MRS. MILLIE DAHLEN

Norwegian Meatballs

1½ pounds round steak
½ pound veal steak
½ pound lean pork
3 egg yolks, beaten
2 to 4 tablespoons minced onion
(optional)
2 tablespoons cornstarch

¼ to ¾ teaspoon ginger
Salt and pepper to taste
1 pint cream (or less)
5 cups beef broth, or 3 13¾-ounce
cans
5 tablespoons cornstarch
½ cup cold water

In a meat grinder, grind the round steak, veal steak, and pork three times. In a bowl, mix meats with egg yolks, onion (if used), cornstarch, ginger, salt, and pepper. Mix well until mixture is sticky. Add cream a little at a time until the meat is of desired consistency (moist but not running). It may not take the full pint. Chill, then form into meatballs. These should be cooked in meat broth slowly, until done (about 15 minutes). After meatballs are cooked, remove them with a slotted spoon to a serving bowl. Dissolve cornstarch in water and stir into boiling broth. Cook until mixture thickens and clears. Drop meatballs into gravy and simmer slowly until hot. Makes about 60 meatballs with 6 cups of gravy, or about 10 to 12 servings.

MRS. ADOLPH RUEN

The following recipes are from *Notably Norwegian* by Louise Roalson (Penfield Press, 215 Brown St., Iowa City, Iowa 52240). Ida Sacquitne of Decorah demonstrates lefse making at the Norwegian-American museum in Decorah and annually for the Nordic Fest. While most recipes insist that you use a special lefse pin and grill, some Decorah cooks confess that they make do without, using a regular rolling pin and skillet instead, with satisfactory results. The lefse, however, are not quite as thin as they would be if rolled out with a grooved pin.

Lefse

5 well-packed cups riced potatoes   *2 cups all-purpose flour*
½ cup (1 stick) margarine   *1 teaspoon salt*
3 tablespoons powdered sugar

Use Idaho russet potatoes. Boil, then mash and rice potatoes. Add margarine while potatoes are still warm. Cool until room temperature. Add powdered sugar, flour, and salt. Mix with your hands, knead well, and then roll into a log. Cut and measure into ⅓-cup portions and make a round ball of each portion. Press it down by hand and it will be easier to keep round while rolling out. Dust the large canvaslike cloth lefse "board" (or pastry board) with flour. Press dough down, turn over, and press down again. Roll as thinly as possible using a rolling pin with a pastry sleeve into 14-inch circles to fit the lefse grill. The secret of making thin lefse is using a covered rolling pin. For the last roll across the dough use a grooved lefse rolling pin, which marks the dough slightly and makes it thinner. Using a lefse stick, roll dough onto stick and transfer to hot lefse grill or griddle. You must use a lefse stick or holes will be made in the dough. (Some cooks use a thin spatula instead.) Bake a minute or two, then turn with lefse stick or spatula. Turn when lefse bubbles and brown spots appear. Fold each lefse in half or quarters. Cool between towels and store in plastic bag. Spread with butter to eat. Some people sprinkle the lefse with brown or white sugar and then roll it up. Makes about 18.

Marilyn Haugen Istad of Decorah says, "This is the recipe used by my daughter Jan and her teenage friends about thirteen years ago to make kringle. As a demonstration in a store window at the Nordic Fest, they rolled and baked these tasty goodies and sold them to the visitors."

Pastry demonstrations at Nordic Fest

Kringle

5¼ cups all-purpose flour
2 teaspoons baking powder
Pinch of salt
⅔ cup margarine
2 cups granulated sugar

1 teaspoon vanilla
2 egg yolks, unbeaten
2 teaspoons baking soda
2 cups buttermilk

Mix flour, baking powder, and salt and set aside. Cream margarine, sugar, and vanilla. Add egg yolks. Add baking soda to buttermilk and add to creamed mixture before foaming stops. Add dry ingredients. Chill at least 3 hours.

Preheat oven to 400 degrees. Place a clean dish towel on a flat surface. Flour well. Drop a teaspoonful of dough onto floured towel. Roll with your hands into a long rope, about ⅜ inch in diameter. Place rolls on greased cookie sheets, making figure eights or pretzel designs with the dough ropes. Bake 4 minutes on bottom shelf of oven, move to top shelf, and bake 2 minutes longer, until lightly browned on bottom. Makes 4 to 5 dozen.

STRAWBERRY DAYS

W hen a curious out-of-towner called the Strawberry Point town hall to find out what happens during Strawberry Days, the town clerk couldn't have been more succinct. "That's the time of year when the whole town turns into a strawberry," she replied matter-of-factly.

She was telling the truth. Throughout this annual June celebration, when strawberries are flourishing, there's a strawberry everywhere you turn in this friendly little town of 1,400. A cluster of giggly little girls in strawberry costumes vied for the title of Little Miss Strawberry in front of the old Franklin Hotel and Cafe. A local politician tossed strawberry-flavored candies to spectators from a basket during the parade. Ladies served strawberry shortcake and homemade ice cream with fresh strawberries in the church fellowship halls. And local merchants offered strawberry give-aways.

But even when the celebration is over and all the strawberry vines have dried up, plenty of evidence of this town's symbol lingers. Strawberries are painted around the border of a local beauty shop's sign, and they appear as trinkets and decorations in the storefront windows of the drug store and soda fountain. The biggest reminder of all, however, is in front of the library, where a Volkswagen-size replica of the fruit towers atop a white pole painted with a green vine. The townspeople proudly refer to it as the "World's Largest Strawberry."

The town's name can be traced back to 1841, when Old Mission Road, a military wagon road, was laid out from Dubuque to Fort Atkinson. It was located on a forty-mile strip of land that included the northern parts of Clayton and Fayette counties known as neutral ground, which served as a protective barrier between the Winnebago Indians and the hostile Sac and Fox tribes. While moving 2,900 Winnebagos from Wisconsin to the safety of Fort Atkinson, the army set up camp near a spring in a point of timber flourishing with wild strawberries. Before leaving, some troop members set out a stake in front of the campsight inscribed with the words "Strawberry Point."

Because of its refreshing spring, the site became a popular resting

place for Eastern immigrants en route to settle claims in the Midwest. Between 1847 and 1853, about twenty of those families set up claims along a segment of Old Mission Road, now known as Mission Street, which runs east and west through town. In 1853, the Stearns brothers platted the town now known as Strawberry Point, although they originally chose Franklin as its name after their hometown of Franklintown, New York. That name was rejected, however, when they learned that an application for the same name had already come from Lee County. So they settled for the inscription they discovered on a wooden stake stuck in the ground a mile west of town.

But not everyone was satisfied with the choice, particularly the railroaders. Indignantly, they decided to call their station Endfield, because they didn't feel Strawberry Point was appropriate. Like it or not, they soon learned they'd have to accept it, because in 1875, the state legislature passed a law requiring the name of the railroad to correspond with the town's original name.

Today you'd be hard-pressed to find a citizen in town who isn't proud to call Strawberry Point his or her home. One such resident is George Fenchel, a retired school administrator and former mayor. Since his retirement he's made his hometown a more colorful place to live while salvaging fading memories by decorating sides of old buildings with murals depicting scenes from early Strawberry Point history. Smaller scenes painted on canvas by Fenchel hang on the walls of the library, the Lutheran church, and a local café. In 1978, he helped write the scripts for a pageant commemorating the town's 125th anniversary, in which some of the most memorable moments in Strawberry Point's history were re-enacted in skits. Perhaps the most earthshaking, literally, was the time the World's Largest Strawberry blew down in a violent storm. Fortunately, the only injury was to the strawberry itself, which had to be repaired before it was erected again.

Strawberry Point is the kind of place where everybody knows everybody and good citizens don't go unrecognized. Several years ago, Fenchel remembered, the town celebrated Doc Anderson Day upon the doctor's retirement from medical practice. "He's been a doctor here since 1936; for years he was the only doctor in town," Fenchel said. In honor of his services the town put on a skit which starred a member of the community dressed up as a stork. "Then each person Doc Anderson had brought into the world walked across the stage."

Much of the town's history is preserved in the Wilder Museum, a state tourist attraction which boasts a collection of more than five hundred antique dolls as well as replicas of a Victorian parlor, child's bedroom, and early museum. The museum is located on the former home site of another Strawberry Point citizen, the late Florence Roe Wiggins, who also played a role in immortalizing part of Strawberry Point's past: its food customs. A former food columnist for the local paper, Mrs. Wiggins compiled her childhood recollections of favorite dishes prepared by friends, neighbors, and relatives in her community in a cookbook entitled *Strawberry Point Kitchens* (Graphic Publishing Co., Strawberry Point, Iowa 52076). For a town so proud of its name, it makes sense that a substantial number of those recipes feature the town's namesake.

Mrs. Gibb's Rhubarb Dessert with Strawberries

1 cup sifted all-purpose flour
¾ cup oatmeal
1 cup brown sugar
1 teaspoon cinnamon
½ cup (1 stick) melted butter
3½ cups cut rhubarb
1 cup granulated sugar

2 tablespoons cornstarch
1 cup water
1 teaspoon vanilla
1 10-ounce box frozen strawberries
2 tablespoons minute tapioca

Preheat oven to 325 degrees. Mix together flour, oatmeal, brown sugar, cinnamon, and melted butter. Pat half in the bottom of a 9-inch square pan. Save rest for topping. Spread rhubarb on crust. Meanwhile, in a saucepan combine sugar, cornstarch, water, and vanilla. Cook and stir until clear. Stir in strawberries and tapioca. Pour over rhubarb while hot. Top with crumb mixture and pat down. Bake in preheated oven 1 hour. Makes 6 to 8 servings.

Mama's Strawberry Sponge

1 3-ounce package strawberry-flavored Jell-O
2 cups boiling water
1 cup chopped nuts (walnuts or pecans)

1 cup crushed strawberries
1 cup whipping cream, whipped
4 egg whites, stiffly beaten
Whipped cream for garnish

Dissolve Jell-O in boiling water. Just before it sets, add nuts and strawberries; fold in cream and stiffly beaten egg whites. Set in a cool place to harden and serve with whipped cream. Makes 6 to 8 servings.

Strawberry Flip

2 cups strawberry juice (made by
   straining crushed strawberries
   through a sieve)
1 cup orange juice

1 cup pineapple juice
1 cup lemon juice
7 cups water
1 cup simple syrup

Combine all ingredients and serve in glasses half-filled with chipped ice. Makes about 13 cups.

Note: To make 1 cup simple syrup, combine 1 cup each granulated sugar and water in a saucepan. Bring to a simmer and stir until sugar is dissolved. Cool to room temperature, then refrigerate in a sealed jar.

Clarice's Berry Bavarian Crown

1 3-ounce package strawberry-
   flavored Jell-O
1 cup hot water
½ cup cold water

2 10-ounce packages frozen
   strawberries, thawed
2 cups whipping cream, whipped
1 large angel food cake
Ruby glaze (recipe follows)

Dissolve Jell-O in hot water. Add cold water and chill until congealed slightly. Beat until fluffy. Drain berries and reserve juice for glaze. Fold berries and whipped cream into Jell-O. Tear cake into small pieces (do not use browned parts of cake). Alternate cake and strawberry mixture in layers in an 8 × 11-inch pan or a 9-inch springform pan. Carefully work strawberry mixture around cake. Chill until firm. Cover with ruby glaze and chill overnight. Makes 12 servings.

Ruby Glaze

1 tablespoon cornstarch
Reserved strawberry juice

1 teaspoon butter
2 or 3 drops red food coloring

Blend cornstarch and juice in a saucepan. Cook until clear (this will take 3 to 5 minutes). Remove from heat and add butter and food coloring. Cool, then pour over cake mixture.

Lorna's Glazed Strawberry Pie

1½ quarts strawberries
½ cup water
1 cup granulated sugar
2½ tablespoons cornstarch
1 tablespoon butter

Few drops red food coloring
1 9-inch baked pastry shell
Sweetened whipped cream,
	flavored with vanilla if desired

Wash, drain, and hull strawberries. Crush 2 cups of the berries and combine in a medium saucepan with water, sugar, and cornstarch. Bring mixture to a boil and cook over simmer flame about 2 minutes, until clear. Add butter and enough red food coloring to give a bright color; strain and cool slightly. Fill baked and cooled pastry shell with remaining berries. Spoon strawberry glaze over berries, making sure that all are covered. Chill. Just before serving, top with whipped cream. Makes 6 to 8 servings.

VEISHEA

Even the staunchest Iowa State supporter may have a rough time telling a visitor what the letters VEISHEA actually stand for. But anyone who's ever been on campus during this long-standing celebration could give his or her own definition. It's a four-day weekend jam-packed with mud volleyball games, canoe races, student-directed theatrical productions, impressive open house displays, and fireworks. It's a spectacular parade of elaborate floats designed and constructed by members of sororities, fraternities, and dormitories. And it's an opportunity to indulge in a VEISHEA cherry pie, if you can make it down to the basement of the Home Economics building before the last of the six thousand pastries is sold, that is.

The VEISHEA cherry pie sale, which predates VEISHEA itself, is one of the most popular yet shortest lived events during the annual spring celebration, which gets its name from the first letters of each of Iowa State's colleges. Long before the doors open for business, customers begin lining up outside the Institutional Management Tea Room, many armed with boxes and crates from home, prepared to stock up on enough of the fruit-filled tarts to feed an army of out-of-town guests or satisfy their own cherry pie cravings until next year. Once the pie committee begins taking orders, it's only a matter of hours until the supply is completely wiped out.

Millie Kalsem, a former dietitian who now lives in Ames, is one of the few alumnae who can remember a time when the cherry pie supply exceeded the demand. She was a member of Omicron Nu, the honorary home economics organization which originated the project in 1921 as part of an all-college Home Economics Day celebration, a forerunner of VEISHEA. "At that time, the celebration was scheduled in the middle of February, close to Washington's birthday," she recalled. "And since cherry pie seemed to be a favorite with almost everyone, we decided it would be the perfect thing to serve." Kalsem, then a senior, was selected chair of the group in charge of making the two thousand pie crusts; an-

---

other classmate headed the pie-filling committee. "I had just finished Miss Bailey's advanced cookery class," she said. "My instructor suggested that we use her recipe for hot water pie crust because it was supposed to be a lot less work. We weighed out a little bit of dough for each crust, rolled them out, and then shaped them on the back of muffin tins."

The pies were served à la mode to each ticket holder who visited the food laboratory along with ham sandwiches, coffee, and a jumbo popcorn ball. In addition to preparing the pies, the Omicron Nus had also made candy to sell at an intersociety soccer game followed by a vaudeville show staged by members of the Home Economics Club. The spectacle surely would have been a big success had it not been for one obstacle beyond their control: weather. "It rained and snowed all day and we didn't get nearly the turnout we'd expected," Kalsem said. "We had several hundred pies left over that we ended up selling at a discount to the director of dormitories to serve to the dorm students." To prevent that predicament from happening again, the pie sales were incorporated into the first annual VEISHEA celebration the following year, which was held at the peak of spring rather than winter. Only during World War II has the Institutional Management Club, which took over the project in 1924, served anything other than cherry pies at VEISHEA. Because of a shortage of sugar and other ingredients, hot breads were served to campus visitors instead.

In the 1960s, the department acquired a tart press, making it possible for students to turn out thousands of pie crusts at a time. Nowadays they're made up in advance and stored in the freezer. Frozen sour bing cherries are used for the filling, which is now dolloped with a special whipped topping prepared by the students. But according to Millie Kalsem, who still tries to sample one of the updated treats every VEISHEA, "They taste quite similar to the ones we baked."

The current VEISHEA cherry pie recipe calls for 405 pounds of flour, 10 pounds of salt, 270 pounds of shortening, 1,380 pounds of frozen cherries, 92 pounds of sugar, 52 pounds of Clear-gel, and 60 quarts of nondairy topping for a yield of 10,000 pies. But a close facsimile can be produced in the home, using arrowroot rather than the institutional product Clear-gel as the thickener. Any pie crust will do, but the original hot water pastry, which tends to be more tender and crumbly rather than flaky, is especially nice.

VEISHEA Cherry Pies

Hot water pastry (recipe follows), or any pastry recipe for an 8- or 9-inch double-crust pie
2 16-ounce cans pitted sour red cherries (water pack)
1½ cups granulated sugar

4 tablespoons arrowroot or cornstarch
Pinch of salt
Whipped cream or topping or ice cream

Preheat oven to 425 degrees. Prepare pastry; roll dough to ⅛-inch thickness. Cut into circles to fit into 3-inch tart tins or over inverted custard cups or muffin tins. Prick bottom and sides with fork. Bake in preheated oven 10 to 12 minutes or until golden.

To prepare filling, drain juice from cherries; reserve ¾ cup juice. Blend sugar, arrowroot or cornstarch, and salt in saucepan. Stir in cherry juice. Cook over medium-high heat until syrupy. Add cherries and continue stirring until very thick and clear. Let stand about 15 minutes. Fill tart shells and refrigerate. Top with whipped cream or topping before serving, or, for old-fashioned VEISHEA cherry pies, serve à la mode with vanilla ice cream. Makes 10 to 12 tarts.

Hot Water Pastry

2 cups sifted all-purpose flour
1 teaspoon baking powder
1 teaspoon salt

⅔ cup shortening or lard
⅓ cup boiling water

Sift flour and remeasure 2 cups. Sift again with baking powder and salt. Add shortening or lard to boiling water and stir until smooth, then add to flour mixture and stir until blended. Roll in waxed paper and chill. Makes enough pastry for 2 8-inch single-crust pies or 10 to 12 tarts.

THE CLEARFIELD CENTENNIAL

O n the Fourth of July in 1982, the citizens of Clearfield, Iowa, had more to celebrate than their country's birthday. They also honored their hometown's hundredth year on the map. The town's entire business district—a single extra-wide street about as long as a football field—was marked off with road blocks, with a banner proclaiming "Celebrate in Clearfield" strung up from one side to the other. Storefront windows were decorated with red, white, and blue streamers.

In a nearby field, a cluster of spectators cheered women contestants in the skillet throw as they tested their ability to decapitate a scarecrow with a basketball for a head with a cast-iron frying pan. Also on the agenda were husband-calling, rolling pin–throwing, goat-milking, and nail-pounding contests. "We were going to have all the ladies' games this afternoon," said Mrs. Mildred Matthews, who was costumed for the occasion in a long gingham dress with matching bonnet. "But they said they'd need at least two days to play all the games they wanted to play." Meanwhile, the men pitched horseshoes, vied for the checkers championship, rosined up their bows for a fiddler's contest, and brushed up their whiskers for the beard judging.

That evening, both present and former citizens crammed under the big show tent to watch community members perform original one-act skits and listen to golden oldies sung by the Centennial Chorus. Throughout the festivities, a gentleman from a neighboring community played tunes such as "Hello, Dolly" on a honky-tonk piano powered by a vacuum cleaner motor while some kids scrambled over a peculiar-looking cubicle made of thick black bars. "That's the old city jail," explained centennial chairman Darl Bell, a retired mail carrier and ambulance driver, as he watched from a wooden bench across the street. "A fellow called up the mayor and offered to clean it up so people could see what it looked like for the centennial."

The last census recorded 437 citizens in Bell's hometown, a number he figures hasn't fluctuated much since 1900. But whatever the community may be lacking because of its small size is compensated for by its big community spirit. "One thing this town's got is cooperation," said Bell. "Whenever the town plans to do anything, everybody helps." That, he added, could explain why at 6:00 A.M. two days before festivities were to begin sixty-six residents were ready to begin sprucing up the main street.

The organization which seems to pump the most life into the community is the Lions Club. Besides remodeling several of the town's rundown buildings, the club is also responsible for putting in a drug store and the Town and Country Cafe, run by Bell's daughter-in-law. "We're an 'eat-out' bunch around here; I don't think there's a woman in town who cooks lunch during harvest season," noted Bell's wife, Margaretta, who helps out in the restaurant with the cooking. The cooks, she said, always receive the most compliments on their slow-cooked roast beef, hamburger gravy over hot biscuits, and array of salads and puddings. "We have a farmer who opens the restaurant at five-thirty or six every morning," Bell said. "The coffee pot's plugged into a timer, so it's already made when he gets there. The only pay he gets is a free breakfast."

Clearfield is, however, proud of its history of creative home cooks, and to prove it the American Legion's auxiliary requested citizens to submit their favorite family recipes to be published in the *Clearfield Centennial Cookbook*. Some of the entries date back to ancestors during the Civil War; others are concoctions of present-day citizens. Here are some of both.

Centennial Cherry Squares

1 cup plus 2 tablespoons all-
purpose flour
1 cup rolled oats
2 cups brown sugar
1 teaspoon baking soda
¾ teaspoon salt
½ cup (1 stick) butter, softened
2 eggs

½ teaspoon almond extract
½ teaspoon baking powder
1 cup shredded coconut
1 cup halved maraschino cherries
½ cup halved pecans
Cherry almond sugar icing (recipe
follows), optional

Preheat oven to 375 degrees. In a mixing bowl, combine 1 cup flour, oats, 1 cup brown sugar, baking soda, ¼ teaspoon salt, and butter. Mix until crumbly. Press into a greased 9 × 13 × 2-inch pan. Bake 10 minutes. In another bowl, beat eggs; stir in remaining 1 cup brown sugar and almond extract. Mix in remaining 2 tablespoons flour, baking powder, and remaining ½ teaspoon salt. Add coconut and cherries. Stir to blend. Pour over mixture in pan and spread evenly. Sprinkle pecans over top. Bake 25 to 30 minutes. Cool. Ice with cherry almond sugar icing and cut into squares. Makes 35 to 40 small squares.

Cherry Almond Sugar Icing

3 tablespoons butter, softened
2 cups powdered sugar
¼ teaspoon almond extract

2 tablespoons (or more) cherry
  juice

In a mixing bowl, cream butter, sugar, and almond extract. Blend in enough cherry juice to thin to spreading consistency.

JEAN ALLEN

Ralph Keller, who runs a welding and machine shop in Clearfield, is well known in the community for the distinctive pancakes he flips at pancake breakfasts for members of the Iowa Blacksmith and Welders Association as well as for his family at home.

Ralph Keller's Bacon Pancakes

3 or 4 slices bacon
3 large eggs, beaten
3 cups milk (about)
3 cups all-purpose flour (whole
  wheat flour, cornmeal, or any
  cereal may be used for part of
  the flour)

3 tablespoons brown sugar
3 teaspoons baking powder
1 teaspoon salt
Reserved bacon grease

Dice and fry bacon in a heavy frying pan until brown. Reserve 3 tablespoons bacon grease. Combine eggs and milk. In a mixing bowl, combine flour, brown sugar, baking powder, and salt. Stir in milk/egg mixture, bacon grease, and diced bacon. Drop by large spoonfuls onto a

medium-hot, lightly greased griddle. Says Ralph: "We make animal shapes (cats or rabbits) with raisins for eyes, nose, and mouth for children." Fry until browned on both sides. Makes 15 to 18 pancakes.

This dish was served to soldiers during the Civil War.

Bubble and Squeak (1861)

½ cup suet or other fat
½ cup chopped bacon or ham
½ cup (1 stick) butter
2 quarts shredded cabbage

8 medium potatoes, peeled and
*   sliced*
Salt and pepper to taste
1 cup hot water

Put fat, bacon or ham, and butter into an iron kettle and bring to a sizzling heat. Add cabbage and potatoes and season with salt and pepper, then add hot water. Cover and cook over slow fire about 1 hour. Makes 10 to 12 servings.

Grandma Anna's Cinnamon Rolls

2 cups milk
¼ cup (½ stick) butter
2 eggs
7 to 8 cups all-purpose flour
1½ teaspoons salt
1 package yeast
½ cup warm water

1 teaspoon granulated sugar
¼ cup melted butter, plus more
*   for greasing pans*
About 2 packed cups brown sugar
Cinnamon
½ to 1 cup chopped nuts
⅓ to ½ cup whipping cream

In a medium saucepan, scald milk; add butter and cool to lukewarm. Beat in eggs. In a large bowl, combine 2 cups flour and salt. Stir in milk mixture. Dissolve yeast in warm water to which 1 teaspoon sugar has been added. When yeast foams, add to milk and flour and beat until bubbles form. Add enough flour to make a dough that will be slightly sticky. Put into greased bowl, cover, and let rise until double.

Preheat oven to 375 degrees. Roll dough out on floured surface to a 12 × 18-inch rectangle. Spread with melted butter, about ¾ cup of the brown sugar, and cinnamon. Roll up and slice in ½-inch slices. Place in shallow pans generously greased with butter and spread with remaining brown sugar and nuts. Pour ½ teaspoon unwhipped whipping cream in between each fold of dough. Cover and let rise again about 30 minutes. Bake until brown, about 25 minutes. Makes 12 to 16 large rolls.

KATHY GORDON BROWN

These delicious and different fruit and spice bars are thick and fluffy, much more like a cake than a bar cookie.

Party Line Bars

¾ cup margarine
2 cups granulated sugar
2 eggs
4 cups all-purpose flour
1 teaspoon baking soda
1 teaspoon baking powder
1 teaspoon cinnamon
1 cup coffee, cooled
1 cup sour milk or buttermilk

2 cups dates, pitted and chopped
½ pound orange slices, seeds and
    white pith removed, cut fine
    (may be chopped in blender or
    food processor)
1 cup chopped nuts
¾ cup coconut (optional)
Brown sugar frosting (recipe
    follows)

Preheat oven to 375 degrees. In a large mixing bowl, cream together margarine and sugar. Beat in eggs. Sift together flour, baking soda, baking powder, and cinnamon. Add to creamed mixture alternately with coffee and milk. Fold in dates, oranges, nuts, and coconut, if used. Pour into greased and floured 9 × 13-inch pan. Bake in preheated oven 40 to 50 minutes, or until cake tester inserted in middle comes out clean. Ice with brown sugar frosting. Makes 2 to 2½ dozen bars.

Brown Sugar Frosting

6 tablespoons brown sugar
6 tablespoons cream or milk

3 tablespoons margarine
Powdered sugar

In a saucepan, bring to a boil brown sugar, cream or milk, and margarine. Gradually blend in enough powdered sugar to obtain spreading consistency.

LOUISE BUSBY

Long before there were McDonald's hamburgers there were Maid-Rites, which are similar to Sloppy Joes; the chain began in Muscatine, Iowa, in 1926. There are still Maid-Rite shops throughout Iowa. Though traditionally made with beef, this home version uses pork.

Pork-Rites

2 pounds ground pork
2 tablespoons vinegar
½ cup water
1 cup ketchup
1 tablespoon brown sugar

1 teaspoon mustard
1 teaspoon salt
¼ cup chopped onion
8 hamburger buns, split and
   toasted

In a skillet, brown pork and drain. Add other ingredients and simmer 20 minutes. Serve on toasted buns. Makes 8 sandwiches.

KATHY GORDON BROWN

If you like apple butter, you'll love this.

Pumpkin Butter

1 1-pound can pumpkin, or 2 cups
   fresh, stewed pumpkin
⅓ cup brown sugar
⅓ cup granulated sugar

¼ teaspoon ground cloves
¼ teaspoon cinnamon
1 tablespoon lemon juice
¼ cup molasses (optional)

Combine all ingredients in a saucepan. Bring mixture to a boil; reduce heat and cook 15 to 20 minutes, stirring often to prevent sticking. Allow to cool. Pour into container(s) to store. Makes about 2 cups.

PATSY GAULE BEADEL

ST. PATRICK'S DAY
IN EMMETSBURG

Any Irishman should feel right at home in Emmetsburg, especially on St. Patrick's Day. Like the natives of its sister city of Dublin, the folks around here insist on paying proper homage to the Irish saint responsible for bringing Christianity to the Emerald Isle. In mid-March, a member of the Irish parliament arrives in Emmetsburg to preside over the weekend's festivities, which include a banquet, a Miss Shamrock pageant, a foot race "O 'Round the Loch," and a parade through the town's business district. An Irish dollar is minted, cans of blarney are sold, mugs of green beer are toasted, and, as Margaret Brennan puts it, everyone there is "either Irish or wishes he was."

Mrs. Brennan is the granddaughter of E. P. McEvoy, who arrived in Emmetsburg in 1871 at the age of nine with his family from Ottawa, Canada. That was only fifteen years after a band of pioneers from Kane County, Illinois, all with names like Mahan, Nolan, Neary, Laughlin, and Jackman, made a new home for themselves and their families along the west branch of the Des Moines River some sixty miles northwest of Fort Dodge. They called themselves the Irish Colony and later named their new settlement after Robert Emmet, the Irish patriot executed by the English in 1803 for fighting for Ireland's independence. The first winter was particularly severe, but endurance was nothing new to these settlers or their predecessors, pointed out Ralph Degnan, a retired farmer from the nearby community of Ayrshire. "My grandpa came over here on a relief ship during the Potato Famine, back in 1847," he said. "People on board were sick and starving and dyin' off like flies."

The ship docked at Ellis Island. With few skills to offer, many of the immigrants were unable to find work, including Degnan's grandfather. So they made their way down to Chicago, "the jumping-off place to the West," Degnan said. Some got jobs in factories; others opened saloons. They lived in the same neighborhoods, attended the same Catholic churches, and always bloc-voted for the Democratic candidate. "Grandpa worked in the Stetson hat factory there 'til he had to give that up. He said it was because he was allergic to wool, but his brother always said it was because he was allergic to work," Degnan said with a wink.

Emmetsburg Publishing Co.

After serving in the Union army during the Civil War, the elder Degnan returned to Freeport, Illinois, to work on the railroad. The tracks eventually led him to Cedar Falls, where he settled down with his family on an eighty-acre farm. "My dad left home when he was nineteen or twenty to start his own farm right here in Ayrshire, only back then it was called the Great Oak Township," Degnan said. Like Emmetsburg, Ayrshire, too, once had a heavy Irish population. "But just about all of them have died off now—all but maybe four or five families," he said.

Degnan became friendly with his future bride, Florence, the butcher's daughter, at the local Irish church and school. "There was lots of singing and dancing at the church, especially back when Father Carroll was our priest," Mrs. Degnan recalled. "We played cards, too, like rummy and 500, but all the money we won was used to keep our convent going. At school the nuns used to teach us old Irish jigs. We'd wear paper hats and put on little programs."

In their younger years the Degnans frequently danced at the Pavillion to tunes like "Roses of Picardy" and "When Irish Eyes Are Smiling." "Ralph was always the best dancer—why, he could dance just like Lawrence Welk!" she declared. St. Patrick's Day was observed even then, although the festivities weren't nearly so elaborate. In the early 1900s it was celebrated with a church dinner and a home talent show, usually with an Irish theme.

In 1961, two local businessmen collected twenty-five dollars to sponsor a city-wide St. Patrick's Day celebration. The following year the Emmetsburg mayor and lord mayor of Dublin officially proclaimed their hometowns sister cities, based on their mutual desire to preserve their Irish heritage. Included in the proclamation was an agreement to join together in commemorating St. Patrick's Day by sending over an Irish dignitary to participate in the Emmetsburg festivities.

Today, a St. Patrick's Day Association with some 260 members begins planning the event nearly a year in advance in a building across the street from the courthouse square where the life-size statue of Robert Emmet, identical to the one in Dublin, stands. The perpetuation of Irish tradition is also evident in some Emmetsburg kitchens, where the simple but hearty stews, freshly baked soda breads, cookies, and confections passed down through generations of avid Irish-blooded bakers are still favorites, particularly around St. Patrick's Day.

One of Florence Degnan's favorite treats while growing up near Emmetsburg was this cookie recipe, passed on to her by her Irish aunt.

Aunt Julia's Rocks (1861)

1 cup (2 sticks) butter or lard
1½ cups brown sugar
3 egg yolks
3 cups all-purpose flour
1 teaspoon baking soda
1 teaspoon cinnamon

½ teaspoon ground cloves
2 cups raisins
1½ cups chopped nuts
1 teaspoon vanilla
3 egg whites, beaten stiff

Preheat oven to 350 degrees. In a mixing bowl, cream together butter or lard and brown sugar until fluffy. Beat in egg yolks. Sift together flour, baking soda, cinnamon, and cloves; add to creamed mixture. Stir in raisins, nuts, and vanilla. Fold in egg whites with fingers. Drop by teaspoonfuls on ungreased cookie sheets. Bake at 350 degrees for 12 to 15 minutes, or until done. Makes 4 dozen.

Florence Degnan recalls: "I always carried Blarney Stones down to the polls whenever I counted votes for our district. The voters always left with frosting all over their fingers and faces!"

Blarney Stones

1 white angel food cake
2 cups powdered sugar
Water to thin

1 teaspoon vanilla
1 cup ground peanuts

Cut cake into 1½-inch cubes. Make frosting by combining powdered sugar, enough water to thin, and vanilla. Dip each piece of cake in frosting, then roll in peanuts. Makes enough to serve 25 to 30 hungry voters.

Aunt Mate's Irish Stew

1½ pounds boneless beef ribs,
    cubed
Hot fat to coat bottom of pan
    (about ¼ cup)
¼ cup all-purpose flour
6 cups water

2 cups carrots, cut into chunks
    (about 5 medium)
3 small onions, peeled and
    quartered
2 cups cubed potatoes
2 cups chopped cabbage
Salt and pepper to taste

Preheat oven to 325 degrees. In a large, heavy skillet, brown ribs in hot fat on both sides. Transfer from skillet to a roaster pan. To the drippings, add flour; cook and stir until smooth and bubbly. Add 3 cups water, raise heat, and stir until mixture comes to a boil. Pour gravy over meat and bake, covered, in preheated oven 1 hour. Add vegetables, 3 cups water, and salt and pepper to taste; bake uncovered 45 minutes more. Makes 4 to 6 servings.

Margaret Brennan passed along this exceptionally rich, delicious soda bread recipe as well as this anecdote:

"A story is told of a young silk-hatted attorney from a city who was traveling in the area with a circuit judge. The year was 1868. Nightfall found them near the Irish Colony and the judge went to the door of one of the houses and asked if they might stay the night. The lady of the house, Mrs. McCormack, assured them that they would be most welcome and directed them to put their horses in the barn. The house was low, with a sod roof and quite unprepossessing appearance. The young attorney was sure that he would be unable to eat any food prepared in such a place and when he found some eggs in a nest in the barn he cracked them and ate them raw. When he and the judge entered the house he found the table set with a snowy linen tablecloth. There was the fragrance of freshly baked bread and of ham frying in a skillet on the stove. Mrs. McCormack excused herself for a moment and went outside. She returned with a puzzled look on her face. 'I wanted to fry you some fresh eggs to go with your ham,' she said, 'but something must have eaten them.'"

Margaret Brennan's
Irish Soda Bread

½ cup shortening
½ cup granulated sugar
1 teaspoon baking soda
1 teaspoon salt

1 egg
3 cups all-purpose flour
1 cup buttermilk
1 cup raisins

Preheat oven to 325 degrees. In a mixing bowl, cream shortening with sugar until fluffy. Beat in baking soda, salt, and egg. Add alternately the flour and buttermilk. Fold in raisins. Place in an ungreased 8-inch round pan. With a floured knife, make a large cross over the top. Bake 50 to 60 minutes, or until cake tester comes out clean when inserted in middle. Makes 1 8-inch loaf.

"I think you'll like this!" Mrs. Brennan wrote at the bottom of the index card with her handwritten recipe for brack, another classic Irish quick bread loaded with plump, tea-soaked raisins. Wrong, Mrs. Brennan. I loved it!

Brack

2 cups cold tea   2 tablespoons orange marmalade
2 cups brown sugar   4 cups all-purpose flour
1 pound raisins   3½ teaspoons baking soda
1 egg, lightly beaten   Dash of salt

In a medium bowl, combine tea and brown sugar. Add raisins, cover, and let soak overnight. Preheat oven to 350 degrees. Stir egg and orange marmalade into tea/raisin mixture. Sift together remaining ingredients and blend into tea/raisin mixture. Grease 2 9 × 5-inch pans. Divide batter evenly between pans. Bake about 60 to 70 minutes, or until toothpick inserted in middle comes out clean. Let cool 10 minutes in pan. Remove bread to rack and let cool completely. Makes 2 loaves.

Note: The flavor of this greatly improves when wrapped airtight and stored at room temperature for at least a day or two before slicing. It also freezes beautifully.

CARROLL'S BAVARIAN FEST

John Wagner couldn't speak much English when he arrived in Carroll, Iowa, from Munich, Germany, in 1961. But some words drew immediate understanding between him and the townfolk. Like polka. And beer. And brats. And 'kraut. That's because an estimated 75 percent of the nearly ten thousand residents of this leading pork- and beef-producing city can also trace their roots back to Wagner's native country.

"People here are proud of their German heritage, and they like to show it," said Wagner, a heavy-set man with a silver pompadour and neatly trimmed goatee and mustache. Wagner, who for years managed the local Elks Lodge, is perhaps best known for his culinary skills as the head chef at every Elks Club dinner as well as for the special bratwurst recipe he helped the proprietors of Bernholz's Meat Lockers develop. "Some people back home make it with hot peppers, but we make ours milder, with oregano instead," he said. The savory pork links are the mainstay of every German-style function in this town, most notably, the Bavarian Fest, which was put on by the city's merchants for the first time in 1982. That year the other featured attractions included a parade headed by Clydesdale horses, tug-of-war contests, free hot-air balloon rides, and numerous polka bands, which kept the crowds on their feet on the concrete slabs in the park until after midnight.

Amid the lederhosen and dirndls, one couple, Harold and Lois Conrad, could be easily spotted in front of one of the three bandstands throughout most of the festival. Garbed in plum-colored velvet capes and jeweled crowns, they were presented the titles of Bavarian king and queen the first night of the event after the townspeople cast their ballots. Conrad came to Carroll from Germany. His wife is a native Iowan. Her German-born parents were baptized in the German church once located seven miles from Carroll. Though fully Americanized, the Conrads still have a few things in common with their ancestors. "We love to dance; we've got our own style of dancing," Mrs. Conrad said enthusiastically. "And we love to listen to polka music, especially if it's the Eddie Skeets Band. And we love the bratwurst the Bernholzes make. Some bratwurst I could taste for days, but theirs we like."

The Bavarian Fest is actually two local celebrations rolled into one: St. Boniface Day and the annual Polka Days Parades. St. Boniface Day, explained local merchant Joe Dalhoff, is a German version of St. Patrick's Day. The latter has always been boisterously observed by the Irishmen of Carroll, who makes up a substantial portion of the population. "We named it after St. Boniface, the German patriarch who lost his life when he took off to conquer the Huns," Dalhoff explained. Free miniature bratwursts were donated by members of the business community "as a goodwill gesture to the public," he added. And there was always plenty of sauerkraut to go with them. "Folks were always trying to outdo each other to see who could make the best 'kraut at the beer and food stands," Dalhoff recalled. "Some would jazz it up by putting a little vinegar in it or some caraway seeds."

But the Carroll citizens don't necessarily wait for an annual festival to party Bavarian-style. At the Elks Lodge there's German entertainment year-round: Oktoberfests, polka dancing, beer-chugging, and a bar maid's contest with an award for "the gal who shows the most dedicated patronage to a certain beverage—and I don't mean milk," Wagner said with a mischievous grin. One year the lodge sponsored a beer belly contest, a spectacle which drew a larger crowd than any other yet turned out to be its biggest flop. Dalhoff, who painted his stomach like a bull's head for the event, was one of the two entrants. "And I lost," the trim Dalhoff confessed. "The other guy was a bricklayer; his belly was a real dandy."

The club members also get together regularly for dinners at the lodge, although Wagner admitted he rarely prepared his German specialties for those events—unless, perhaps, it was an entrée featuring bratwurst and 'kraut.

Though most frequently served on a bun with lots of mustard, some people, like Wagner, frequently dress up bratwurst in other ways. "At home we eat bratwurst with eggs in the morning or cooked on the grill with 'kraut on the side. You have to be careful that you don't overcook it, though, or the skin will burst and the juice will run out." Mary Bernholz, whose husband, Dale, and brother Lyle have run Bernholz's Meat Lockers for more than twenty-five years, says she's "tried it every which way, warm or cold. Sometimes I boil it a little and put it in a barbecue sauce; other times I might put in a little water with potatoes and sauerkraut and cook it in the microwave."

One of Wagner's favorite uses for bratwurst is in this hearty casserole.

Bratwurst-Vegetable Medley

3 tablespoons butter or margarine	*1 10-ounce package frozen*
4 tablespoons all-purpose flour	*broccoli, thawed*
¼ teaspoon salt	*1 10-ounce package frozen*
2 cups milk	*cauliflower, thawed*
1 cup shredded sharp cheddar	*1 10-ounce package frozen*
cheese	*brussel sprouts, thawed*
	6 links fully cooked bratwurst

In a saucepan over medium-low heat, melt butter or margarine. Blend in flour and salt; cook and stir 2 minutes. Add milk, raise heat to medium, and cook and stir until mixture thickens and bubbles. Remove from heat; stir in cheese until smooth.

Preheat oven to 350 degrees. Cook broccoli, cauliflower, and brussels sprouts just until crisp-tender. Arrange in a buttered 1½ quart casserole and cover with cheese sauce. Arrange bratwurst links over vegetables. Cover and bake 15 to 20 minutes, or just until bratwurst is heated. Makes 6 servings.

Sauerkraut Supreme

1 tablespoon butter
1 medium onion, diced
¼ pound ground ham (optional)
1 quart sauerkraut, homemade or
  commercial

2 teaspoons caraway seeds
2 tablespoons brown sugar
½ cup water

In a 2-quart kettle over medium heat, melt butter. Add onion and ham and cook until browned. Rinse sauerkraut with cold water and drain. Add to onion and ham. Add caraway seeds, brown sugar, and water. Simmer, covered, over low heat for 2 hours or longer (the longer it cooks, the more mellow the flavor). Makes about 6 servings.

These two sauerkraut recipes were featured in the *Catholic Daughters of the Americas Cookbook* (Route 1, Box 125, Carroll, Iowa 51401). Mrs. James Houlihan submitted this refreshing, tangy-sweet rendition flecked with red and green, a terrific accompaniment to grilled bratwurst.

Sauerkraut Salad

1 27-ounce can sauerkraut
1 cup granulated sugar
½ cup vinegar
½ cup salad oil
1 small onion, chopped

½ cup chopped sweet pickle
½ green pepper, chopped
2 ounces chopped, drained
  pimientos, for color

Rinse sauerkraut with cold water and drain. In a saucepan, mix the sugar, vinegar, and salad oil together and boil. Pour the boiled ingredients while still hot over the sauerkraut and remaining ingredients. This salad tastes better if left to chill in the refrigerator overnight. Makes 7 cups or 14 to 16 servings.

State treasurer Bev Klein contributed this recipe, which is a tasty meal in itself.

Kraut Casserole

1½ pounds lean ground beef   *½ cup uncooked rice*
3 medium onions, chopped   *3 tablespoons brown sugar*
1 quart sauerkraut, well drained   *Salt and pepper to taste*
1 quart home-canned tomatoes,   *Chinese chow mein noodles*
  or 1 28-ounce can

Preheat oven to 350 degrees. In a heavy skillet over medium heat, brown beef and onions. Drain grease. In a 2-quart casserole, mix all ingredients except chow mein noodles. Cover and bake in preheated oven for 1½ to 2 hours. Sprinkle noodles over the top just before serving. Makes 6 to 8 servings.

THE NATIONAL HOBO CONVENTION

There are no Marriotts or Hiltons with fancy suites in Britt, Iowa. Yet the members of the organization which holds its annual convention there every year couldn't find the accommodations more to their liking. With a cozy spot right next to the railroad tracks, a banquet prepared by the master of Mulligan stew, and hospitality provided by some of the friendliest folks in the United States, what more could they ask for? For more than fifty years, Britt has been the site of the National Hobo Convention. Each August, homeless travelers from all over convene for four or five days at this special "hobo jungle" in the middle of the country, normally occupied only by an abandoned boxcar. Every night they stay up until the wee hours around a blazing campfire, telling jokes and exchanging adventures about life riding the rails. Each year they attend a special eulogy service conducted by a local Catholic priest for the Hardrock Kid, who passed away on a park bench in Ogden in 1977. The popular five-time King of the Hoboes was buried at the Evergreen Cemetery in Britt when friends discovered he had left no survivors.

On Saturday, visitors from all walks of life—twenty thousand or so—unite in paying homage to this seldom-recognized brotherhood. The special events include a foot race, an art show, country music by nationally known entertainers, a feast of Mulligan stew and—for the grand finale—a parade preceded by the coronation of the new King and Queen of the Hoboes. Many flock to hobo jungle afterward to get autographs or perhaps a snapshot taken beside some of the most distinguished guests of honor: Slow-Motion Shorty, Frying Pan Jack, Cinderbox Cindy, Mountain Dew. But the hobo who always manages to attract the most attention is Steamtrain Maury Graham, a jovial, white-bearded man with the looks and charisma of a shopping mall Santa in tatters. Graham, who has maintained hobo royalty with queens Long Looker Mic and Lu the Lush, garnered quite a bit of media publicity in the early 1970s when he began delivering good hobo cheer to patients in veterans' hospitals all over the country. He's also earned culinary recognition for the Mulligan stew he mixes up with a wooden stick in an iron pot at various local celebrations. As a special treat to the hoboes during the convention, he sometimes prepares his other specialty: a "boiled dinner" consisting of one potato, an onion, hot pepper, two eggs, and a sausage link—all boiled whole.

Until 1900, the conventions of the "Tourists Union #63," as the hoboes were then called, were held in Chicago, "'til it started turning into such a big metropolis," Graham explained. Police interrogated them. City folks taunted them. Some even threw rocks. So they decided to seek "some small, friendly place in the middle of the country" for their conventions instead, he added. Not long afterward, Britt citizens Thos. A. Way, T. A. Potter, and W. E. Bradford read about the convention in the Chicago newspapers. They then wrote a letter to the "Grand Head Pipe," Charles Noe, and invited him to bring the convention to Britt. Not only did they view the invitation as a goodwill gesture to the hoboes; they also saw it as a novel way of giving their little town a distinction which would set it apart from the rest of the nation. They paid the leader's carfare to Britt to inspect the site, and it met with his approval. Banners were strung up across the streets, a fife and drum corps clad in patched uniforms played ragtime tunes, and a barbecued ox was served to everyone at noon. Reporters from major cities all over the country were given a sight-seeing tour behind a team of horses to view the town's major attractions: the round elevator at M.&L. St., the arch over the cemetery gate, the town pump, the Salvation Army barracks.

More than thirty years passed before the second hobo convention in Britt was held. Yet it just couldn't seem to shake its reputation for being a "hobo town." So in 1933, several years after the demise of the county fair, Hobo Day was revived in its place. Hairbreadth Harry was crowned King of the Hoboes, a title he kept for three years. The honor so moved him, in fact, that he was inspired to write a book entitled *Inner Tubes Come Clean.* Ramblin' Rudy Phillips, another author who retired from railroad riding to run a barbecue business in Shawneetown, Illinois, was on hand at the 1982 convention to take part in the festivities and to push his book *A Hobo Lives Again* by wearing it clipped to his belt. In the book he not only relates his personal experiences as a wanderer but also defends the hobo's dignity. "Most people lump hoboes with bums and winos. But you know where hoboes got their name?" he quizzed. "They were once migrant workers, and their bosses called 'em 'hoe boys' for short. The wheat farmer couldn't have harvested his crop if it hadn't been for the thousands of hoboes who drifted west to help him."

Phillips, like any other hobo, has been snubbed by society on more than one occasion. But never in Britt. He first set foot in the town more

than fifty years ago. "I knocked on a back door, hoping to get a bite to eat in exchange for a little work. And I got a 'sit down'—finest dinner of chicken and mashed potatoes I ever had," he recalled. A "sit down," he explained, is a meal the hobo is invited to share at the dinner table with the family. Though they're always appreciative of a "knee-shaker," a plate of food given to them on a back porch, "a sit down is the sweetest word a hobo's ever heard. Never will I forget how friendly and nice the people of Britt, Ioway, are," he proclaimed.

Arthur Parker, alias Slow-Motion Shorty, travels from California to attend the conventions. The stubbly-faced, slightly stooped hobo retiree, wearing dark, round glasses, trousers upheld by suspenders, and a black felt hat pulled down low over his ears, has been a regular at the convention off and on since 1937. "I was passin' through Des Moines and saw the convention advertised on a sign," he remembered. "I was pretty tired and hot, so I decided to stop over and see what was going on." It was there that he earned his nickname. "I was carryin' a big gunnysack over my shoulder and I couldn't move too fast. So one of 'em says, 'Hey, I think we oughta call you Slow-Motion Shorty.'" Parker rode the rails into town for most of the events since, "'til I had a pretty bad heart attack. In '78 I took a bus, and this year I got to fly out. I'm just plain wore out from all that travelin'." Only a handful of hoboes still ride the rails these days. "It's just plain too dangerous," said Steamtrain Maury Graham, who now does most of his traveling in a dusty old van with a flat tire on the back. "Us hoboes are a dying breed." Even so, neither the hoboes nor the townspeople of Britt have any intentions of doing away with the convention. Graham said he believes that "when there aren't any hoboes left, the convention'll be held in their memory. Everybody will have a chance to be a hobo. It'll be America's biggest cookout."

And for just as long as you can count on a hobo convention in Britt, you can also bet there will be a big pot of Mulligan stew. Every year, a club or scout troop helps chop the ingredients for the feast, which tastes a little different each time depending on who's doing the cooking. "Now I ain't trying to brag, but I make the best hobo stew in America," vouches Graham. "It's something us hoboes have learned and learned and learned."

There's never a set recipe to follow for Mulligan stew, he explained. Whoever was "crumb boss" would tell a couple of guys to go find some vegetables and go to the meat market for some bologna butts or bacon butts. Each had his favorite way of seasoning it. "See those brown bushes over there?" he asked, pointing his hand-whittled walking stick to a clump of shrubbery by the railroad tracks. "That's dill. It's very aromatic;

you put some of that in, and the flavor just springs up all over your mouth." The main secrets to his formula, he said, "are cutting up the right kind of meat and vegetables into bite-size pieces, seasoning it with bottles and bottles of soy sauce and Kitchen Bouquet, and thickening it with cornmeal instead of flour."

Here's his basic idea, cut down for a family of six.

Steamtrain Maury's Mulligan Stew

1½ pounds fine-cut stew beef
3½ quarts water or stock
2 medium carrots, chopped
2 medium potatoes, chopped
1 medium onion, chopped
½ cup chopped celery
½ head cabbage, chopped
1 rutabaga, chopped (optional)

1 tablespoon soy sauce (or more)
1 tablespoon Kitchen Bouquet (or more)
1 bay leaf
Handful chopped fresh dill (if available)
1 to 2 tablespoons cornmeal
¼ cup cold water or stock

Place beef and water or stock in a heavy, lidded kettle. Bring slowly to a boil. Reduce heat at once and simmer, about 1½ to 2 hours. Add vegetables and seasonings. Simmer about 45 minutes or longer over very low heat, stirring frequently. To thicken, make a paste by blending the cornmeal with about ¼ cup of cold water or stock. Pour the paste slowly into the stew while stirring. Simmer and stir 5 to 10 minutes. Makes 6 to 8 servings.

INDEX